Praise for *Sustainability*

'A comprehensive guidebook for corporations ... ut shifting to more equitable, ecologically-sustainable operations.

Hazel Henderson, leading futurist and author of
Beyond Globalization.

'Australia is emerging as a world leader in the debate about corporate sustainability. As Dexter Dunphy and Jodie Benveniste say in introducing this fascinating book, sustainability is emerging as "the focus of a new value debate about the shape of the future". With business playing an ever-greater role in our globalizing economies, the wisdom and experience of the authors collected here make essential reading for business people determined to combine values and value creation in the new century.'

John Elkington, Chairman, SustainAbility Ltd.; member, European Union Consultative Forum on Sustainable Development; author,
Cannibals With Forks: The Triple Bottom Line
of 21st Century Business.

'The authors of *Sustainability* have done a remarkable job of summarizing the status of the worldwide corporate movement toward sustainability, with an intelligent blend of practical examples and guiding theory. This is an important work and CEOs everywhere should read it to gain a jump start in their own companies.'

Ray C. Anderson, Chairman and CEO, Interface Inc.

'For a corporation to truly be a good Corporate Citizen, not only must it deliver a "triple bottom line" today but it must also work out what is its distinctive contribution to a Sustainable Future. What is its contribution to ecological sustainability? To sustainable human progress? To sustainable wealth creation?

Sustainability gives us the charts we need—we in business must now navigate towards a sustainable future!'

Greg Bourne, Regional President/Director,
BP Amoco Australia/New Zealand

'The sustainability paradigm requires a new way of thinking for managers—those not attuned will find that they risk losing competitive commercial advantage. The wisdom contained in this book provides the impetus to develop and implement the organisational vision, strategies, structures and processes that are essential for a sustainable corporate future. Human resource managers will find the guidance required to ensure their companies are prepared to support a new way of working.

Beyond management "faddism", *Sustainability* is essential reading for all members of our community including legislators, business leaders, environmentalists, managers and all those who care about the long term survival of our home planet.'

**Dr Barbara Penson, Vice-President, Human Resources
Placer Dome Asia Pacific—a company committed to
a sustainable future**

'This is a most timely book. Most thinking leaders have become aware that commercial success in organisations is no longer sufficient. We need to create organisations that also acknowledge the humanity of those that work there. We need also to ensure our effort to pursue economic progress today does not impinge on the earth in such a way that it threatens the reasonable aspirations of future generations. This book nicely integrates the thoughts of some of Australia's seminal thinkers in the area of sustainability. I commend it to leaders and managers . . .'

Ted Scott, CEO, Stanwell Corporation

SUSTAINABILITY

The Corporate Challenge of the 21st Century

Edited by Dexter Dunphy, Jodie Benveniste,
Andrew Griffiths and Philip Sutton

ALLEN & UNWIN

First published in 2000

Allen & Unwin
9 Atchison Street
St Leonards NSW 2065
Australia
Phone: (61 2) 8425 0100
Fax: (61 2) 9906 2218
Email: frontdesk@allen-unwin.com.au
Web: http://www.allenandunwin.com

National Library of Australia
Cataloguing-in-Publication entry:

Sustainability: the corporate challenge of the 21st century.

Bibliography.
Includes index.
ISBN 1 86508 228 7.

1. Social responsibility of business. 2. Quality of life.
3. Sustainable development. 4. Business planning.
I. Dunphy, Dexter C. (Dexter Colboyd), 1934– .

658.408

Set in 11/12.5 pt Adobe Garamond by DOCUPRO, Sydney
Printed by Kin Keong Printing Co. Pte Ltd, Singapore

10 9 8 7 6 5 4 3 2 1

Contents

Figures, tables and boxes

Figures

Tables

Boxes

Contributors

JODIE BENVENISTE Jodie is an organisational psychologist, a social researcher and a writer. Her research focus has included issues of work/family balance, women and work, young people and work and work/life balance. Her book, *Woman, Work Child: Women Talk About Balancing Work and Family* was published in 1998 by Simon & Schuster. Previously, she worked as a management consultant, consulting on a range of human resource issues including organisational change, training, performance management, recruitment and selection, psychological assessment and remuneration to both the public and private sectors. She has also written extensively for *Business Class* magazine, a women's business magazine, and is currently a researcher at the University of Technology, Sydney in the Business School.

MARK DIESENDORF Mark is Professor of Environmental Science and Director of the Institute for Sustainable Futures at University of Technology, Sydney. He is a researcher, lecturer, consultant and facilitator of social and organisational change. Originally educated as a physical scientist, he has broadened out into the transdisciplinary areas of sustainable energy, urban transportation, greenhouse response strategies in general, theory of sustainability and processes for achieving ecologically sustainable and socially just development. He is a member of the Editorial Board of the international journal *Environmental Science and Policy* and is co-editor with Clive Hamilton of the book *Human Ecology, Human Economy: Ideas for an Ecologically Sustainable Future* (Allen & Unwin, 1997).

DEXTER DUNPHY Dexter is Distinguished Professor at the University of Technology, Sydney. Dexter's main research and consulting interests are in the management of organisational change and human resource management. His research is published in about sixty articles and fifteen books, including the Australian best sellers (with Doug Stace) *Under New Management: Australian Organizations in Transition* (McGraw-Hill, 1990) and *Beyond the Boundaries: Leading and Re-creating the Successful Enterprise* (McGraw-Hill, 1994). Dexter's most recent book *The Sustainable Corporation: Organisational Renewal in Australia* (co-authored with Andrew Griffiths) was published by Allen & Unwin in 1998. Dexter was formerly Professor of Management and Foundation Director of the Centre for Corporate Change at the Australian Graduate School of Management (AGSM).

PAUL GILDING Paul is Founder and Chairman of Ecos Corporation, which provides strategic support and advice to corporate clients and partners seeking commercial advantage through a focus on sustainability. Since forming Ecos in 1995 he has advised a range of leading international and Australian corporations including Placer Dome, BP, DuPont, Lend Lease, Pacific Power, Suncor Energy, the Queensland Timber Industry and WMC. Paul is a former Executive Director of Greenpeace and in 1997 he received the prestigious *Tomorrow Magazine* 'Environmental Leadership Award' for outstanding leadership in the field. In 1994, Time International listed Paul in its '*Time*'s global 100 roster of young leaders for the new millennium' and in 1992, the influential World Economic Forum (WEF) appointed him a Global Leader for Tomorrow at its annual meeting in Davos, Switzerland.

PAUL GOLLAN Paul (BA Hons (NSW), MBA (Nottingham, UK), MSc Econ) teaches Human Resource Management and Industrial Relations at the London School of Economics. He was previously a Lecturer in Management at the Graduate School of Management, Macquarie University, a Senior Researcher at the Australian Centre for Industrial Relations Research and Training (University of Sydney), and a senior researcher at the Australian Graduate School of Management (University of NSW) Centre for Corporate Change. Paul has recently published *Globalisation and its Impact on the World of Work, Future of Work: Likely Long Term Developments in the Restructuring of Australian Industrial Relations* and *Employee Relations in the Press* (published in 1997). He is co-author (with V. Campling) of a book on non-union workplaces titled *Bargained Out: Negotiating Without Unions in Australia* (Federation Press, 1999). He is presently completing his doctoral thesis 'Non-union forms of Employee Participation and Involvement' at the London School of Economics.

ANDREW GRIFFITHS   Andrew is currently a researcher and lecturer in the School of Management, Faculty of Business at Queensland University of Technology. He specialises in the areas of Strategic Change Management and Innovation; Organization Design and Environmental Management. Prior to this, he worked at the Centre for Corporate Change, Australian Graduate School of Management at the University of New South Wales. Andrew recently released his first book, *The Sustainable Corporation* (Allen & Unwin, 1998), which was co-authored with Professor Dexter Dunphy. He has also published work in leading management journals and conferences internationally. Andrew has consulted and researched extensively in leading manufacturing and service firms both in Australia and overseas. He recently submitted his Doctorate at the University of New South Wales.

MOLLY HARRISS OLSON   Molly is Director of Eco Futures, an Australian-based international policy firm working on building sustainable strategies with business, government and civic leaders. Molly is national convenor of Australia's Business Leaders Forum on Sustainable Development, an eminent group of over 100 Australian and international CEOs providing critical leadership on sustainability issues. Molly worked in the White House as the inaugural Executive Director of President Clinton's Council on Sustainable Development and was the first chair of King Carl Gustaf's Environmental Symposium, Stockholm, Sweden, in 1996. She was the distinguished Bates Scholar at Yale University where she received her Master of Environmental Studies and the Myerhoff Visiting Scholar on Global Civic Responsibility at Goucher College. In January 1995, Molly was selected to be a member of the World Economic Forum's prestigious Global Leaders for Tomorrow program, and in January 2000 she addressed over 2000 multinational corporation CEOs at Davos as the first sustainability expert in the opening plenary of the World Economic Forum's annual meeting.

ALAN PEARS   Alan originally trained as a mechanical engineer. Through the 1970s he worked at various times as a secondary school teacher, community educator, community activist and junior academic. Since the late 1970s, he has worked on energy issues, with particular focus on their interaction with people and the environment. Alan managed Melbourne's Energy Information Centre in the early 1980s, before working in the Victorian government's energy department. There, he helped to develop a number of innovative energy efficiency programs and policies. Since 1991, Alan has been co-director of the environmental consultancy, Sustainable Solutions. His work has spanned design of environmentally-improved household appliances and buildings, policy and strategic analysis, public education booklets, industry development policy and program development.

VIV READ Viv has over twenty-five years experience as a consultant and manager in organisational transformation and renewal, human resource management and workplace relations, for both the public and private sectors in Australia and South-East Asia. She has been involved with industries as diverse as manufacturing, mining, the waterfront, water and electricity authorities, hospitality and service, community organisations and all levels of government. She is a Fellow and the immediate past National President of the Australian Human Resource Institute, a member of an International Advisory Group for the State of the Art and Practice (Strategic Human Resource Management) Research Project, and Patron of the Johnson & Johnson New Leaders Foundation. She is based in Sydney.

PHILIP SUTTON Philip is the founder and Director of Policy and Strategy of Green Innovations, a non-profit environmental policy think tank and consultancy organisation promoting the achievement of global and local ecological sustainability. Philip's work is focused on environmental management systems for sustainability-promoting organisations and on strategies for an ecologically sustainable economy. Philip was the architect of the Victorian Flora and Fauna Guarantee legislation passed in 1988. He worked for a year in 1991 in the Victorian Office of the Environment on strategies for achieving a successful green economy. He was selected in 1991 by the *Age* Newspaper/Melbourne University Politics Department 'Agenda Project' as being one of the twenty most influential people in Victoria in the environmental policy arena. Philip is a member of the editorial board of the UK-based journal *Greener Management International*.

HARDIN TIBBS Hardin is a management consultant with extensive international experience. He is CEO of Synthesys Strategic Consulting, a Canberra-based management consulting firm. Hardin specialises in futures analysis and strategy development, and is an experienced scenario planner. Before moving to Australia he was a senior consultant with Global Business Network (GBN), a research and consulting firm in California, and he continues to work with GBN in Australia and the Asia–Pacific region. In addition to his strategy work, Hardin has made significant contributions on issues involving technology and environment, and he is the author of an influential paper defining industrial ecology, a new approach to industrial sustainability. Before joining GBN, Hardin was a consultant at Arthur D. Little, Inc., the international management, technology and environmental consulting firm based in Cambridge, Massachusetts.

PHILLIP TOYNE   Phillip is one of Australia's best known conservationists and Aboriginal rights lawyers. Until recently, Phillip has held key leadership positions in the Commonwealth Government, environment and Aboriginal organisations. He was Deputy Secretary in the Commonwealth Department of Environment, where he played a major role in the international policy arena on issues such as biodiversity, sustainable development and climate change. Phillip was Executive Director of the Australian Conservation Foundation, where he led successful campaigns to protect areas of global conservation significance including Kakadu, the Wet Tropics and Antarctica, and began the long process of merging green and Aboriginal partnerships. He also developed the National Landcare program with National Farmers Federation head Rick Farley, a movement which has radically changed land use practices in Australia and which is now moving to Africa and America. As the first legal council to the Pitjantjatjara Aboriginal people of the Central Desert, Phillip negotiated the return of native title for Uluru (Ayers Rock) National Park to its traditional owners. This was a world first and became a role model for environment and indigenous partnerships worldwide. In partnership with his wife, Molly Harriss Olson, Phillip is Director of Eco Futures, an Australian-based international policy firm working on building sustainable strategies with business, government and civic leaders. They advise a range of leading Australian and international organisations including the Commonwealth Minister for the Environment, the OECD, Visy Industries, Cape York Land Council, ICM International, Boral Energy, Collex, the Fred Hollows Foundation, the Australian Conservation Foundation and the World Wildlife Fund.

Part I
Introduction

1

An introduction to the sustainable corporation

Dexter Dunphy and Jodie Benveniste

This book arose out of two small but exciting conferences organised by the Centre for Corporate Change at the Australian Graduate School of Management (AGSM), University of New South Wales, Sydney, Australia.[2] These conferences brought together experts and innovative thinkers from a number of disparate fields of study in the natural and social sciences. What the participants had in common was a growing commitment to finding a way to involve corporations in increasingly adopting practices that contribute to sustaining and renewing the quality of life of their workforces and the community and adding to the richness and diversity of the biosphere. For those corporations operating in the private sector, we sought to achieve this with no loss of profitability and preferably with a positive contribution to the bottom line.

What we present on these pages is a product of the exciting interchange of ideas that emerged at these conferences and through subsequent active networking in person and online. This book is both an outcome of that dialogue and a contribution to continuing it in a wider forum.

An unusual feature of this book is that it brings together in dialogue specialists in fields that historically have been seen as unrelated. On the one hand are social scientists, social researchers, human resource managers and corporate change consultants with a commitment to creating a more fully human and humane society and world of work. On the other are natural scientists, ecological consultants and 'green' activists with a commitment to maintaining the biological integrity of the planet. We have discovered that what we have in common is a conviction that a sea change is needed in corporate values, a fundamental shift in how most corporations interpret their role in society, in order to create a more sustainable world.

In particular we are looking for new strategic initiatives that go beyond mere compliance to the minimal standards of health and safety regulations, environmental legislation and community expectations. In contrast we are seeking to encourage a proactive strategy which positively pursues the highest standards of corporate citizenship—for its own sake, because it is right, and also because it is a more effective way of doing business.

We are not simply prophets crying in the wilderness here for we are increasingly encountering organisations that are already moving down this path. We report some of these corporate initiatives. What is becoming clear, however, is that we are seeing a fundamental shift in the dominant economic paradigm. For example, some organisations are ushering in a new way of thinking about resource use. This new view accepts that neither society nor the natural world are boundless reservoirs of fresh resources that can be used up and thrown away as the corporation reaches out to take more. The new view accepts that we are reaching, in the case of some resources have already reached, a point where the supply of the resource, whether oil, fish or skilled professionals, is diminishing at the very time the need for these resources is increasing.

In the face of these limits to growth, where to from here?

The leading-edge organisations are increasingly adopting proactive strategies for sustaining and renewing key resources. For example, standard linear supply chains progressively exhaust the reservoir of non-renewable resources and excrete waste, noxious substances and pollution along the chain, producing 'bads' as well as valued 'goods'. So some organisations are moving to replace supply chains with virtuous cycles of resource use which create 'supply loops' that eliminate polluting substances and effluent and redefine the remaining 'waste' as valuable resources to be reclaimed, recycled and reprocessed (as in nature itself). Similarly with human resources, some organisations have used people as industrial cannon fodder to be exploited, burned out, used up and divested. In the new world of work, people are seen as the prime source of wealth and as having value in and of themselves. In the knowledge-based society, commitment, knowledge and skills are vital to corporate success. It therefore makes sense to invest in the development of all corporate members in order to build the human capabilities that create continuing innovation and high performance.

In order to understand the sea change at work, it is instructive to look back at the paradigm that dominated the twentieth century. The central preoccupation of the twentieth century was on harnessing the industrial revolution, initiated in the nineteenth century, for national wealth creation. As some nations succeeded in dramatically increasing their wealth through industrialisation, they faced another issue: 'How should the wealth be distributed?' The conflicts of fascism and democracy, communism and capitalism represented the working out of a collective answer to the themes of wealth creation and wealth distribution. The organising concept around which people's emerging hopes, aspirations and ideologies clustered in the twentieth century was 'progress', of which the most important element was economic progress. The concept focused the minds of generations on the communal task of forging a more affluent society, for themselves and their children. There were major conflicts about what progress meant in practice but general agreement that all should work to maximise the potential of a productive society.

Key issue for the twenty-first century

What issue will dominate the twenty-first century? What organising concept will emerge as the central focus of human consciousness? In an ambitious attempt to improve research and thinking about the future, a worldwide survey for The Millennium Project identified fifteen global issues that will dominate the future. The foremost issue identified was 'achieving sustainable development' and the survey writers comment on it as follows: 'Never before has world opinion been so united on a single goal as it is on achieving sustainable development' (Glen & Gordon, 1998).

Why sustainability? First, we have seen enterprises widely acclaimed one year as high performers only to fail the next and we have also seen a similar phenomenon with nations. This raises the issue of how we can develop organisations and societies that are able to sustain highly productive performance indefinitely. Second, it is becoming increasingly clear that sustained economic success and quality of community life depends on developing a different relationship with the natural environment. To the extent that we have generated economic affluence, this has been achieved in many cases by using global resources at a rate that is unsustainable into the future.

What is sustainability?

More a symbol than a scientific concept, sustainability is a focus for a new value debate about the shape of the future. It is a signpost pointing to a general direction we must take, while the debate is engaged about the best path to lead us forward.

Sustainability results from activities which:

- enhance the planet's ability to maintain and renew the viability of the biosphere and protect all living species
- enhance society's ability to maintain itself to solve its major problems
- maintain a decent level of welfare for present and future generations of humanity
- extend the productive life of organisations and maintain high levels of corporate performance.

In addition we make a distinction between ecological and human sustainability. By ecological sustainability we are referring to redesigning organisations to contribute to sustainable economic development and the protection and renewal of the biosphere. By human sustainability we are referring to building human capability and skills for sustainable high level organisational performance and for community and societal well-being. Ecological and human sustainability encompass the main tenets of sustainability, including what is commonly termed the triple bottom line—that is, economic, social and environmental outcomes. These distinctions also reflect our conviction that commitment to human and societal well-being is as important to the sustainability debate as ecological commitment to the planet. We must preserve a planet fit to live on and also create organisations that sustain the quality of social life.

If we are to have a desirable future, we must promote sustainability actions globally and at all levels of society while eliminating actions which lead to the deterioration of our physical and social environment. Unfortunately, many of our mundane ways of living and working detract from sustainability rather than contribute to it. The process of reorienting ourselves to the emerging issue of sustainability is beginning but it represents a revolution in the traditional ways of thinking about ourselves, our world and the way we work. In this process, modern corporations and their leaders have a large role to play.

We depend on corporations for the products and services we need to sustain our lives. However, some corporate practices have been, and still are, contributing to the deterioration of the quality of life and to environmental waste, degradation and pollution. Corporations are the core of modern society; as such they are a large part of the problems we are now encountering and they must therefore be part of the solution.

Fortunately, the basis of corporate performance and productivity is changing. We are moving from a world where wealth was based on material production and the acquisition of material possessions, to a world where wealth is increasingly based on knowledge production and the availability of services. In the past it may well have been accurate to posit a clash between the push to increase productivity and the need to protect the environment. Now, however, corporations are discovering that they can be even more successful in business terms while making substantial contributions to the quality of life of their employees and the community, and sustaining and renewing the natural environment. How is this possible?

The importance of people

In the last few years, business literature has been increasingly concerned with how performance can be sustained in the face of massive and often unpredictable change. The globalisation of business, economic deregulation and new technologies have transformed markets, created intense international competition and made survival dependent on rapid organisational reshaping and continuous transformation. In the developed nations, the initial response was to seek survival by drastically cutting costs, particularly through corporate downsizing and restructuring. Much of this has been underpinned by an ideology of economic neo-liberalism and a 'market forces' view of strategy that is particularly well summarised in the work of Michael Porter at Harvard Business School. We have seen a feeding frenzy of takeovers and mergers, radical downsizings, repeated restructurings, and a pressure for short term returns as CEOs move on at two to three year intervals. In the past twelve years, for example, Australian organisations have retrenched one in two full time employees. Many other Western countries followed a similar path, particularly the UK and the US. How effective has this approach been?

Research in the US and elsewhere now shows that the majority of these attempts failed in business terms, particularly if repeated in the same organisation. Downsizing and restructuring bring no automatic benefits and frequently represent a loss of the firm's intellectual capital and skill base. These strategies only work to the firm's advantage when they are part of its overall strategy to shift and upgrade the skill mix of its workforce.

This raises the question: What is the basis for performance in developed economies? Downsizing and restructuring are usually desperate attempts to compete on costs, but few firms in the developed economies can compete on cost alone. Since the fall of the iron and bamboo curtains, 1.5 billion cheap workers have been added to the world's workforce. Competing on cost alone is a game we in the developed countries cannot win. The real competitive battles are being fought on added value, speed and flexibility of response to changing market demands. In these areas, the knowledge and skills of employees become critical to achieving and maintaining high performance. A recently published study by Professor Dennis Turner and Mike Crawford shows definitively that high performance derives from systematically building corporate competencies; in other words, investing in human capability—intellectual capital (Turner & Crawford, 1998). In particular, the competencies associated with effectively reshaping the organisation are critical to future success. A US study of firms with sustained long term performance supports this view—corporations that invested more in building human capital and supporting technologies outperformed the US stock market by a factor of fifteen and their performance was six times that of comparable companies that didn't make this investment. Investing in people is generally more effective than divesting them.

A recent book by Stanford Professor Jeffrey Pfeffer (1998) carefully reviews the research evidence on the characteristics of high performing organisations. He concludes that the most critical factor is their human resource practices. The prime basis for sustainable performance is investing in people and systems. Sustaining long term performance depends increasingly on creating learning organisations that reshape themselves for future challenges and which systematically build the human and technical capital base to support this. If the world's corporations acted on this insight, however, their performance would still not be sustainable in the longer term. As we move into the next century, our very success is threatening the world's life support system which we have taken for granted in the past.

A planet under threat means the end of business as usual. So we must rethink our approach to wealth creation, in particular, moving from an exploitative to a regenerative mode, reducing resource use, recycling products and eliminating waste. In addition, we must undo much of the damage that has been done. This can be costly—for example, it has cost A$137 million to clean up Homebush Bay in Sydney for the Year 2000 Olympics. Corporations have to rethink all phases of their productive activity to ensure they are sustainable—in other words, compatible with maintaining a healthy workforce, society and natural environment.

Is sustainability good business?

Von Weizsäcker and others have written a book (*Factor 4: Doubling Wealth—Halving Resource Use*) that contains many examples of businesses which have more than quadrupled their productivity while halving their resource use. Far from reducing productivity and profits, an increasing number of corporations are finding that fostering sustainability actually increases these outcomes. To give an Australian example, Pacific Power owns and operates the Eraring Power Station on Lake Macquarie in NSW. Some of the immense amount of water it requires was previously purchased from the local water board. Pacific Power involved its employees in looking for ways to make its operations more environmentally friendly. It established quality teams, one of which looked at ways to reduce water usage. Eraring now takes sewage from the area's water treatment plant which it filters using a Memtech filtration plant and a reverse osmosis plant installed at a cost of A$4.5 million. The filtration water is used for the production of electricity at the power station. As a result, plans to construct an expensive ocean outfall for the area have not gone ahead. There have been large savings for Eraring, the government and the local community. This is a win–win situation for all concerned.

Some companies have strenuously pursued a goal of zero emissions, in other words eliminating all waste or recycling it. The Nagoya Plant of the Kirin Brewery company in Shinkawa, Japan, reached zero emissions in 1997. Beer dregs are used as livestock feed, yeast is recycled for pharmaceuticals. Much of what was formerly thrown away is now sold to other firms (Ota, 1998).

It is possible to reduce the footprint of our activities on the planet. One way of doing this is to eliminate the concept of waste by understanding that our waste may be someone else's resource. R-recycle Australia is using innovative US technology to process worn truck and car tyres. The result is a highly versatile product that offers improved performance in items such as retreads, shoes and conveyor belts while cutting materials costs by up to 30 per cent. With eighteen million tyres thrown away in Australia each year, the waste represents a valuable new resource (Hooper, 1998).

Steps to corporate sustainability

There is an enormous difference in the readiness of various corporations to move toward sustainable practices. Some firms are highly advanced in terms of having invested in the capabilities, knowledge and skills of their workforce, but have given little or no thought to ecological sustainability. Others are the reverse of that. We need some measure of organisational progress in this regard and we need to develop appropriate change strategies for organisations to advance steadily toward ful sustainability . Within the corporate sustainability research project at the Centre for Corporate Change, AGSM, we have developed a model to allow us to make systematic comparisons between organisations, and units within an organisation, of such progress. We refer to this model as 'Phases in the development of corporate sustainability' (see Appendix 1.1).

The 'phases' represent what social scientists refer to as a set of 'ideal types', that is, they are an intellectual framework for analysing some aspect of reality. In this case, they are meant to be a tool that we can use to make meaningful comparisons between organisations about their relative levels of commitment to the two kinds of sustainability that we are concerned about (human and ecological). The phases outline a set of distinct steps organisations can take in progressing to sustainability. It is a progression from active antagonism, through indifference, to a strong commitment to actively furthering sustainability values, not only within the organisation itself but within the industry and society as a whole.

We can use the phases to characterise the organisation's current strategic stance, that is, its characteristic way of treating the human and natural resources that it uses. We can also use it to trace the historical trajectory that the organisation has taken in getting to where it is. We do not assume that a firm necessarily progresses through the phases step by step on an 'improving' trajectory. To the contrary, it is quite possible for an organisation to leapfrog phases or to regress, that is to move back down the ladder. (This is likely to be triggered, for example, by the appointment of a new CEO or major changes in the firm's economic environment.)

Similarly, an organisation may adopt a different strategic stance on sustainability (that is, be in a different phase) in the human and the ecological areas. The organisation as a whole may, for instance, have relatively enlightened human resource strategies (HS5) yet be simultaneously pursuing an unsustainable ecological strategy (ES2). An example of this might be a mining company that invests strongly in the training and development of its employees and subcontractors but which operates environmentally polluting mining operations. Different divisions or strategic business units within the organisation may also vary in terms of the phase of sustainability they are at. For instance, one division may have adopted an HS5 approach while another may have adopted an HS3 approach.

Overall, the phase model allows us to make systematic comparisons between organisations or organisational units in terms of how sustainable their strategies are and the kind of contribution they are making (or not making) to the sustainability movement. Having categorised the organisation's current position, the framework then suggests an appropriate direction for the organisation to move to increase its contribution to sustainable practices.

The way forward

The encouraging fact is that an increasing number of organisations are finding that investing in people rather than divesting them, and renewing natural resources rather than wasting or degrading them, also makes sense in business terms. These corporate strategies are the secret to creating the high performance organisations of the future—and will inevitably contribute to the sustainability of society and our general way of life. This book is a trumpet call to arouse all who work for modern corporations, or consult to them, to actively contribute to this shift in corporate consciousness and to create the practices that will promote a healthy way of life for the planet and those who inhabit it.

We turn now to an overview of the chapters that make up this book.

An introduction to the chapters

This book represents a diversity of opinions and perspectives on the sustainability debate. Each chapter reflects the individual author's sphere of knowledge and personal background as a social scientist, change agent, human resource professional, environmental scientist, ecological consultant or 'green' activist. The book consists of four parts. Part I serves as an introduction to corporate sustainability. Parts II and III focus on specific aspects of human and ecological sustainability respectively— aspects such as corporate capabilities, technologies and processes, and issues of quality and strategy. Finally, Part IV incorporates material on new organisational architectures, guiding principles and implementation strategies for achieving corporate sustainability.

In Chapter 2, 'Sustainability and sustainable development', Mark Diesendorf addresses such fundamental questions as: 'Why do we need sustainable development?; 'What are sustainability and sustainable development?'; and 'What roles do corporations play in pathways toward sustainable and unsustainable futures?' His chapter outlines a framework for understanding sustainability and for pursuing sustainable development. The framework includes underlying ethical principles, broad goals, measurable objectives and a broad strategy for the implementation of sustainable deveopment. His chapter reminds us that although human society has made dramatic technological advances over the past two centuries, we remain totally dependent for our survival upon the continued functioning of natural systems.

In Chapter 3, 'Sustainability—doing it', Paul Gilding discusses the 'how' of sustainability—that is: 'What are the drivers and processes?'; 'Who are the main players and what are their roles in furthering the transition to a more sustainable world?' Gilding explores the historical development of sustainability and other broad trends driving change in the economy and discusses how 'self-interest' positions different players in the sustainability debate, including business, activists and governments. He argues that sustainability has become a competitive issue and that those corporations that recognise this will be rewarded not only by increased shareholder value but also by way of a more satisfied and motivated workforce and a more sustainable and robust corporation.

Chapter 4 is the first of three chapters focusing on specific aspects of human sustainability. In 'Human resources, capabilities and sutainability', Paul Gollan addresses such questions as: 'How do organisations currently utilise and apply human resources?'; 'How do organisations deteriorate or renew these resources and what are the implications of such approaches for employers and employees?'; and 'How can we redefine the ways organisations use their human resources in order to ensure human sustainability?' He argues that true sustainability requires the organisation to recognise and place value on human capabilities and that this entails taking a more holistic and integrated approach to people management.

In Chapter 5, 'Technologies and processes for human sustainability', Viv Read explores ways that technologies and processes are able to enhance workplaces and work spaces, provide environments where people enjoy working and learning, and assist in building and sustaining meaningful relationships with stakeholders. She considers the meaning of sustainability from the perspective of the employer and the employee and outlines a framework for a sustainable work environment. Read does warn, however, that the glitter and glamour offered by new technologies have the potential to obscure the real challenge for human sustainability—that of developing and sustaining effective relationships and ensuring the psychological health and well-being of all stakeholders.

In Chapter 6, 'Quality of work, home and community life', Jodie Benveniste explores the wider context in which corporations operate and argues that corporations have an important societal as well as economic role to play in the knowledge economy. She outlines, in particular, five areas requiring corporate attention. These include re-envisaging the corporation as: (1) providing community employment; (2) ensuring work/life balance; (3) pursuing and promoting diversity; (4) being an active member of community; and (5) being driven by values incorporating human and ecological sustainability. Benveniste argues that corporations that remodel themselves along these lines will be the backbone of the new economy, and those that don't face the prospect of failure.

Chapter 7 is the first of three chapters focusing on specific aspects of ecological sustainability. In 'Building corporate capabilities to promote ecological sustainability', Philip Sutton considers the broad capabilities and more specific competencies that corporations may need if they are to be effective in promoting sustainability and in meeting their commercial objectives. These include mindsets and values, thinking, technical and management skills and new knowledge. The remainder of the chapter focuses on a fictional 'case study', 'Paradyme Corporation', which illustrates how capabilities and competencies of direct relevance to ecological sustainability can be orchestrated and deployed in a real life setting.

Chapter 8, 'Technologies and processes for ecological sustainability', is a parallel chapter to Viv Read's Chapter 4, on technologies and processes for human sustainability. In Chapter 8 Alan Pears considers the role technology and processes play in moving toward ecological sustainability. He outlines a practical approach to moving toward ecological sustainability by asking a number of pertinent questions such as: 'How does my business impact on the environment?'; 'How, and to what extent, can I influence these environmental impacts?'; and 'Can I envisage a scenario in which my business is ecologically sustainable?' Pears provides two examples of businesses, one a service provider, the other a manufacturer of appliances, which illustrate how technology and environmental improvement can lead to ecological sustainability.

In Chapter 9, 'The technology strategy of the sustainable corporation', Hardin Tibbs argues that the modern-day organisation is the product of global industrial development where a corporation's main objective was to achieve maximum economic output and growth. This was a socially acceptable objective during the exponential phase following the industrial revolution. In contrast, the sustainable corporation is the prospective future form of the corporation after the physical expansion phase of industrialisation decelerates. In this chapter, Tibbs outlines how a new technology meta-strategy for the corporation can envisage not only a sustainable corporation but a sustainable society in a post-industrialist world.

In Chapter 10, 'New organisational architectures: Creating and retrofitting for sustainability', Andrew Griffiths considers the issue of corporate structure and its relation to sustainability. In particular, he asks: 'How can current organisational architectures, practices and routines impede the development of sustainable organisations?'; 'What kinds of corporate architectures will characterise the sustainable corporation?'; and 'How do we transform corporate architectures to create sustainable practices?' Griffiths examines the limitations of current corporate architectures and considers new alternatives such as network organisations, virtual organisations and organisations as communities of practice.

In Chapter 11, 'Guiding principles: The way ahead', Molly Harriss Olson and Phillip Toyne discuss the important concept of guiding principles for corporate sustainability. A wide range of examples of sustainability principles already in operation are discussed including the

Natural Step, William McDonough's 'four R's', and the Coalition for Environmentally Responsible Economies' principles for assessing socially responsible investments. This chapter illustrates how guiding principles can serve as a compass to steer a course toward a new paradigm for the corporation and in doing so, move the organisation toward sustainability.

In the final chapter, 'Implementing the sustainable corporation', Dexter Dunphy considers strategies for implementing the sustainable corporation by suggesting ways to bring new organisational forms into being and by considering the social context required for change. Dunphy considers both evolutionary and transformative approaches to change, outlines a number of key success factors in corporate change programs and discusses the role of change agents in the change process. Dunphy parallels corporate change with the need for an inner transformation, that is, the role of individual consciousness and personal action in creating the sustainable corporation.

Considered together, the chapters create a debate about the nature of corporate sustainability and the ways it can be achieved. We have sought no consensus among the authors—to the contrary, we have encouraged a diversity of views. The result is, in our opinion, a significant contribution to the construction of a new world view—a world view which will determine the future pattern of our global civilisation and whether, in fact, our civilisation has a sustainable future at all. This is not an idle academic debate but a serious and profound discussion of the conditions for the survival of human and other species on this planet. We urge you to read this book, join the debate and participate in the action.

Endnotes

1 Part of this chapter appeared in the winter 99 issue of *AGSM*, the magazine of the Australian Graduate School of Management, under the title, 'Sustainability: The secret of high performance'.

2 The '1st Corporate Sustainability Conference' was held from 17– 19 July 1998. The '2nd Corporate Sustainability Conference' was held from 9–11 April 1999. Both conferences were hosted by the Centre for Corporate Change at the AGSM. Conference participants were all members of the Corporate Sustainability Network.

Appendix 1.1 Phases in the development of corporate sustainability

1 REJECTION

Human sustainability (HSI)

Employees and subcontractors are regarded as a resource to be exploited. Health and safety features are ignored or given 'lip service'. Disadvantages stemming from ethnicity, gender, social class, intellectual ability and language proficiency are systematically exploited to advantage the organisation and further disadvantage employees and subcontractors. Force, threats of force and abuse are used to maintain compliance and workforce subjection. Training costs are kept to a minimum necessary to operate the business; expenditure on personal and professional development is avoided. The organisation does not take responsibility for the health, welfare and future career prospects of its employees nor for the community in which it is a part. Community concerns are rejected outright.

Ecological sustainability (ESI)

The environment is regarded as a 'free good' to be exploited. Owners/managers are hostile to environmental activists and to pressures from government, other corporations, or community groups aimed at achieving ecological sustainability. Pro-environmental action is seen as a threat to the organisation. Physical resource extraction and production processes are used which directly destroy future productive capacity and/or damage the ecosystem. Polluting by-products are discharged into the biosphere causing damage and threatening living processes. The organisation does not take responsibility for the environmental impact of its ongoing operations nor does it modify its operations to lessen future ecological degradation.

2 NON-RESPONSIVENESS

Human sustainability (HS2)

Financial and technological factors dominate business strategies to the exclusion of most aspects of human resource management. 'Industrial relations' (IR) or 'employee relations' (ER) strategies dominate the human agenda with 'labour' viewed as a cost to be minimised. Apart from cost minimisation, IR/ER strategies are directed at developing a compliant workforce responsive to managerial control. The training agenda, if there is one, centres on technical and supervisory training. Broader human resource strategies and policies are ignored as are issues of wider social responsibility and community concern.

Ecological sustainability (ES2)

The ecological environment is not considered to be a relevant factor in strategic or operational decisions. Financial and technological factors dominate business strategies to the exclusion of environmental concerns. Traditional approaches to efficiency dominate the production process and the environment is taken for granted. Environmental resources that are free or subsidised (air, water, etc.) are wasted and little regard is given to environmental degradation resulting from the organisation's activities. Environmental risks, costs, opportunities and imperatives are seen as irrelevant or not perceived at all.

3 COMPLIANCE/RISK REDUCTION

Human sustainability (HS3)

Financial and technological factors still dominate business strategies but senior management views the firm as a 'decent employer'. The emphasis is on compliance with legal requirements in IR, safety, workplace standards etc. Human resource functions such as training, IR, organisation development, total quality management (TQM) are instituted but there is little integration between them. Basically the organisation pursues a policy of legal compliance plus benevolent paternalism, with the expectation of employee loyalty in response. Community concerns are addressed only when the company faces risk of prosecution or where negative publicity may have a damaging impact on the company's financial bottom line.

Ecological sustainability (ES3)

Financial and technological factors still dominate business strategies but senior management seeks to comply with environmental laws and to minimise the firm's potential liabilities from actions that might have an adverse impact on the environment. The most obvious environmental abuses are eliminated, particularly those that could lead to litigation or strong community action directed against the firm. Other environmental issues, which are unlikely to attract litigation or strong community action, are ignored.

4 EFFICIENCY

Human sustainability (HS4)

There is a systematic attempt to integrate human resource functions to reduce costs and increase efficiency. Human resource functions are integrated into a coherent HR system. People are viewed as a significant source of expenditure to be used as productively as possible. Technical and supervisory training is augmented with human relations (interpersonal skills) training. The organisation may institute programs of teamwork around significant business functions and generally pursues a value adding rather than an exclusively cost reduction strategy. There is careful calculation of cost/benefit ratios for human resource expenditure to ensure that efficiencies are achieved. Community projects are undertaken where funds are available and where a cost benefit to the company can be illustrated.

Ecological sustainability (ES4)

Poor environment practice is seen as an important source of avoidable cost. Ecological issues that generate costs are systematically reviewed in an attempt to reduce costs and increase efficiencies by eliminating waste and by reviewing the procurement, production and distribution process. There may be active involvement in some systematic approach such as total quality environmental management (ISO 14001). Enviromental issues that are not seen as generating avoidable costs or increasing efficiencies are ignored.

5 STRATEGIC SUSTAINABILITY

Human sustainability (HS5)

The workforce skills mix and diversity are seen as an integral and vitally important aspect of corporate and business strategies. Intellectual and social capital are used to develop strategic advantage through innovation in products/services. Programs are instituted to recruit the best talent to the organisation and to develop high levels of competence in individuals and groups. In addition, skills are systematised to form the basis of corporate competencies so that the organisation is less vulnerable to the loss of key individuals. Emphasis is placed on product and service innovation and speed of response to emerging market demands. Flexible workplace practices are strong features of workplace culture and contribute to the workforce leading more balanced lives. Communities affected by the organisation's operations are taken into account and initiatives to address adverse impacts on communities are integrated into corporate strategy. Furthermore, the corporation views itself as a member of the community and as a result contributes to community betterment by offering sponsorship or employee time to participate in projects aimed at promoting community cohesion and well-being.

Ecological sustainability (ES5)

Proactive environmental strategies supporting ecological sustainability are seen as a source of strategic business opportunities to provide competitive advantage. Product redesign is used to reduce material throughput and to use materials that can be recycled. New products and processes are developed that substitute for or displace existing environmentally damaging products and processes or satisfy emerging community needs around sustainable issues (reforestation; treatment of toxic waste). The organisation seeks competitive leadership through spearheading environmentally friendly products and processes.

6 IDEOLOGICAL COMMITMENT

Human sustainability (HS6)

The organisation accepts responsibility for contributing to the process of renewing and upgrading human knowledge and skill formation in the community and society generally, and is a strong promoter of workplace diversity and work/life balance as workplace principles. It adopts a strong and clearly defined corporate

Ecological sustainability (ES6)

The organisation becomes an active promoter of ecological sustainability values and seeks to influence key participants in the industry and society in general. Environmental best practice is espoused and enacted because it is the responsible thing to do. The organisation tries to assist society to be ecologically sustainable ethical position based on multiple stakeholder perspectives and seeks to exert influence on the key participants in the industry and in society in general to pursue human welfare, equitable and just social practices, and the fulfillment of human potential for all.

society to be ecologically sustainable and uses its entire range of products and services to this end. The organisation is prepared to use its influence to promote positive sustainability policies on the part of governments, the restructuring of markets and the development of community values to facilitate the emergence of a sustainable society.

References

Collins, J. and Porras, J. 1994 *Built to Last: Successful Habits of Visionary Companies*, Century, London.

Glenn, J. R. and Gordon, T. J. 1998 *State of the Future Report: Issues and Opportunities*, American Council for the United Nations University: The Millennium Project, Washington.

Hooper, N. 1998 'Recycled rubber hits the road to success', *Business Review Weekly*, 3 August: http://www.brw.com.au/content/030898/brw12.htm

Ota, M. 1998 'Cutting edge: The zero emissions challenge', *Aichi Voice*, vol. 9: http://www.pref.aichi.jp/voice/9_cutting_edge.html

Pfeffer, J. 1998 *The Human Equation: Building Profits by Putting People First*, Harvard Business School Press, Boston.

Turner, D. and Crawford, M. 1998 *Change Power: Capabilities that Drive Corporate Renewal*, Woodslane, Sydney.

2

Sustainability and sustainable development

Mark Diesendorf

Introduction

The aim of this chapter is to provide a framework for discussing the fundamental questions:

- What are sustainability and sustainable development?
- Why do we need sustainable development?
- What roles do corporations play in pathways towards sustainable and unsustainable futures?
- What is the difference between the sustainability of a corporation and the promotion of sustainability by a corporation?
- In broad terms, how can corporations implement sustainable development?'

The reasons why there is a need for sustainable development are summarised in the second section. Then the concepts of sustainability and sustainable development, in forms that can be readily applied to both the planet and human society, are introduced. The role of corporations in sustainable development is outlined in the fourth section while in the fifth section a framework for understanding sustainability and pursuing sustainable development is presented. This framework sets out explicitly the underlying ethical assumptions, broad goals, measurable objectives and action measures for implementation, and integrates ecological, social and economic aspects of sustainability. The last main section outlines a broad strategy for implementation of sustainable development, drawing on examples from the possible role of corporations.

The need for sustainable development

In the twentieth century human societies made amazing technological achievements, such as skyscrapers, agro-food industries, personal computers, heart transplants, jumbo jets and landing people on the moon. However, the achievements have blinded us to our limitations. The Biosphere 2 experiment in the US has shown that, despite the expenditure of hundreds of millions of dollars, we cannot as yet keep an artificial ecosystem, including a small group of people, alive in a self-sustaining manner under an airtight dome on the surface of the earth. Despite the expenditure of billions of dollars, we cannot as yet keep alive in a self-sustaining manner a single astronaut in a satellite orbiting the earth. Despite our technological achievements, we humans are totally dependent for our survival upon the continued functioning of natural systems.

Unfortunately, many of us, especially those living in cities, share the delusion that we are somehow independent of nature. We forget about the free but essential services that nature provides for us. For instance, plant life provides the oxygen we breathe and, directly and indirectly, the food we eat. (Even human meat eaters depend on plant-eating animals.) The natural, bio-geochemical cycles ensure that water, carbon, oxygen and essential elements, such as phosphorus and nitrogen, are recycled. It is true that a few natural systems are replaceable by artificial ones, but only at enormous economic cost. For instance, we could continue to sacrifice our topsoil and in theory grow all our food by hydroponics. However, in practice this would be extremely expensive—we cannot live off tomatoes and lettuces alone.

Over the past four decades, many important books have been written by scientists and other scholars about the adverse impacts of humans on their life support systems (for example, Carson 1962; Commoner 1972; Birch 1975; Ehrlich & Ehrlich 1990; Boyden, Dovers & Shirlow 1990; McMichael 1993; World Resources Institute 1994; Brown et al. (various years)). In addition, warning statements have been issued to humanity by large groups of eminent scientists (for example, Union of Concerned Scientists 1992; Science Summit 1993). On a large scale the principal impacts of humans on the environment are:

- changes, possibly irreversible, to the composition of the atmosphere and therefore to earth's climate
- destruction of stratospheric ozone and therefore increased damage to living organisms from ultraviolet light in sunshine
- degradation of topsoil and increases in desertification
- loss of biological diversity

- damage to photosynthesis and nutrient cycles
- widespread pollution of air, rivers and oceans
- depletion of artesian water storages.

In the socio-economic aspects of sustainability, there are several major areas of concern, especially when we consider international trends over the past 20–25 years:

- A large body of evidence exists to suggest that the gap between rich and poor has been increasing, both between countries and within many countries. This gap has even increased in countries that were recently regarded as great powers—such as the UK, the US and the former Soviet Union.
- Human rights violations are still endemic in many countries. Although there has been great progress in human rights in most developed countries, there are still quite serious problems in some, such as the US and Australia. Grounds for concern include the racial composition of prison populations, the unaccountability of internal security agencies, the funding of dictatorships in developing countries by government agencies in developed countries, and the denial of basic human rights to refugees and illegal migrants.
- Debt and economic slavery are still prevalent. With the erosion of minimum working conditions and wages in several developed countries, the rise of sweatshops appears to be a growing problem in the US and Australia.
- A large proportion of the world's population has inadequate diet, nutrition and access to drinking water.
- A large proportion of the world's children live in poverty. Ethnic groups, indigenous people and other minorities in nominally rich countries are generally at risk.
- Preventable and treatable diseases are prevalent. In the poor countries, infectious diseases are still widespread, while in 'rich' countries the diseases of civilisation—diseases of the circulatory system, cancer and mental illness—are prevalent, while minorities still suffer severely from infectious diseases.
- A large proportion of the world's population is still illiterate.
- There are still many refugees resulting from war, political persecution, environmental destruction and economic hardship.
- Despite significant overall advances made during the twentieth century, the status of women is still generally below that of men, even in the US and Australia.
- The dominant economic system leads to inequities in the access to resources.

The evidence supporting these points is set out in Tabatabai (1993); UNICEF (1994); UNDP (1996); UNHCR (1997); Ellwood (1998); and World Bank (1999).

Clearly, sustainable development, involving improvements to the natural environment and in the social and economic domains, is needed in the 'rich' countries as well as in the 'poor'.

What are sustainability and sustainable development?

We take the view that sustainability and sustainable development are contestable concepts, like democracy, truth and justice (Jacobs, 1991). They cannot be defined in the same way that physical scientists might define the standard metre. Indeed, discussion and debate about the concepts of sustainability and sustainable development provide a focus for contact between contending positions (Myerson & Rydin, 1996) and so become essential parts of the practical process of working towards sustainability.

Nevertheless, some kind of description of the concepts is necessary to establish the broad domain of discussion. For instance, many proponents of sustainability, sustainable futures and sustainable development might not wish these concepts to be applied to the economic success of a company which manufactures weapons of mass destruction, or to the maintenance of the futures market for stocks and shares.

Sustainability and sustainable futures are treated here as the goals or endpoints of a process called 'sustainable development'. A sustainable society is considered to be a society that has reached sustainability through this process. So, it remains to define 'sustainable development'.

The well-known broad definition in the Brundtland Report (WCED, 1987) is: 'Sustainable development is development that meets the needs of the present without compromising the ability of future generations to meet their own needs.' This definition emphasises the long term aspect of the concept of sustainability and introduces the ethical principle of achieving equity between the present and future generations. The context in which the definition is embedded indicates that 'needs' include a sound environment, a just society and a healthy economy. Sustainable development is not intended to mean sustaining practices, industries and organisations that are harmful to these three requirements.

While providing a valuable perspective on sustainable development, the Brundtland Report's definition is limited in several ways. As part of a political document (in the sense of involving power structures in international relations), the definition appears to equate 'needs' with 'wants' and to assume that economic growth is necessarily part of development. Because it does not clearly distinguish between different types of economic structure, it appears to support growth in the use of materials and energy, a form of economic growth that damages the natural environment. The definition does not mention the natural environment explicitly, focusing only on human needs or wants. However, the report as a whole makes it clear that these 'needs' include the conservation of the natural environment.

Our broad definition of sustainable development is: 'Sustainable development comprises types of economic and social development that protect and enhance the natural environment and social equity.' This broad definition conveys explicitly that there are three principal aspects—ecological, economic and social—and that the ecological aspect and social equity are primary. Furthermore, this description does not support trade-offs between environment, economy and society. It says that any type of social or economic development is sustainable, *provided* that it protects and enhances the environment and social equity.

'Development' as used here covers social and economic improvement in a broad sense, as summarised below. It may or may not involve economic growth. The emphasis is not on economic growth per se but rather on 'qualitative improvement in human well-being' or 'unfolding of human potential', as discussed by the ecological economist, Herman Daly.

Protecting the natural environment is not intended to mean 'freezing' ecosystems to the extent that natural evolutionary and ecological processes cannot occur, but rather means 'keeping changes at non-catastrophic, pre-human rates'.

The importance of ecological sustainability follows from the fact that the economy and society depend ultimately on the integrity of the biosphere and the ecological processes occurring within it. As mentioned in the previous section, nature provides human societies and economies with a complex life support system, comprising among other things air, water, food and a suitable climate for survival, as well as the physical resources which are currently the foundation of economies. We interfere with these natural systems at our own risk. For this reason, our broad definition of sustainable development makes the ecological aspect a constraint on types of economic and social development.

In Australia, the adjective 'ecologically' is normally placed before 'sustainable development' to indicate the primacy of the ecological aspect of sustainability and to remind us that the concept of sustainable development is not intended to support the development of environmentally damaging industries. A more accurate term would be 'ecologically sustainable and socially equitable development'. However, in this chapter, this is shortened to the well-known international term, 'sustainable development'.

Box 2.1 Some components of human well-being

- Access to clean air and water
- Adequate diet
- Adequate dwellings
- Personal security, both physical and emotional
- Opportunities for learning
- Opportunities for cooperative small-group interaction
- An emotional support network
- Opportunities for creative behaviour
- An appropriate pattern of physical exercise
- An environment and a lifestyle that do not promote a sense of alienation, of anomie, of being deprived, of boredom, of loneliness or of chronic frustration

Source: After Boyden & Dovers, 1997

Social equity is used here in the sense of 'equal opportunity' rather than 'equality'. With this interpretation, sustainability could, in principle, exist under some forms of capitalism and some forms of socialism.

In subsequent chapters of this book, the economic and social aspects of sustainability are combined into a single aspect called 'human sustainability'. However, here we keep these aspects separate in order to emphasise the importance of the non-economic, social aspects of sustainability. In our broad definition of sustainability, these enter through social equity and many components of human well-being that cannot be described by economic indicators alone (see Box 2.1).

Together, these and other conditions may be considered to describe a state of human health. While they all can be influenced to some degree by economic conditions, they are clearly determined to a large degree by social structure and institutions.

Role of corporations in sustainable development

In this chapter a corporation is considered to be 'an association of individuals, created by law or under authority of law, having a continuous existence irrespective of that of its members, and powers and liabilities distinct from those of its members' (*Macquarie Dictionary*, 1981). A corporation is one element of an economy, and the economy is one element of a society. So, corporations contribute to the sustainability or unsustainability of a society and the planet as a whole, but do not totally determine it.

Corporations impact on the natural environment, their own work-forces and society at large and so affect the sustainability of the planet and society. They make these impacts through their choices of raw materials and suppliers, land use, geographic locations, manufacturing processes including creation of wastes and pollution, organisational structures, financial arrangements, management systems, employment and work practices, customer services, community activities, uses of information and lobbying. Their social impacts are both direct (for example, those following from the locations of their offices and factories) and indirect (for example, by creating models of consumption which are copied in the community at large).

It is sometimes argued that corporations operate on behalf of consumers and so it is consumers alone who are responsible for the impacts of corporations. This view treats corporations as the passive instruments of consumer demand. In reality, corporations shape consumer demand and the market in various ways. For example, they create consumption by advertising and marketing. They acquire and store knowledge that is not always publicly available and then release it selectively. In this way, they also define 'goods' and 'services' and create new products. This can influence sustainability, for better or worse, as shown by the example in Box 2.2.

Corporations also lobby governments to create laws and other conditions that are favourable for their operations and products. For instance, they may have limited liability, tax deductions for investments, infrastructure provided by government, subsidised energy and patent protection. Clearly, corporations are important players in the sustainability scene. Therefore, creating a sustainable society must involve changes to corporations as well to other social institutions.

In pursuing the goal of sustainable development, the most obvious contribution that corporations can make is to improve the quality and efficiency of their own internal operations, without changing the kinds of products they sell. For example, a car manufacturer might practice this aspect of sustainable development by:

- implementing cleaner production processes, including design for disassembly
- replacing a 'fordist' production line with work teams
- making buildings energy efficient
- reducing noise and local air pollution within the factory and beyond its boundaries

Box 2.2 Should utilities supply energy or energy services?

This example shows how defining goods and services affects sustainability. Until the 1980s, the emphasis in the energy sector was on energy supply. This emphasis was part of the old paradigm that the more energy we use, the better off we are. Utilities supplied energy, in the form of electricity or oil or natural gas. Consumers were taught to seek the cheapest energy in terms of the cost of a kilowatt-hour of electricity, or a megajoule of natural gas, or a litre of petrol. However, recently, the concept of 'energy service company' (ESCO) has emerged. ESCOs supply energy services such as warm houses in winter, cold food and drink, clean clothes and hot showers. In a least cost approach, an energy service is generally provided by means of a combination of energy supply and efficient energy use. For instance, the least cost warm home may include passive solar design, insulation and draught exclusion, and the least cost hot shower usually involves a water-efficient showerhead. In this approach, it is not the cost per unit of energy that is important, but rather the total energy bill. By reducing the number of energy units used wastefully, the consumer can often pay more for a unit of energy and still have a lower energy bill. By changing the concept of the product from 'energy' to 'energy services', corporations and the rest of society can simultaneously improve economic efficiency and improve the natural environment.

- building new plant in an industrial ecology park close to a railway station and offering public transport travel passes as part of employment packages
- placing strict environmental and social equity requirements on suppliers
- consulting with local community about noise, pollution, transport, parking, working hours and the provision of public facilities by the corporation.

A more challenging aspect of sustainable development is a corporation's decision to stop producing certain types of products and services, because of their negative environmental and social impacts. Should a corporation refrain from making cars, even cleaner ones? If it does, would another corporation fill the alleged niche? If we take the view that corporations help create demand for something by marketing it, then the decision to stop marketing it may reduce demand for it. In this way the decision by a large corporation could change the market and hence, in a small way, the structure of the national economy, so that 'bads' become less popular than 'goods'.

Following a suggestion by Philip Sutton in this book (see Chapter 7), a corporation which is successfully integrating sustainable development into its strategy, both in terms of its operations and the kinds of 'goods' or 'bads' it sells, is called here a 'sustainability-promoting corporation'. Of course, the degree to which the corporation is promoting sustainability will have to be taken into account. Some corporations may be simultaneously promoting and damaging sustainability: for example, an oil company which has invested substantially in renewable energy; a tourist company that provides both traditional tourism (with substantial negative impacts on biodiversity) and genuine ecotourism.

The term 'sustainable corporation' is avoided here, because its most obvious meaning is simply a long-lived corporation. Long-lived corporations do not necessarily produce an ecologically sustainable planet and a socially equitable society. Do we really want to sustain corporations based on child labour, or making weapons of aggression, junk food and cigarettes? However, there is some evidence that corporations which build sound, responsive relationships with all their stakeholders—including employees, suppliers, customers, investors and local communities—tend to be longer lived and more successful as businesses in the long term than other corporations (Wheeler & Sillanpää, 1997).

For this reason alone, a corporation may choose to become sustainability-promoting. However, there are other business reasons as well for becoming a sustainability-promoting organisation:

- To reduce the risk of litigation and consumer boycotts resulting from perceived bad practice. Examples are the ongoing litigation experienced by tobacco corporations; the severe boycotts experienced in Europe by Shell as fallout from its plan to dispose of the Brent Spar oil rig and its perceived role in the environmental and social damage in Nigeria; and the ongoing boycotts experienced by Nestlé, for its promotion of artificial milk formula in less developed countries.
- To reduce production costs through more efficient use of energy and materials, and turning wastes into resources or marketable products. (But note that this is not always the case—sometimes there can be significant additional costs.)
- To secure market advantage and product differentiation for products and services produced in environmentally sound and socially just ways.
- To enhance customer loyalty by adapting to changing community expectations for better practice with respect to sustainability.

Before considering some of the ways in which corporations can become sustainability-promoting, we set out a general framework for understanding sustainability and for implementing sustainable development.

Figure 2.1 Model of sustainability and ecologically sustainable and socially equitable development

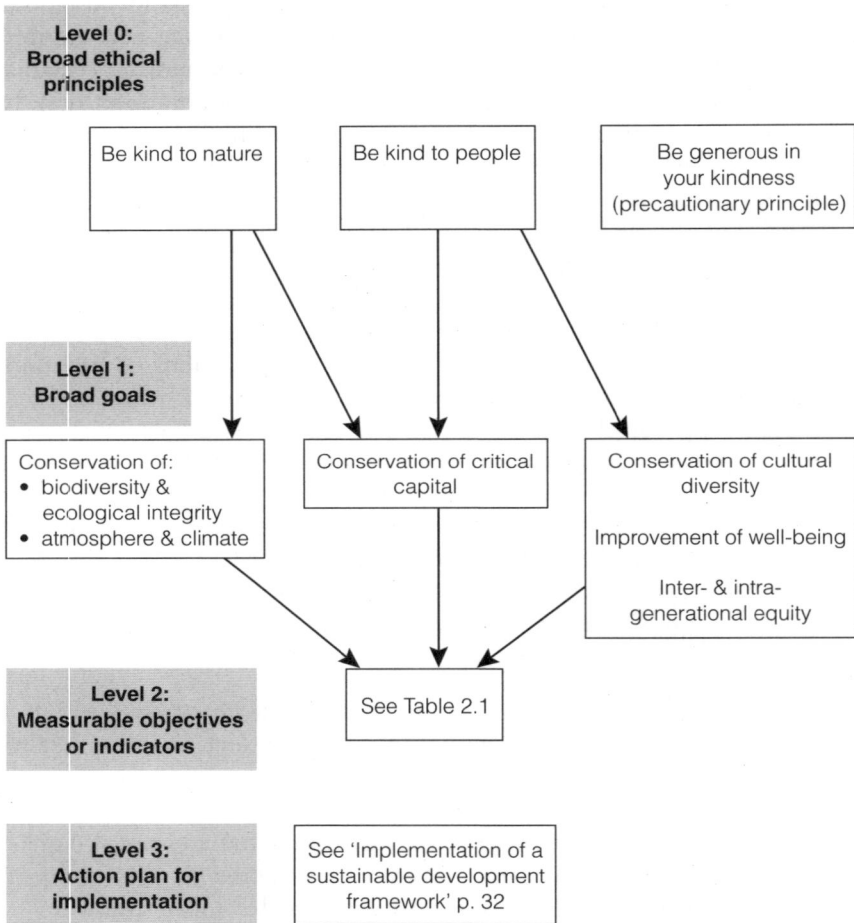

Level 0: Broad ethical principles		
Be kind to nature	Be kind to people	Be generous in your kindness (precautionary principle)

Level 1: Broad goals		
Conservation of: • biodiversity & ecological integrity • atmosphere & climate	Conservation of critical capital	Conservation of cultural diversity Improvement of well-being Inter- & intra-generational equity

Level 2: Measurable objectives or indicators	See Table 2.1

Level 3: Action plan for implementation	See 'Implementation of a sustainable development framework' p. 32

Framework for sustainability

As shown in Figure 2.1, the framework or model (Diesendorf, 1998) has four logical levels:

- Level 0, comprising the broad ethical principles
- Level 1, comprising broad goals arising from these principles
- Level 2, comprising measurable objectives or indicators
- Level 3, comprising the action plan for implementation of ecologically sustainable and socially equitable development.

Level 0

At Level 0 there are three principles:

- respect nature
- respect humans
- be generous in our respect.

The last is the Precautionary Principle. One version of this principle is given in the Australian Intergovernmental Agreement on the Environment (Australian Government, 1992): 'Where there are threats of serious or irreversible environmental damage, lack of full scientific certainty should not be used as a reason for postponing measures to prevent environmental degradation.'

These broad principles are actually ethical requirements. By ethics, we mean pertaining to questions of right or wrong, or good or bad. In the past, consideration of values and ethics was not popular in the business world. However, there are signs that this may be changing: for example, the World Business Academy and its journal *Perspectives on Business and Global Change*, published by Berrett-Koehler in San Francisco. Those who are uncomfortable with starting from an ethical position might consider that the above ethical principles are essential for the long term viability of the economy and society. Therefore, they could be seen as enlightened self-interest on the part of individuals and corporations planning for a long term future.

Level I

At Level 1, the broad goals to conserve or enhance inter- and intra-generational equity, human well-being, biodiversity and ecological integrity are widely supported ones in the sustainability literature. To these goals the 'conservation of cultural diversity' has been added here as a social analogue to the 'conservation of biodiversity'. It is implicit in several approaches to sustainability and can be justified in a similar way to the latter (Diesendorf, 1997). To find pathways to ecological sustainability, the dominant cultures of the early twenty-first century could learn something from pre-industrial cultures which are rapidly disappearing. We do not have to become hunter-gatherers or shifting agriculturalists to understand and in some cases to implement the general features of those societies that contributed to sustainability. Driven by necessity, they evolved appropriate social organisations, decision making processes, spiritual beliefs (including a conserver ethic), food harvesting processes and other appropriate technologies.

The goal of inter-generational equity is the basic thrust of the

Brundtland definition of sustainable development. If we accept this goal, then it can be argued that we must also accept the need for intra-generational (that is, social) equity. It should be recalled that, in this chapter, 'equity' does not mean 'equality', but rather 'equal opportunity'.

The 'conservation of natural capital', widely used in some models of sustainability, has been replaced here by the 'conservation of critical capital', because the former overlaps strongly with 'conservation of biodiversity and ecological integrity' and, even where it does not, there are vast quantities of some forms of natural capital (for example, sand) which are not in urgent need of conservation. 'Critical' capital facilitates a focus on those forms of natural and human-made capital which are threatened with damage, destruction or dispersion (for example, phosphorus, archaeological sites).

Conservation of atmosphere and climate is not normally included as a sustainability goal. However, in view of the seriousness of the present threat and the fact that the potential effects of climate change impact on biodiversity, ecological integrity and human health, it has been listed explicitly here alongside critical capital.

Level 2

There is a rapidly growing literature on sustainability indicators (for example, Daly & Cobb, 1990; Hamilton, 1997; Hart, 1998; Sustainable Seattle, 1995). Some examples of measurable objectives or sustainability indicators for a society are given in Table 2.1. Several of the indicators are really categories rather than indicators themselves, so further refinement is still needed. For example, in 'rate of materials flow' it is necessary to specify which materials and what kinds of flows.

Standard criteria for indicators in general are that they should be measurable, relevant, simple to use and understand, reliable, reproducible, and timely for decision making. Several authors suggest that sustainability indicators should, in addition, reflect something fundamental to the environmental, economic and social/cultural health of a community over generations (Hart, 1998).

The categories of indicator—'ecological', 'economic' and 'social'—are presented in quotes because there is considerable overlap between categories. For instance, vehicle kilometres travelled per capita (or VKT) has ecological implications from greenhouse gas emissions and local air pollution; economic implications for a city (for example, high VKT suggests urban sprawl and hence high infrastructure costs) and social implications in terms of isolation of people who do not work outside the home (especially women and young children) in outer suburbs and physical divisions through communities by major roads. This overlap

Table 2.1 Examples of some measurable objectives or sustainability indicators

'Ecological'	'Economic'	'Social'
Rate of materials' flow	Genuine progress indicator	Basic services within walking & cycling distances of dwellings
Rate of energy use	Distribution of household & personal income	Availability of day care for under 5s
Total & per capita rate of greenhouse gas emissions	Per cent of income needed to pay for basic 'needs' of a person	Levels of education, including literacy & numeracy
Vehicle kilometres travelled per capita	Per cent of children living in households with no adult earner	Life expectancies at birth and at age 20
Human population & growth rate	Mortgage repayments & rents relative to median income in region	Morbidity rates
Area of land degraded & polluted	Employment by top 5 companies in the region	Crime rates
Water pollution		Homelessness
Air pollution		Teaching of indigenous languages in schools

may be a useful criterion for a sustainability indicator, as opposed to an ordinary ecological or social or economic indicator. In devising sustainability indicators, we also try to put the observed quantity into a sustainability context: for instance, mortgage repayments and rents are related to the median income in the region.

It must be recognised that the measurable objectives are strongly dependent on cultural viewpoints. Some of these measurable objectives are only useful when applied to the whole planet, while others are appropriate only for specific regions, for example, 'developed' countries or bio-regions or municipalities. The development of indicators is still a non-trivial exercise. For the internal operations of a corporation, it is quite a specialised activity, especially for social indicators.

Sustainability indicators have an important place in the concept of sustainability and the process of sustainable development. Indicators are required for monitoring progress and are valuable for motivating action. However, they do not in themselves produce good policy and actions to implement it. To avoid creating inappropriate indicators, policy is first developed by asking the question: 'What behaviour am I seeking?' and then creating indicators to serve that policy (see below).

If we take the analogy of sustainability as a tree, the main trunks are now the broad ethical principles (Level 0), the main branches are the broad goals (Level 1), and the secondary branches are the measurable objectives (Level 2). The model will evolve with time, so we need not be disturbed that some major branches and many branches, twigs and leaves are only sketched in lightly or are even not yet visible. There is already plenty to do.

Implementation of a sustainable development framework

The foregoing section has examined a framework for answering the question: 'What is the scope of sustainability and how can we present it in a systematic manner, distinguishing between ethical principles, broad goals and objectives which are actionable and measurable?' This is illustrated in Levels 0–2 of Figure 2.1. To this sustainability framework must be added a systematic process for implementing it and for assessing progress towards it (Level 3).

The approach proposed in this chapter is to combine the most relevant and appropriate elements from the Ottawa Charter on health promotion and the set of action principles known as the Bellagio Principles (IISD, 1998). The Ottawa Charter arose from the first International Conference on Health Promotion, held in Ottawa in 1986 (WHO, 1997). Most of the charter can be readily applied to the health of the environment as well as to the health of people. Drawing on the Ottawa Charter and the Bellagio Principles, the following steps towards the implementation of ecologically sustainable and socially equitable development are proposed. Examples are drawn from business.

Step 1: Present a guiding vision, goals and scenarios

This essential step is identified in the Bellagio Principles. Without it, the other steps cannot be taken, at least, not in the direction of ecologically sustainable and socially equitable development. In practice this step involves both research and the facilitation of participatory processes. These can be combined into participatory action research (Carr & Kemmis, 1983; Cunningham, 1993; Toulmin & Gustavsen, 1996).

On some issues there are already quite clear visions, goals and scenarios for approaching sustainable systems: for example, sustainable energy scenarios based on the efficient use of renewable energy sources. For some businesses, the vision may simply involve an improvement in existing operations and products: for example, a manufacturer of electrical appliances may develop a refrigerator which is energy efficient, has reusable parts and is reliable. For other businesses, the vision may involve a change in products, for example, from building coal-fired power stations to wind farms.

Step 2: Develop sustainability policy in all sectors, at all levels, with all types of instrument

Policy is a means of coordinating collective action for change. It is made by governments, businesses, trade unions, professional organisations and community organisations. Sustainability policy has some special features, due to the pervasiveness of uncertainty, irreversibility, non-linearity of systems, and broad spatial and temporal scales (Walker, 1994; Dovers, 1995). Sustainability policy must foster environmental protection and social equity; identify barriers to sustainability and ways of overcoming them (and so have a research component); and involve both the power structure and ordinary people.

The instruments for implementing sustainability policy may include:

- economic (taxes, charges, bounties, rebates, and targeted expenditure)
- regulatory (laws, codes, product certification and standards)
- education, communication, information and training
- institutional change (which is a combination of regulatory and economic instruments).

For example, using such instruments, a corporation could implement environmental policies for energy and water conservation, communication by email and by internal mail in reusable envelopes, ordering consumables, ordering components of goods to be manufactured, and solid waste minimisation based on the hierarchical principles of 'reduce, reuse and recycle'. It could also develop social policies on its interaction with the local community, ethical investment of its profits, and improved service for customers.

Step 3: Create supportive environments

Such environments may be physical, institutional or psychological. They include living and working conditions, technologies and facilities, plans and programs, and cultural support (for example, from films, theatre and songs). For example, a corporation could reduce the environmental and social impacts of motor car use by its employees and customers by locating its offices at a public transport node, by providing secure bicycle parking and showers, by offering executive packages that include yearly public transport tickets, and by organising car pooling.

Sustainability targets and indicators are required for this step. They are best developed through a consultative process involving a wide range of members of the community and the implementing organisation.

Step 4: Strengthen community action

Community action has an important role to play in social change processes, because it may facilitate bypassing the barriers erected by vested interests, empower the majority of stakeholders, provide a mutual learning experience, cross sectoral boundaries and, by involving all stakeholders, facilitate the implementation of decisions.

Community action may occur in a wide range of tasks: for example, in setting priorities, making decisions, planning strategies and participating in implementation. To do this effectively, members of the community require access to information and funding (or, within business, time off normal work).

In the case of a corporation, the 'community' may consist of all employees or even all stakeholders.

Step 5: Develop personal and organisational skills

These skills are developed by communication, education, information and training. They provide both personal and collective empowerment for social change. They may be acquired in school, home, work and community settings. They may be assisted by educational institutions, governments, employers and community organisations. For example, businesses could use training programs run by their human resources units, with inputs from external consultants. Such skill development is generally referred to as 'capacity building'.

Step 6: Reorient the system

This involves changing organisational structure and operations, whether the organisation concerned is a business, industry, government or United Nations program. The changes require sustainability policies and all the instruments listed in Step 2. These are institutionalised into a new system, which is a more supportive environment for ecologically sustainable and socially equitable development (Step 3). For example, the transformation of some energy supply utilities into energy service companies in the 1980s and 1990s, discussed in Box 2, required policies, legal constraints, 'cultural' changes to organisations, new programs and projects, and new financial mechanisms.

In some corporations on the pathway towards sustainability promotion, large changes in structure and work practices may be appropriate, for example, from production lines based on large teams of unskilled single-task workers to small teams of multi-task workers.

The above six steps add up to an action plan for the implementation of sustainable development. They can be applied to both the internal operations of a corporation and to the goods/bads and services they produce. Discussion and debate are an important aspect of all steps. The steps do not necessarily comprise a linear system, because each step may be revisited in a 'cycle of learning' in which an evaluation process provides the link between each cycle (see the action research literature cited previously). Indeed, Step 6 is really a combination of Steps 2 and 3, taken at a more general and powerful level.

The Bellagio Principles contribute some useful guidelines on how these steps should be implemented—namely with a holistic approach of adequate scope, a practical focus, broad participation, openness, ongoing assessment and adequate support.

Conclusion

Sustainability is treated here as the goal or endpoint of a process called 'sustainable development' or 'ecologically sustainable and socially equitable development'. Sustainable development comprises types of economic and social development which protect and enhance the natural environment, social equity and human well-being.

The concept of sustainability can be readily applied to the planet and to human society. However, in the case of corporations, it is more meaningful to consider the degree to which they are sustainability-promoting or sustainability-impeding. There are several good business reasons why corporations should follow the former path.

The model of sustainability presented in this paper integrates ecological, social and economic aspects without accepting trade-offs. It has four logical levels: ethical principles, broad goals, measurable objectives or indicators, and a broad strategy for implementation. It offers both a comprehensive theoretical framework and a six-step implementation strategy, involving action by government at all levels, business and community organisations. In essence, this strategy involves facilitating community participation and empowerment in order to create a vision and scenarios, to develop sustainability policy and to implement ecologically sustainable and socially equitable development by changing the system. Only then will we see major progress towards a sustainable society and planet.

References

Australian Government, 1992 *Intergovernmental Agreement on the Environment*, Department of the Environment, Canberra.

Birch, C. 1975 *Confronting the Future: Australia and the World: The Next Hundred Years*, Penguin, Harmondsworth.

Boyden, S., Dovers, S. and Shirlow, M. 1990 *Our Biosphere under Threat: Ecological Realities and Australia's Opportunities*, Oxford University Press, Melbourne.

Boyden, S. and Dovers, S. 1997 'Humans in the biosphere' in M. Diesendorf and C. Hamilton (eds), *Human Ecology, Human Economy: Ideas for an Ecologically Sustainable Future*, Allen & Unwin, Sydney, pp. 3–34.

Brown, L. R. et al. (various years) *State of the World Reports*, W. W. Norton, New York, annually from 1984.

Carr, W. and Kemmis, S. 1983 *Becoming Critical: Knowing through Action Research*, Deakin University, Waurn Ponds, Victoria.

Carson, R. 1962 *Silent Spring*, Houghton Mifflin, Boston.

Commoner, B. 1972 *The Closing Circle*, Bantam, Toronto.

Cunningham, J. B. 1993 *Action Research and Organisational Development*, Praeger, Westport, Conn.

Daly, H. E. and Cobb, J. B. 1990 *For the Common Good*, Beacon Press, Boston.

Diesendorf, M. 1997 'Principles of ecological sustainability' in M. Diesendorf and C. Hamilton (eds), *Human Ecology, Human Economy: Ideas for an Ecologically Sustainable Future*, Allen & Unwin, Sydney, pp. 64–97.

——1998 'Models of sustainability and sustainable development', *Beyond Growth: Policies and Institutions for Sustainability*, Proceedings, 5th Biennial Conference of International Society for Ecological Economics, Santiago, November.

Dovers, S. 1995 'A framework for scaling and framing policy problems in sustainability', *Ecological Economics*, vol. 12, pp. 93–106.

Ehrlich, P. and Ehrlich, A. 1990 *The Population Explosion*, Hutchinson, London.

Ellwood, W. (ed.) 1998 *The A-Z of World Development*, New Internationalist Publications, Oxford.

Hamilton, C. 1997 *The Genuine Progress Indicator: A New Index of Changes in Well-being in Australia*, Australia Institute, Canberra.

Hart, M., 1998 *Hart Environmental Data Website* (accessed 20 May 1998): http://www.subjectmatters.com/indicators/

International Institute for Sustainable Development (IISD) 1998 website (accessed 6 September 1998): http://iisd1.iisd.ca/measure/bellagio1.htm/

Jacobs, M. 1991 *The Green Economy*, Pluto Press, London.

Macquarie Dictionary 1981 Macquarie Library, Sydney.

McMichael, A. J. 1993 *Planetary Overload: Global Environmental Change and the Health of the Species*, Cambridge University Press, Cambridge.

Myerson, G. and Rydin, Y. 1996 'Sustainable development: The implications of the global debate for land use planning' in S. Buckingham-Hatfield, & P. Evans (eds), *Environmental Planning and Sustainability*, John Wiley & Sons, Chichester, pp. 19–34.

Science Summit on World Population 1993 *Joint Statement by Fifty-eight of the World's Scientific Academies*, National Academy Press, Washington, DC.

Sustainable Seattle, 1995 *Indicators of Sustainable Community*, Available from Metrocenter YMCA, 909 Fourth Avenue, Seattle WA 98104, USA: email sustsea@halcyon.com

Tabatabai, H. 1993 *The Incidence of Poverty in Developing Countries: An ILO Compendium of Data*, International Labour Office, Geneva.

Toulmin, S. and Gustavsen, B. (eds) 1996 *Beyond Theory: Changing Organisations through Participation*, John Benjamins, Amsterdam & Philadelphia.

UNHCR 1997 *The State of the World's Refugees*, Oxford University Press, Oxford.

UNICEF 1994 *The State of the World's Children*, Oxford University Press, Oxford.

Union of Concerned Scientists 1992 *World's Scientists' Warning to Humanity*, Union of Concerned Scientists, Washington, DC.

United Nations Development Program (UNDP) 1996 *Human Development Report 1996*, Oxford University Press, Oxford.

von Weizsäcker, E., Lovins, A. B. and Lovins, L. H. 1997 *Factor 4: Doubling Wealth, Halving Resource Use*, Allen & Unwin, Sydney.

Walker, K. J. 1994 *The Political Economy of Environmental Policy: An Australian Introduction*, New South Wales University Press, Sydney.

Wheeler, D. and Sillanpää, M. 1997 *The Stakeholder Corporation: A Blueprint for Maximizing Stakeholder Value*, Pitman, London.

WHO, 1997 Website of World Health Organisation, Division of Health Promotion, Education & Communication (accessed on 2 September 1998): http://www.who.int/hpr/hep/documents/ottawa.html

World Bank 1999 *World Development Indicators 1999*, World Bank, Washington, DC.

World Commission on Environment and Development (WCED) 1987 *Our Common Future*, Oxford University Press, Oxford.

World Resources Institute 1994 *World Resources 1994–95: A Guide to the Global Environment*, Report in collaboration with the UN Environment Program and the UNDP, Oxford University Press, New York & Oxford.

3

Sustainability—doing it

Paul Gilding

Introduction

There is a divide that always occurs as a new idea moves through society from the edges to the centre. There are those who continue to focus on getting the question and answer right, and there are those who jump ahead and start doing it, without a clear idea of where it will end up. Both approaches are essential to a successful outcome. In this context, the decades of debate about definitions of sustainability and what it means to society have been important. But they won't count for much unless we get down to doing something about it.

This chapter is about 'doing' sustainability. Not because it's more important than developing the theory around sustainability, but because that is the business I and my colleagues are involved in. We work with major corporations around the world trying to apply sustainability in practice. Therefore that's what we know most about and hopefully where we can add most value to this book's overview of these issues.

I say 'we' because even though I'm writing this chapter and take responsibility for it, these ideas are all co-developed. They have been argued about and debated through by our team of people that work with corporations on these challenges. They are also therefore the ideas of our clients. Together, we try things out. Some things work, some things don't, and from those lessons we try to work out better ways of moving forward. We are a group that doesn't claim to have the answers, just some experience in the process of trying to work them out.[1]

The world in which we work is the world of business. It is the world in which shareholder value still rules supreme and where sustainability is only relevant if it can help to build this value. It is the world of trial and error, success and failure. Therefore it is about compromise, not about building the idealised sustainable corporation. It is about the inch by inch transition of getting companies a little closer to the ideal. This, in our view, is the sharp end of sustainability.

This chapter, therefore, is not about what sustainability is, although we'll touch on this a little in a business context. This chapter is about how we believe the transition to a more sustainable world will occur. What are the drivers? What are some of the processes? Who are the different players and what roles might they play? It is a commentary therefore not on sustainability, but on the *process* of the transition towards it.

The sustainability debate: a beginner's guide

There are many views and explanations of sustainability. They tend to vary relative to the proponents' values, belief systems and self-interests. This is hardly surprising. The question: 'What is sustainability?' could just about be substituted with: 'What kind of society would you like to live in?'

Looking at it in its simplest form, sustainability means to 'keep in existence'. This is a concept with pretty broad appeal! Most people would like to see our society continue on; our people develop and grow; our businesses exist in some form; our environment continue to nourish us. While in the current complex debate this may seem like oversimplifying the issue, it is an important base line from which to begin and should not be moved on from lightly.

'Keeping in existence' is in one sense a very low ranking objective for society. We would like to do more than simply stay in existence. In fact, impetus for a focus on sustainability was the widespread recognition that, with business as usual, there actually was a risk of no longer 'keeping in existence'. In other words the practical problems facing the world, like climate change, biodiversity loss, soil degradation and issues around poverty and developing economies were threatening our world's continued development. Therefore the call to action was heard, at least at a theoretical level.

There are certainly still many differences of opinion around sustainability, but there are also many points of agreement. Perhaps the overriding consistency is that sustainability requires an integrated approach to social, environmental and economic concerns in decision making, recognising that all three areas are important.

The ongoing debate is largely about the details of how to interpret and implement these generally agreed ideas, in the context of different values, beliefs and needs. There are also the attendant battles over turf and self-interest, given that any major change in society leaves winners and losers.

Despite the acceptance of sustainability as a set of values, the moves toward action by the business community have been at best patchy in their success. It is our view that much of the difficulty stems from taking sustainability in isolation, as a new idea that needs to be incorporated into policy or business strategy.

Difficult as that is, it is still not enough. It is our experience in working with business that the idea of sustainability only begins to make sense when you consider it in the context of a broader evolution of the economy. It is also only then that moving from policy to implementation of sustainability begins to work as the actions taken can be designed to integrate with these broader trends.

It is certainly no surprise in the context outlined above, that so many business leaders are actively involved in this debate. Major corporations like Shell, BP-Amoco, Johnson & Johnson and DuPont are analysing and interpreting these new ideas and seeking business benefit from leadership in the area. After all, sustainability is questioning how business operates and challenging traditional attitudes about the role of business in society. This is happening just at a time when on the surface, 'the market economy' is becoming the dominant model of how global society is organised. There are others in business who, in this context, see sustainability as a Trojan horse. They fear that activists using the 'motherhood' appeal of the values involved will work their way into business culture and somehow corrupt all that is 'good and free' about market economics and a focus on shareholder value. This is an indication that the debate has a long way to run yet.

It is also no surprise that social and environmental activists are actively involved in the sustainability debate, often moving into questions of the market and how it works. With the retreat of government and the dominance of business as an organisational vehicle in our society, anything that encourages a more holistic view by business is worth a closer look. They are examining the implications for social change, seeking to understand how to use the market to shift attitudes and behaviour and having internal debates about the extent to which they should work with commercial interests in partnership. They are understandably cautious about cooperation and being accused of selling out.

These are just a few examples of the interests at work, and it is these interests that are framing the transition towards sustainability. Before we go too far down the path of what these different views of sustainability are, let's go back and understand how we got to this point.

We will explore the historical development of sustainability and other broad trends that are driving change in the economy. We will do so to more fully understand our present state and to help develop the understanding business leaders need to apply principles of sustainability to their daily work. We will then look at different viewpoints of sustainability that have arisen from different sectors and the reasons behind their respective analyses.

This will help us understand why this whole issue is arguably one of the key issues for business leaders at the beginning of the twenty-first century. It will also help us to understand how to approach implementing sustainability in an integrated way, and in a way which builds shareholder value.

Historical context

The last twenty years have seen profound changes to the economy. Many commentators have referred to the arrival of the environmental issue in the mainstream of business life. More recently the arrival of social issues into the business debate has gained attention and is being seen by some as 'the next wave'. These two trends are often put forward as being what sustainability is about—the integration of social and environmental issues into our decision making as a society.

We would like to argue that while this analysis is correct, it needs to be broadened in two ways. First, it needs to be broadened so that rather than 'adding on' environmental and social issues to decision making, there is an integration of economic, environmental and social considerations into a single approach, seeking added value to all three areas. It should not be a question of trading off competing interests with the assumption of costs, but an attempt to increase value through creative approaches and innovative outcomes. This creativity is what the market is good at.

Second, the analysis needs to be broadened to take into account some very significant global trends beyond sustainability. As we said in opening, it is our experience that only by taking into account these broader trends can decision makers come up with action plans that will work in the real world beyond policy concepts. We would summarise these trends by saying there is an evolution of society and the economy underway, which has sustainability as a component. One of the key outcomes of this evolution is a changing role for business in society. Another is a shift in how change occurs in the economy when social values change.

One of the reasons this is important is because when we see sustainability as only the incorporation of environmental and social questions into decision making, we miss many of the complexities of sustainability and the subtleties of implementing the changes it requires. If we examine it in the context of some broader shifts in society, then responding to it becomes not only easier, but also an opportunity with a series of benefits.

First, let us briefly examine some of the major shifts that have occurred over the last few decades that relate most directly to these issues. The seven major areas we outline include the major drivers of the sustainability debate but also the major drivers of the broader evolution of the economy referred to above.

If we compare the mid-1970s with the mid-1990s, we get a sense of how dramatically our society has shifted. In that time:

- The environmental issue has moved from the fringe to the mainstream. It has shifted from being an 'issue' which needed to be addressed, and into a basic part of society's values and beliefs. This is what we refer to as the victory of environmentalism. While this is an idea shift rather than a widespread behaviour change at this stage, it is nevertheless of enormous long term significance.
- Capitalism, or to put it more fully, 'liberal, free market democracy', has won the ideological battle over communism. This 'victory of capitalism' is far more significant than the so-called 'defeat' of the Soviet Union. The world's people have decided, pretty much whenever they're given the chance, that they prefer some form of the Western model of democracy and the market over the alternatives. This puts 'business' as an organisational form very much at centre stage of any debate about the future shape of society.
- Government has retreated, or at least changed its role. Some argue this is an ideological shift—the dominance of economic rationalism in Western countries forcing government out of historical roles and removing resources from it. While this is partly the case, there is also an element of democratic choice—people are realising that competition and market forces are often a better mechanism for getting a desired result. Therefore they elect governments of this persuasion. There is also an element of struggling for relevance: How can governments apply command and control techniques to global capitalism, when capital can simply slip away to a different jurisdiction?

■ Civil society has matured into the role of mainstream player in policy debates and in controlling business excesses. With the retreat of government, and the rise of the global corporation, there has not been a commensurate increase in the authority of international institutions. In this context, civil society has risen to the challenge and is increasingly taking a direct policing role through the market and a direct democratic role in international fora such as UN treaty negotiations. At a local level, communities are demanding and getting a much greater direct say in what types of developments occur in their local region. They are also framing what 'market based democracy' means in their country. We are effectively seeing the rise of the ultimate 'global regulator'.

■ Broad-based globalisation has gained unstoppable momentum. However, this is far more than the rise of free trade and the spread of global capital. It is about a shift in the way we think as a society. It is not just capital that flies around the world at the press of the button. It is information between activists, best practice among public administrators, news stories to media outlets and so forth. This shift in how we think is inexorably linked to two other trends. First, the victory of environmentalism, which has taught us to think in terms of global interdependence. Second, the Internet, which is rapidly becoming an enabling technology for globalisation. The Internet means dramatically reduced 'barriers to entry' to becoming an international business. It also means communities in developing countries can gather information on any large multinational that they seek to monitor. This is broad-based globalisation.

■ Technology has shifted from being an exciting source of new products to make our lives easier and more interesting, to being the creator of revolutions with the power to transform our society and take us dramatically forward (or backward). Examples include the Internet, with its capacity to transform the way we use, develop and share information and knowledge, and how we conduct business. Another is biotechnology with its capacity, depending upon how we use it, to both solve many of our most pressing environmental and social problems and to create many more. Our current energy system, the source of arguably our most pressing environmental problem, climate change, is now on the way to being transformed into a decentralised, small unit-based and clean system, using new technologies. Technology is changing everything.

■ There has been a communications revolution, driven by globalisation and technology shifts, which has transformed the way the media affects our lives. A particularly relevant impact here is the way companies are held accountable around the world for their actions anywhere in the world. As many refer to it, there is now 'nowhere to hide'. It is now possible for a community group in a developing country with just a few thousand dollars to take broadcast quality video images and send them around the world on the Internet. It also means that any 'good story', such as the conflict between Shell and Greenpeace over the disposal of the Brent Spar oil rig, soon gets global coverage, turning what used to be local or regional issues quickly into global ones. This has brought brand and reputation centre stage in the debate around sustainability and business strategy.

What do these shifts mean?

Most importantly these shifts mean that just about every assumption that the industrial economy was built upon has changed. We are in transition to a new economy, a knowledge economy. Command and control, whether it be inside companies or across communities, no longer works. Knowledge becomes king. This can be either knowledge that is commercialised into intellectual property based products, or knowledge that is business process focused, such as how a mining company can effectively operate in a developing country. This in turn means that the role of the employee shifts, from being part of the command and control industrial machine to being part of the knowledge capital of a company. People in many cases stop becoming cost centres and start becoming knowledge assets.

A knowledge economy is a fast moving, global one in which 'it is not the big that eat the small, but the fast that eat the slow'. This is a profound shift, which many major industrial corporations are struggling with. After all, it threatens some of the foundations of our current economy and poses some real challenges to business leaders whose experience and training have been based on a model that is fast fading.

Another of the implications of these trends is that they require responding to the sustainability challenge with a truly integrated approach. It's not just about taking into account the social or environmental concerns of stakeholders. It is rather recognising that several interrelated shifts are occurring that, when taken together, are changing the nature of the economy in significant ways.

Perhaps the best way to describe this is to talk about the difference between doing things better and doing different things. If an oil company concerned with sustainability defined the issue as social and environmental, it would see its challenge as being to produce and distribute oil in ways which took into account high standards of social and environmental performance. This is the model pursued by business in the 1980s and 1990s. If, however, the trends mentioned in previous paragraphs were incorporated into the company's strategic thinking, then the oil company would realise that the old model wasn't going to be enough. There is no point being an advanced producer of oil if the economy is moving away from the consumption of oil. With technologies being developed that can address climate change, with globalisation and with a strong civil society ensuring rapid take up of any financially viable solution, there is a major strategic shift occurring. It means that it's not just stakeholder expectations that are changing, but the market fundamentals on which business is based.

Another implication of the changes outlined above is that brand and reputation catapult to centre stage in importance. This is because in a knowledge economy, the sources of competitive advantage change. For example, rather than maintaining low production costs, the object may be to attract and retain the best knowledge workers. Rather than strong relationships with regulators and politicians, the object may be a positive reputation with community stakeholders. And rather than relying on government to arbitrate disputes with communities, it is more likely that a company will form a partnership with a community organisation to seek a solution before a conflict arises. With the economy shifting away from material intensity and into knowledge intensity, partnerships between traditional industrial companies and younger knowledge companies may also be a crucial transition strategy.

There are many other examples, but these provide enough of an indication for us to start discussing some of the different interpretations and views of sustainability. In summary, the above tells us that we are seeing a number of significant and parallel trends acting synergistically to create a wide ranging evolution of our economy. In this new era many of the assumptions on which our current society was built are rapidly fading in relevance. We are in effect in the middle of a transition, from an industrial economy to a knowledge economy.

Understanding the sustainability debate: follow the self-interest

So what's driving this transition? Is it market opportunity? Activist campaigns? Government regulation? Values shift? And how will the change be driven from here on? Who are the players and what are the different approaches they are taking?

To understand many debates, following the self-interest is a useful starting point. There are not many of us sufficiently developed as people to genuinely put aside self-interest and come to an objective conclusion on what is best for most of the people most of the time. There is nothing inherently wrong with self-interest, despite the bad name it's been given. After all, it is right that one should defend one's interests and it's certainly right that one should have them. In reality, much of our democratic process is based on a full and free debate between competing self-interests. A strong society is one where this debate can occur without undue influence being given to any one interest due to financial or political muscle.

One way to sort through different views on sustainability is to understand the various 'self-interests' at work. Each of these various elements of society need to respond to the shifting values of society as they occur. That's how change happens. Given that society has generally accepted that sustainability is basically a good idea—something we should strive for—then the various interests in society start to incorporate this idea into their activity. However the process is not a smooth one. Like any change, there is conflict and resistance along the way. Inside the traditional breakdown of interest groups, such as business, community groups, and government, for example, there are widely varying opinions on what the best way forward is for those particular interests.

In our view, the trend that is most synergistic with sustainability is the transition to a more knowledge-based economy. Increasing the knowledge intensity of our economy is a prerequisite to solving the environmental crisis that underpins our current lack of sustainability. The assumptions we are making about the way change is going to occur stem from that belief. This is because it is our conclusion that, based on the seven drivers referred to earlier, the change process towards a knowledge economy is going to be driven by market forces (including consumer attitudes) rather than by public pressure applied through regulation or ethical pressure.

If this is correct, and we certainly accept that it is a potential outcome rather than inevitable, then it divides the debate in a different way than it has previously been divided. Rather than dividing the 'sides' of the debate into business versus social change advocates, it divides between those who believe the change will come through the market versus through traditional drivers like regulation and ethical pressure.

So that's what we think.

We will now apply this analysis to two broad frameworks of viewpoints. As always with generalisation there will be exceptions and arguments about the way this applies. Nevertheless we find these two ways of seeing the debate as useful in understanding the way change has and will occur.

The ideological analysis sees sustainability (for or against) as a political or moral cause, a transition that is being forced onto society through social action and political pressure. Its proponents fall into two categories. First, the proponents of change. These are various social movements and holders of belief sets that can be broadly characterised as being interventionist—a belief in strong controls on, and intervention in, the market. Second, there are those who are the opponents of this group; generally certain sections of big business and ideologies of the right. Both sides see the struggle for sustainability as a moral battle between forces in society, the other side of which must be beaten and cannot be converted.

The pragmatic analysis sees sustainability as an inevitable response to a scientific, social and market reality. It sees real environmental and social problems. It accepts that these problems threaten societal health, both social and economic, and therefore need to be responded to. It arises broadly from more pragmatic sections of various social movements and from the less ideological, more market responsive sectors of business. It is not primarily driven by the great moral debates, but is rather more interested in achieving market advantage in the case of business and practical change in the case of social change activists.

These are fundamentally different models because they make significantly different assumptions about how change will occur and who will lead it. It certainly makes it far more complex than business versus environmentalists or left versus right. There are believers in each model in business, in environmental and social activism, in science, in politics and so on.

The self-interest of the proponents of each model is a useful starting point in understanding the models. We should be clear, however, that we are not arguing that self-interest is the only influence, just an important one.

Business views

We will start with business. For business leaders, the self-interest depends on what type of business culture you work within. It also depends upon what business you are in. It is fairly obvious that if you're in the solar energy business, you're going to be an advocate of change towards renewable energy. Where it is less obvious is if you are in, for example, the oil business. There it is more likely to break down your business culture.

There is a new business culture developing around the knowledge economy. This is the culture of assumption of constant change, of comfort with new technology, of the need to change business strategy on the run as developments occur, of knowledge workers, of partnerships and alliances, of corporate values beyond profit, of a desire to deliver social value. This is a corporate culture very comfortable with sustainability, in fact one that welcomes it as a business opportunity. While it is easy to see such a culture in a new business area like the computer industry, it is also developing elsewhere.

BP, for example, is developing a corporate culture, led by CEO John Browne, which is focused on a range of forward thinking concepts in business. Browne is often quoted as a leader on general business theory, as well as being an advocate for a progressive position on climate change. A relevant example is his arguments on the importance of knowledge and the need to adapt corporate culture to capture and develop it. In the context of our comments above on a range of trends leading to the transition to a knowledge economy, we start to see how BP's self-interest is in promoting a greater focus on sustainability. Sustainability is a very knowledge-intensive business opportunity. Companies that understand knowledge management are more likely to succeed in this area.

Another example is DuPont. Under new CEO Chad Holliday, DuPont sees knowledge intensity as being the basis of its transition into the twenty-first century. Holliday sees change as a constant, with the challenge being how to develop, in a large traditional business, a corporate culture that can learn to benefit from this reality. The company recently set itself a series of challenging business goals in this area—recognising the transition will be crucial to long term growth.

If the winners in a commercial competitive sense are the fast and nimble— those most readily adaptable to fast change, to a greater focus on knowledge intensity, to a complex and ambiguous series of stakeholder relationships—then those who know they will be the winners have a self-interest in encouraging that change. BP is clearly more adaptable than say Exxon, so its commercial interest is best served by rapid change. If DuPont can succeed in its current transition from being a chemical company into being a knowledge intensive science company, then it will grow faster and more consistently than competitors stuck in the old model. Companies like BP and DuPont see sustainability from within this pragmatic analysis.

On the opposite end are those companies that are conservative and comfortable with the status quo. They seem resistant to new cultural ideas, and have a defensive position on most social issues. They are often quite ideological in analysis of change and therefore see sustainability as a threat. They are proponents of the ideological analysis outlined above. They are not just acting, however, out of ideology, they are acting out of self-interest as well. The culture of these companies does not make them adaptable to change.

Examples include Australia's BHP in the first half of the 1990s (prior to the recent changes in executive management) and global players like Exxon. They see the world in simple terms, which were appropriate during the industrial age where volume of material production and efficiency of mechanical processes determined profitability. So Exxon, for example, helps to finance and lead lobby groups like the extremely conservative Global Climate Coalition to lobby against action on climate change. This is in their self-interest, not because they are in the oil business (so is BP who broke ranks with this group), but because they have an industrial age corporate culture. It does not yet consistently translate into good or bad commercial performance. In the two examples of Exxon and BHP, the score is one all. BHP's old management led the company into disastrous financial territory, while Exxon continues to perform. The challenge will come when the speed of change really picks up.

Activist views

Environmental and social movements tend to break down in similar ways, though arguably they have a stronger ideological driver as well. Despite public positions advocating radical change, many environmental and social change organisations are internally very conservative. Conservative not in the sense of political positions, but in terms of capacity to adapt and change. So while some organisations, notably, for example, the World Resources Institute (WRI) and the Environmental Defense Fund (EDF) in the US, embrace change, many others are very cautious and sceptical of new ideas. Their cultures are so steeped in an anti-business role that they find it difficult to then embrace new ideas involving the market. These organisations tend to be focused on using government-forced change, such as regulation and international treaties.

While they are important, the proportional influence of these mechanisms is in rapid decline. These types of groups are therefore not comfortable and are less trusting with market or community based systems of control. They arguably resist change because their self-interest is served by the status quo. Other groups, like the EDF and the WRI, not only feel comfortable with such change; they actively experiment with it. The EDF, for example, is partnering with BP to develop carbon-trading trials.

It should not be misinterpreted from these comments that working *with* business is the natural choice of the pragmatic approach. For example, the recent furore over genetically modified organisms (GMOs), which has had such a dramatic influence on the market for these products, has been a traditional confrontational campaign. However, its application, by groups such as Greenpeace in the UK, to a significant degree has been through the market, rather than through government regulation. Greenpeace in the UK has long been an advocate of market based campaigning and in this case successfully forced retailers like Sainsburys to cease stocking GMO food products. This put a large plug into the growing market for genetically modified crops in just six months, whereas a government driven response would have taken years.

Government views and attitudes to regulation

With the retreat of government, there is much confusion and debate in government circles regarding the role of the market in achieving change. It is not just government, however. For some industries, noticeably those that are most progressive on these issues, more regulation can bring competitive advantage. DuPont, for example, has been very effective at reducing its toxic waste emissions from the very high levels recorded in the 1980s. While the culture of the US business sector is very anti-regulation, it is arguable that DuPont's self-interest would be best served by tighter regulations on their industry's toxic waste discharges. After all, like the BP example above, once a company becomes adaptable to change, further change becomes a benefit to the company compared to slower reacting competitors.

In government circles, this confusion over the role of the market is clear. There is great experimentation with voluntary agreements and this trend is clearly increasing. While initially promoted in Europe, it has now become far more widespread, noticeably in the US and countries like Australia. This is resisted, as you would expect, by the advocates of the ideological model in both business and activist circles. Ideological activists resist it because they see it as a cop out from the 'real action' forced by regulation. Ideological business resists it because it starts to drive the market in a direction they feel uncomfortable with. So, for example, while opposing forced regulatory action on climate change, some US business circles are now even opposing legislation which gives credit for voluntary early action on CO_2 reductions. They don't fear action on climate, they fear change—they are scared of the market actually working!

Many in government also resist change, again often based on self-interest. If their culture and power comes from their capacity to regulate the market, then a different approach can be quite threatening. If we go back to the broad trends discussed above, for example, we see the rise of civil society and the retreat of government. In this context, we see more partnerships between progressive business and the community sector (for example, the EDF and BP as above). It can be quite threatening for the government regulatory community if a major focus of change becomes direct relationships between the community and the market.

Conclusion

Sustainability is here to stay as a driver of change. It will develop different names and interpretations, but the fundamental idea—that we will keep our society first in existence and second developing—will persist. To achieve this outcome, we will learn to incorporate an integrated understanding of the social, environmental and economic implications and value of what we do as a society. This understanding will drive our decision making.

One of the strongest conclusions we draw from the above analysis is the clear synergy between the sustainability requirements to reduce negative environmental and social impacts and the overall trend towards the knowledge economy. An alignment between sustainability and the knowledge economy would see a very powerful mobilisation of resources and market action.

The knowledge economy, learning to manage knowledge workers, dematerialisation of the economy, and the development of a new business culture to suit this need, are now all ideas that are well established and will continue to grow.

There are some interesting threads that are starting to emerge between proponents of different analyses of sustainability. One of the most ironic is the commonality of views between conservative business circles and some activist groups. It is like an informal alliance to keep the status quo, where change is driven not through the market and the community, but by government regulation guided by pressure groups, resisted by business.

We are seeing an effective realignment of societal forces. What is fading is the sector-based assumptions—where business, environmentalists, government and social change advocates have more unity among themselves than with the other sectors. What is emerging are alliances where some activists have more in common with some business leaders than with other activists and, similarly, some business leaders share more with activists than their fellow CEOs. This realignment is happening around the ideological and pragmatic analyses we referred to above.

One of the interesting results of this is the formal alliances between some businesses and activist organisations. These partnerships are developing as new ways of advancing social causes while delivering competitive advantage to the businesses involved. It is effectively an alignment of self-interest among the parties involved.

It is also clear that it is not possible to act on sustainability in isolation. Without incorporating the synergistic implications of other trends, like globalisation, the communications revolution and new technologies, it is inevitable that business in particular will make major strategic errors in developing their response strategies.

If there were one single most important conclusion from our analysis, it would be that sustainability has become a competitive issue. Gone are the old models about social change. It is no longer the case that change is advocated by activists, resisted by business and arbitrated by government. The mainstreaming of sustainability is about its integration into our society and therefore the arrival of real competition among companies who see the world in transition to a new economy. Those that work this out and develop the tools needed to succeed in this transition will be rewarded in the old way—increased shareholder value—and in a new way—a more satisfied and motivated workforce and a more sustainable and robust corporation.

Endnote

1 The 'we' used throughout this chapter refers to the members of Ecos Corporation.

Part II

Towards human sustainability

4

Human resources, capabilities and sustainability

Paul Gollan

Key questions

In this chapter we address the following key questions:

- How do organisations currently use and apply human resources?
- How do organisations deteriorate or renew these resources and what are the implications of such approaches for employers and their employees?
- How can we redefine the ways organisations use their human resources in order to ensure human sustainability?
- To what extent do corporations need to exercise social responsibility as well as economic responsibility?
- How can employers balance the interests of different stakeholders in organisations while maintaining a sustainable work environment for employees?

Introduction

Consider what are commonly believed to be the seven key industries of the next few decades—microelectronics, biotechnology, the new materials industries, civil aviation, telecommunications, robots plus machine tools and computers plus software. All are brain power industries. Each could be anywhere on the face of the globe. Where they will be located depends upon who can organise the brain power to capture them. In the century ahead comparative advantage will be man-made (Thurow, 1993: 45).

An article in a prominent UK management magazine *Management Today* highlighted the problem confronting many companies. It argued 'years of corporate lip service to the importance of people are finally catching up. Payment is now due in full, and in kind: for once you have rationalised and reorganised everything else, people really are the only asset' (*Management Today*, 1995). Failure to comprehend the truth of this statement has been reflected in recent years in significant job losses and increases in long term unemployment.

However, with a growing emphasis on customised-quality consciousness in world business and increased use of new technologies, a new form of worker has emerged from the cost-cutting and downsizing regime of the 1980s and 1990s. These new workers are often labelled 'knowledge workers' and they possess certain key characteristics: they are highly skilled, qualified, trained and experienced in new and growing areas of business. In essence, they can be defined as workers who deal with a high degree of complexity and uncertainty which requires a high degree of judgement (De Lacy, 1999). In the new knowledge based society of the 1990s the notion of commitment has also been redefined: the maintenance of intellectual capital or the 'corporate memory' is now seen as dependent on employee commitment and satisfaction. The intellectual capital of organisations is the knowledge, experience and ideas of employees which management attempts to codify and formalise to produce greater organisational value.

The cost-cutting regime associated with many organisational change strategies of the 1980s and 1990s has resulted in the breakdown of the old employment relationships. In a world where loyalty and commitment are no longer seen to be rewarded, those individuals who have increased their marketability and employability are taking control of their own future. As a result, many managers have to come to terms with a new employment relationship based on a contingent or temporary contractual culture which they helped to create. This has reinforced the importance and value of building corporate human capability and ensuring sustainability in the new employment relationship.

This chapter will outline a number of issues for organisations to consider when pursuing sustainable human resource outcomes in the workplace: those outcomes that reinforce corporate profitability and corporate survival and those that satisfy employee aspirations and needs in the workplace. The chapter suggests that developments in human resource management (HRM) in recent years have shifted the emphasis away from human management to a new focus on resource management. It argues that the needs, potential and aspirations of individuals must take centre stage in the workplace. If employers do not bridge the current gap between their rhetoric and workplace reality, then the likely outcome will be an exodus of bright and enthusiastic people to organisations that do. For true corporate sustainability, an organisation must recognise, value and promote the capability of its people. The chapter also examines and provides evidence of the link between workplace effectiveness and humanistic work structures in organisations and shows how reinforcing this link increases productivity and profits.

The state of play

Careers as we have traditionally known them no longer exist. They were predicated on progression through an organisational hierarchy, by seniority and/or merit and on security of employment. Instead, careers are now becoming self-managed. Individuals assess their own worth and think strategically about placing themselves in the best possible employment position, acting as their own agent in a competitive, market driven environment. This being so, companies are suddenly finding themselves in a position where much of the management skeleton that held the edifice together and the cultural 'oil' of loyalty that enabled this machine to function smoothly have largely disappeared. The market liberalism often espoused by many management gurus has entered the internal domain of organisations and individuals, where market driven premiums are paid to motivate formerly committed and loyal employees. As Studs Terkel has suggested 'the worker has become a robot and is [as] dispensable as Kleenex' (Christy, 1998: 8). Consequently the employment relationship is reduced to a financial contract.

A survey entitled 'Enterprise Bargaining in Australia' released by the Commonwealth Department of Industrial Relations in 1995 provided employees in Australia with an opportunity to voice their views about employee relations and their employment conditions in the previous twelve months (DIR, 1995). It reported that, overall, employees had experienced a decline rather than an improvement over a range of employment conditions and issues. In the twelve months prior to the survey, employees reported lower levels of satisfaction with management, weakening levels of job security, widespread increases in the amount of stress on the job and growing dissatisfaction with their ability to balance work and family commitments and responsibilities. Employees report working harder and longer hours than previously and feeling disillusioned with the current workplace.

The recent release of the 1995 Australian Workplace Industrial Relations Survey (AWIRS95) has reconfirmed these results. This survey shows increased employee effort, more job-related stress, and a higher work pace for employees than in the twelve months prior to the survey.

The survey indicated that 59 per cent of employees had increased their effort, 50 per cent had been subjected to increased stress, and 46 per cent had increased the pace at which they had worked (Morehead et al., 1997).

At the same time as surveys like this appear, new management philosophies stress that workers should be seen as empowered members of firms rather than antagonists in a confrontation between capital and labour. This view of the world also stresses that firms are social organisations embedded in a complex skein of rights and obligations, and if employees are reduced to commodities to be bought and sold on the stock market, that undermines the trust and reciprocity of obligation on which a long term positive relationship between management and worker thrive (*Guardian Weekly*, 1996).

Some employees, and indeed what remains of middle management, may counter such schizoid demands with indifference, humour or cynicism. Nevertheless, the effect of such demands is likely to be the entrenchment of 'low trust' employment relations where employees feel they are only a cog in a machine—simply a necessary component in the return on investment equation. With their expectations lowered, a more unforgiving mentality begins to emerge.

To reinforce the point, the 1997 Towers Perrin Workplace Index surveyed 2500 people employed in large private sector US organisations with more than 500 employees. The evidence from the survey suggests that employees accept personal responsibility for maintaining skills and applying those skills in the areas most critical to profitable growth. However, they are only willing to do this in return for training, participation, career development and continuing employment. They are increasingly sceptical that organisations are living up to these obligations. The study suggests that this is beginning to erode employees' faith in management. The study states:

> when employees doubt there is reciprocity and fairness, their work ethic
> and motivation appear to suffer. Thus, over time, negative feelings
> about the company will erode positive feelings about work itself. And
> that, in turn, can adversely affect productivity and performance (Towers
> Perrin, 1997: 7).

For example, employees who feel they can have a full career with their company are far more motivated to contribute, with 91 per cent stating that they are motivated to help their company succeed, compared to just 48 per cent who do not see a future with the company (Towers Perrin, 1997: 19).

The danger for organisations is that power and knowledge are now invested in more people outside the traditional confines of the management hierarchy. Corporate knowledge and experience, the strategic competitive advantage in most organisations, are now located at the lower levels of the organisation in a great many more people. In successful organisations today, such as Microsoft and Netscape, almost all of their assets are people. For example, of Microsoft's market valuation of US$85 billion at the end of 1996, less than US$1 billion was made up of physical assets. The rest of the assets walk out of the front door each evening. Charles Handy has added to the debate by suggesting that on average the intellectual assets of most organisations are usually worth three or four times tangible book value (Stewart, 1994: 35; Handy, 1997). Organisations need to understand that employees have the knowledge that is essential for the organisation's success, and so have the potential to shift the balance of power away from management and back to themselves. To understand these developments the next section identifies the influences on human resource sustainability, suggesting that a number of factors are important for organisations in implementing a more sustainable approach.

Factors and influences in human resource sustainability

Figure 4.1 represents the major factors, influences and outcomes of human resource sustainability in organisations. While not intending to be exhaustive, it identifies five major factors in the debate about human resource sustainability. Essentially, the model defines human resources sustainability in terms of capacity of organisations to create value in their organisations, thereby having the ability and capacity to regenerate value and renew wealth through the application of human resource policies and practices. This will entail investment in human knowledge through continuous learning, and the application and development of such knowledge through employee participation and involvement. In addition, the model identifies four main drivers for organisations trying to achieve corporate human resource sustainability and examines their impact on employee satisfaction and commitment and on the traditional organisational objectives of increased productivity and profits.

Consultation and employee involvement

Consultation and participation are important requirements which ensure that the interests of all employees are considered in major changes occurring in the workplace. Moreover, actively involving employees in

Figure 4.1 Factors and influences in human resource sustainability

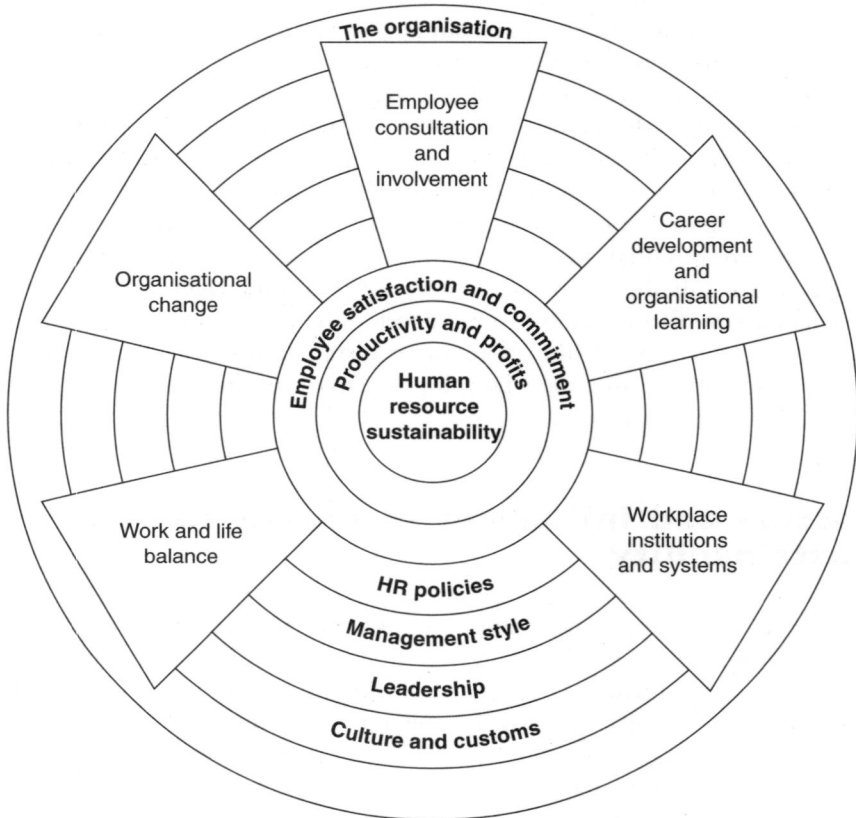

The organisation

Employee consultation and involvement

Career development and organisational learning

Organisational change

Employee satisfaction and commitment

Productivity and profits

Human resource sustainability

Work and life balance

Workplace institutions and systems

HR policies

Management style

Leadership

Culture and customs

the consultation process is also a factor in convincing employees of management's commitment to conduct corporate change in a fair and equitable way.

A number of studies in recent years have highlighted the importance of giving employees 'a say' at work (Morehead et al., 1997). These studies report that employees have taken on increased responsibility at work, but that this has not brought a greater willingness by employers to trust employees or provide more opportunities for greater participation and involvement in organisational decision making processes. To the contrary, there is some evidence of even greater intensification by management of traditional authoritarian control systems (ACIRRT, 1999). However, other evidence indicated that greater consultation and involvement of employees at work through direct and indirect methods produce not only a more satisfied and productive workforce but also a more committed employee to the organisation, producing real financial benefits for the organisation (Gollan, 1998; Gollan & Davis, 1999; Patterson et al., 1997; Patterson & West, 1998).

The latest AWIRS95 survey (Morehead et al, 1997) has added to this debate and highlighted the need for employers to regain the focus of employee involvement and participation in the workforce. Significantly, the survey indicated that where such practices existed, the overwhelming majority of managers indicated that greater employee participation had a positive impact on the workplace, with four out of five workplaces indicating improvements in management–employee communication, and the majority of managers indicating greater ease with the introduction of change, improved quality and increased workplace performance.

In addition to these figures at least 80 per cent of managers surveyed said work groups or quality circles also led to improvements in workplace performance, product or service quality, communication between management and employees and easier introduction of organisational change (also see following section on human resource sustainability and the bottom line).

However, despite such increases in participative decision making, many employees still feel that their level of influence over the way their workplace is managed or organised and over decisions that affect them is limited. Up to 66 per cent of employees indicate no or only very limited influence over management (some 43 per cent indicated that they had no influence at all) and 58 per cent of employees indicated no or only a little influence over organisational decisions in their workplaces.

Research by Campling and Gollan (1999) further highlights the link between employee participation programs, greater employee motivation and improved organisational performance. The case study and survey evidence in their research suggests communication of employee grievances and concerns were major issues and often affected the ability to introduce change and organisational commitment.

Recent research has reinforced this data, suggesting that the growth of employee involvement and participation programs can be directly correlated with improved organisational performance (Gollan & Davis, 1997). This occurs because management recognises that the improvement of company performance is based on the integration of human resource management with product and market strategies on improved understanding of the needs of employees and employers at the workplace and on making better use of their skill and ingenuity. Strategies designed to achieve a more comprehensive use of the employee's human potential, desire to learn, flexibility and personal responsibility deliver higher levels of performance.

Career development and organisational learning

In recent years many organisations have focused almost exclusively on cost-cutting measures. In the process they have diminished their most vital resource—the key skills of their employees—which are so critical in a competitive environment. One of the greatest difficulties faced by human resource and personnel managers is to demonstrate to an organisation's decision makers, especially in times of cost-cutting and downsizing, the economic benefits and the real added value of training employees and building corporate human resource capabilities.

In this regard, recent US and European studies have shown a strong link between a company's investment in its employees and stock market performance and profits. Evidence from the latest American Management Association (AMA) (1996) survey of more than 1000 large and medium-sized US companies paints a different picture of companies that increase their training budgets at the same time as trimming their workforce. It is suggested that these companies are creating new environments to respond to new business conditions. The AMA survey highlighted a remarkably strong correlation between increased training budgets and larger profits and productivity flowing from workforce reductions.

Over the long term, firms that increased their training budgets after workforce reductions were 75 per cent more likely to show increased profits and nearly twice as likely to improve worker productivity than firms that had cut their training expenses. However, only 32 per cent of companies cutting jobs since 1990 reported a long term increase in training budgets. A recent OECD (1999) report also argued that higher training rates have been associated with higher levels of education, productivity and wages.

However, most compelling is the evidence from 100 German companies which reveals a strong link between investment in employees and stock market performance (Bilmes, Wetzker & Xhonneux, 1997). The Boston Consulting Group research team undertaking the study found that companies which build employee capacity at the core of their strategies produced higher long term returns to shareholders than their industry peers. Significantly, the study found that the shares of companies that focus resources on the development of their workforce, out perform competitors who give human resources a low priority. The research examined ten industrial sectors over a seven-year period from 1987 to 1994 (Bilmes, Wetzker & Xhonneux, 1997).

In every industry examined by the researchers, those companies that produced a greater total shareholder return (TSR) than their competitors also scored most highly on such measures as: expenditure per employee; contribution of employees as reflected in mission statements; recruitment; performance evaluation and feedback; promotion opportunities; flexible work hours; prevalence of teams; opportunities to learn skills; and the extent to which employees share in company performance through profit sharing, performance pay and bonus. The TSR is the sum of share price increases and dividends over a given period. The researchers also reviewed a shorter four-year period. This also confirmed that the degree to which a company invests in people is a good predictor of stock market success. Interestingly, the study found that these companies also created the most jobs, with three-quarters of the companies with above average TSR producing a net increase in jobs (Bilmes, Wetzker & Xhonneux, 1997). It seems that these policies are not only good for the company, they are also good for society as a whole.

Downsizing: what's the real cost?

Since the late 1980s, corporate and economic life has been dominated by downsizing, or what is euphemistically referred to as right-sizing, re-engineering or even, a career realignment scheme (CRS). While social scientists, executives, union officials and politicians debate the ethical and moral obligations of organisations to society and the economic welfare of the community, they may be unaware of the hard facts about the real economic cost of downsizing and restructuring to the organisation itself. Only now after the last decade of downsizing has the evidence started to emerge. It is even reported that Stephen Roach, the management crusader credited with starting the fashionable downsizing regime, recently said that it was all a big mistake. But there is no mistake that corporate change and restructuring with various forms of reengineering are continuing to take a heavy toll on employment and creating widespread job insecurity.

A recent paper by Freeman (1996) has suggested that while downsizing continues, there is an increasing tide of opinion that the process of job reductions to cut costs has gone too far in many organisations, especially larger businesses. Moreover, he argues that companies which downsize simply to reduce costs and boost short term profits, or in other words 'slash and burn', may well be putting the longer term viability of their organisation at risk. According to Cascio (1993) downsizing through extensive job layoffs misleadingly inflates the company's reported profits, diverting management and shareholder attention from solving the underlying problems that are undermining an organisation's promise and potential.

Firms pursuing downsizing strategies had thrown away the experience network and knowledge of what made their organisations work effectively, destroying the informal networks which are so vital for success. The central problem for organisations is that once this happens, it is difficult to rebuild such essential contacts and customer relationships when the committed employees or 'gatekeepers' are no longer there. The studies indicate that customers desert a firm long before these relations can be re-established.

The AMA (1996) found downsizing had not brought long term benefits for many organisations. In fact, the figures are devastating for those of the 'slash and burn' corporate mentality. Fewer than half (44 per cent) of the companies that had cut jobs since 1990 reported increased operating profits in the year following the reduction. A similar percentage (45 per cent) reported an increase in operating profits in the longer term (that is, more than a year after the cuts). Surprisingly, even fewer (30 per cent) indicated an immediate increase in worker productivity, and only 40 per cent cited improvements in the longer term.

In addition to these results a US study in the late 1980s examined the effects on share values after downsizing. They found that on the day that the announcement was made stock prices generally increased, but then usually began a long, slow slide. Within a two-year period, over half of the companies surveyed were trading below the market by up to 48 per cent, and two-thirds of the companies were below comparable firms in their industries by 5 to 48 per cent (Dorfman, 1991).

Study after study shows that following downsizing surviving employees become narrow-minded, self-absorbed and risk averse. Morale also sinks, productivity drops, and survivors distrust management. In fact, this constellation of symptoms is so common that Cascio has coined it 'survivors syndrome' or 'anxiety intensification through downsizing' (AIDS) (Cascio, 1993; Littler, Wiesner & Vermeulen, 1997), which reduces commitment and decreases work performance.

These surveys also paint a picture of overwork, stress and insecurity in organisations. The problem for organisations pursuing such strategies is that they will not win commitment to building a new culture in the organisation if employees fear they may lose their jobs. The success of a company depends not only on its skills and knowledge but also on its collective experiences of successes and the shared meaning people give to their life at work. Downsizing disrupts the informal networks of an organisation, the contacts and relationships between employees or teams of employees, and the unofficial routines and processes that underlie most operations. Recent research into organisational change in Australia has found that the emphasis on cost-cutting at 410 big Australian companies had slumped from 68 per cent in 1993 to 56 per cent at the end of 1998 (Kirby, 1999).

Getting the balance right

Another consideration for organisations trying to achieve corporate sustainability is getting the balance right between work and life outside work. Today many workers who have jobs are working long hours, with an increasing number of employees working more than 48 hours a week. However, as the trend to work longer and harder continues among the generation that has discovered the meaning of downsizing, it should not be surprising that a new generation is developing different attitudes to work.

There is evidence of the emergence of a new 'get-a-life' generation in a 1996 survey. This survey covered more than 1200 business students from 30 of the world's leading universities in 10 countries including Australia, and was carried out for accountants Coopers & Lybrand in 1996 by Universum International (1996), a Swedish-based research organisation. The overwhelming conclusion from the study was that this new generation of future managers is demanding a more balanced lifestyle and a rewarding life outside work.

When asked about their future career goals, the students considered a balanced lifestyle, financial rewards, and a challenging international career as their most important priorities. In fact, 45 per cent of the students surveyed named a balanced lifestyle and a rewarding life outside of work as one of the top three priorities (Universum International, 1996).

When choosing their first employer, the number-one priority was the ability to achieve a balanced lifestyle. Long term employment security was low on the list of aspects important to these students. Again, when asked about future life priorities, the theme was reinforced, with personal development and growth, a career, spending time with close friends and relatives, and building a family being most important. In yet another key finding, over 70 per cent of students strongly disagreed with the notion that a person's career is more important than personal and family relationships (Universum International, 1996).

Another survey of 1000 young professionals in 73 countries found that 40 per cent planned to leave their existing employer within two years. The survey uncovered widespread disappointment at the dearth of company investment in their personal development with many considering starting their own business (Donkin, 1999: 19). This finding was further reinforced when the survey revealed that 41 per cent of respondents would value more choice over working hours with many wanting to spend more time with friends and family and slow down enough to keep healthy and balanced (Donkin, 1999: 19). Moreover, a study conducted by Gemini Consulting of 10 300 employees in ten countries found that only 27 per cent of those surveyed felt their organisations were preparing them for successful futures. As a consequence 44 per cent of respondents said that they would leave their jobs tomorrow for a job that would provide them more opportunity for advancement (Gemini Consulting, 1998: 13).

One company that has recognised this situation and is developing policies to handle it is the UK bank Lloyds TSB. As part of its drive to instil leadership and trust in the organisation, it introduced a number of initiatives to make employees' lives more manageable and to help change the culture of long hours (Maitland, 1999). It has nearly 17 000 employees working flexible or reduced hours. In fact, employees no longer have to explain to their managers why they want to change their working hours. A decision is made purely on whether it makes business sense. The company has set a target of 25 per cent of its workforce, senior managers as well as junior employees, to be working flexible hours compared to some 22 per cent currently. Significantly, the new procedures allow employees to choose from a range of options, including job-sharing, reduced hours, a compressed working week (four days instead of five), variable starting and finishing times, and working from home one to three days a week. The only prerequisite is that those seeking these conditions must explain how they will fulfil their duties and how colleagues and customers will be affected. The drivers for the initiatives were increasing competition and the requirement for 24-hour banking in many operations. As such the bank needed to attract and retain employees, 66 per cent of whom are female. They noted also that before the changes were introduced, some 15 per cent of staff taking maternity leave did not return to the bank. The estimated cost of recruiting and training a junior employee can be £10 000. As the head of the Equal Opportunity function suggested, 'Everybody has a life outside work, whatever it might be' (Maitland, 1999).

To reinforce the importance of achieving a work and life balance, a study on the quality of working life (Worrell & Cooper, 1998) of over 1300 managers found nearly 60 per cent indicated that long hours were having a negative impact on their health. Just over 70 per cent said it affected their relationship with their partner and encroached on the time spent with their children, and some 55 per cent of managers suggested that it made them less productive at work. In addition, over half of the respondents felt a sense of 'powerlessness' and lack of control in their work environment, with less than one in five respondents agreeing that they had enough time to fulfil the requirements of their job. When respondents to the survey were asked what one piece of advice they would give to top management of their organisation, 40 per cent of comments referred to the poverty of organisational communication and consultation strategies. The second most important piece of advice identified was for the organisation to value and appreciate employees as the organisation's most important assets (Worrell & Cooper, 1998).

A study by the International Centre for Health and Society at University College London has suggested that the lack of control at work and job insecurity has contributed to ill-health, disease and mortality. The study highlighted that the lack of control at work was the single largest contributing factor to disease incidence, more important than smoking, diet or obesity. In addition, the study indicated that labour market deregulation and other social policies needed to be reassessed in the light of evidence that workplace change had a negative psychological impact, especially when work practices gave workers little or no input into the content of work and flexibility (Long, 1999).

Julie Macken (1999), from the *Australian Financial Review*, has highlighted the dilemma facing many organisations caused by the transition from the manufacturing age to knowledge and information, where the brain cannot function at an optimal level for eight to ten hours a day. Macken cites the example of Hewlett-Packard which, in 1997, had an attrition rate of 20 per cent. More than half of the employees surveyed said that they experienced excessive work pressure. As a consequence Hewlett-Packard introduced policies to reduce and redesign workloads, encouraged employees to set goals for leisure, discouraged working on weekends and holidays, and introduced a 40-hour week. It was suggested that this has improved retention rates and attracted high potential recruits (Macken, 1999).

These findings also highlight the need for businesses to take account of other, non-financial factors when attracting and retaining people in their organisations. Only by acknowledging the importance of work and family, and of the need for personal and social networks outside work, will organisations be able to attract and retain competent and committed employees.

The institutions for a sustainable future

The real question arising from this evidence is whether there can be any real progress towards corporate sustainability without a fundamental overhaul of the structures that underpin existing institutions and systems of employment. A recent report by Valerie Bayliss (1996) of the Royal Society for the Arts (RSA) may hold some clues. The RSA's report challenges traditional assumptions and calls for the dismantling of employment structures and education systems that have supported the traditional working model of a '40/40 job'. This model assumes that people (mostly men) work 40 hours a week for 40 years. The report suggests that this outdated model was based on the growth of public administration in the 1930s and mass production in factories, supported by the concept of the job for life in the same organisation. The problem, as identified in the RSA report, is that if people work less than 40 hours (or in some cases 35 hours) they are described as 'part-timers', peripheral and in fundamentally insecure employment relative to the main 'core' full time workforce.

As the RSA report states, there are unlikely to be enough paid permanent full time jobs to go around (Bayliss, 1996). The paradigms have changed, from where a majority of people will be employed in 40/40 jobs to where a majority of people will be working flexible hours in the temporary labour market. People themselves will be responsible for their working patterns, their education and training and redefining their own work.

The report addresses five important issues for HR sustainability: Can the economy generate a consistently high supply of employment opportunities, however they are structured? Can the intermediate labour market develop and maintain opportunities for all those who need it? Do the nation's education and training systems meet the needs for a sophisticated and competent society? Does the country's infrastructure support people in and out of work, and match the needs of the new world rather than the old? Do individuals recognise their responsibility to develop their own employability, and is the right support available to assist and encourage them? (Bayliss, 1996).

An Australian report by Gollan, Pickersgill and Sullivan (1996) highlights the increasing acute socio-economic polarisation between the highly skilled and the poorly skilled. Those that are highly skilled will be increasingly overworked and working long and anti-social hours, while the poorly skilled will be either unemployable or have their wages driven down to a point that renders them the 'working poor' or 'ghettoised' workers. There will be an industrial relations system that offers few substantive protections for those that are in work, and a social security system that does not adjust to the change in working time arrangements and so creates inequitable outcomes for citizens, thus eroding the social fabric and well-being of society as a whole (see Table 4.1) (also see ACIRRT, 1999). This will produce a society where the social dislocation and hostility we are now seeing will intensify, with the prospect of 'two nations' emerging within society. The danger has been highlighted in a recent editorial in the *Harvard Business Review* (1999: 8) where it is

Table 4.1 Characteristics of the polarised workforce

Workforce	The 'ghettoised' working poor	The knowledge 'gold collar' worker
Social	▪ Social security benefits ▪ Working poor ▪ Income assistance ▪ Declining real incomes ▪ Government social housing ▪ Low quality education	▪ High labour markets ▪ Affluent family structure ▪ Private home ownership ▪ High quality private education
Organisation	▪ Taylorist job design ▪ Cost driven agenda ▪ Limited training and career development ▪ No control over work ▪ Strict workplace supervision ▪ Casual, temporary or part time employment ▪ Service and retail sectors	▪ Internal labour market ▪ Global career horizons and advancement ▪ IT, education, publishing, banking and finance industries ▪ Teamwork and multiskilling ▪ Empowered
Individual	▪ Limited workplace mobility ▪ Limited education ▪ Non-English speaking ▪ Low paid ▪ Job insecurity ▪ Regular unemployment	▪ Highly mobile ▪ Highly educated and skilled ▪ Highly paid elite ▪ Employability and secure employment

even feared that knowledge workers will walk away from deep involvement with society as a whole. After all many of these workers already live in privately policed communities and send their children to private schools.

An OECD (1999) report also highlighted the challenge of reconciling job security for workers with the need of organisational flexibility. The report suggests that, while nations have concentrated in the 1990s on easing restrictions for temporary forms of employment to increase the degree of flexibility and thus the creation of employment, this link is not particularly strong. In fact, the report suggests that the risk of becoming unemployed is lower in countries with stricter regulation through employment protection legislation. However, once unemployed there is a greater risk of remaining unemployed for an extended period of time. In other words, the report argues that employment regulation produces more stable jobs, less labour turnover and fewer unemployed. Conversely the lack of employment regulation and training may intensify existing inequalities in the labour market.

Some organisations have acknowledged these concerns and have introduced volunteer programs in which employees help the less fortunate in society. Such initiatives reflect a shift in corporate attitudes towards the community. For example, Royal Mail and Whitbread Brewing have introduced community action programs. Royal Mail suggests that it is good for business because volunteering helps personnel development, especially in morale, motivation and working with other people, and in the introduction and deployment of new skills (Slavin, 1999: 16). Such actions, however, may ameliorate the social distress caused by current trends in employment but will not eliminate it.

Other organisations have introduced 'social reporting' where companies solicit the opinions and views of employees, suppliers, customers and the communities in which they operate (Slavin, 1999: 16). A survey of the UK's FTSE 100 companies found that 79 reported on social and community issues. As an example, PriceWaterhouseCoopers and KPMG undertake independent audits of their social performance. As Terry Slavin has suggested, for companies 'one of the biggest motivations for the new trend is in enhancing their reputations at a time when it has never been more difficult to recruit—and retain—good graduates' (Slavin, 1999:16). In addition, Slavin suggests that social reporting opens up new channels of communication with employees with the objective of enhancing two-way communication and thus high levels of trust building loyalty and commitment (Slavin, 1999: 16).

Human resource sustainability and the bottom line

> To build a company that is profitable and will live long, managers take care to create a community. Processes are in place to define membership, establish common values, recruit people, develop employees, assess individual potential, live up to a human contract, and establish policies for graceful exits from the company (Arie de Geus, 1997: 58).

We often hear from people at the top echelons of business that 'people are our greatest asset'. In reality, however, despite this rhetoric many organisations seek to cut costs through downsizing and job enlargement. However, evidence now demonstrates that companies that do invest in people, rather than just talk about it, show positive financial outcomes.

For example, a comprehensive study, *Impact of People Management Practices on Business Performance* (Patterson et al., 1997) in the UK has reconfirmed the importance and linkage of good people management practices to productivity and profits. The report showed that the management of people had a greater effect on a business's performance than the combined effect of its strategy, product or service quality, manufacturing technology and expenditure on R&D. The researchers also indicated that satisfaction and organisational commitment explain up to 5 per cent of the difference between the profitability of companies. These results demonstrate the importance of the relationship between employee attitudes and company performance and as such indicate the more satisfied workers are with their jobs, the better the company is likely to perform in terms of profitability and, particularly, productivity.

However, the study's most important finding was the linkage between 'good' HRM practices and profitability and productivity. The report suggested that overall, HRM practices (that is, appraisals, training and development, employee involvement and team working etc.) explain 19 per cent of the variations in profitability and 18 per cent of differences in productivity between companies and within organisations. As the researchers state, this is the most convincing demonstration in the research literature of the 'link between the management of people and the performance of companies' (Patterson et al., 1997).

A follow up study of 5000 employees in 42 UK manufacturing companies conducted by Patterson and West (1998: 2) also suggests a strong link between employee satisfaction and productivity and profitability. In fact, they indicate that aggregated job satisfaction within a company predicted up to 25 per cent of the variation between companies in performance and 12 per cent of profitability one year later. They argue that no other factor (such as competitive strategy, technology, market share, total quality management or R&D strategy) could so effectively predict company performance (Patterson & West, 1998: 3).

Similar results have been found by the Institute for Employment Studies in the UK (Barber, Hayday & Bevan, 1999; Bevan & Barber, 1999). Their survey of 65 000 employees and 25 000 customers in almost 100 retail stores showed a strong link between employee commitment and customer satisfaction and increased sales. The survey data indicated that a one point increase in employee commitment led to a monthly increase of £200 000 per store.

Human resources, capabilities and sustainability: a way forward

The future capabilities in the organisation and, as a consequence, the improvement in performance is premised on the belief that it is necessary to develop a new workplace culture, which emphasises the role of employees as assets rather than merely as a costly factor of production. Importantly, human sustainability is based on organisations pursuing an integrated strategy in which employee relations policies are integrated

Figure 4.2 Human resources, capabilities and sustainability: a way forward

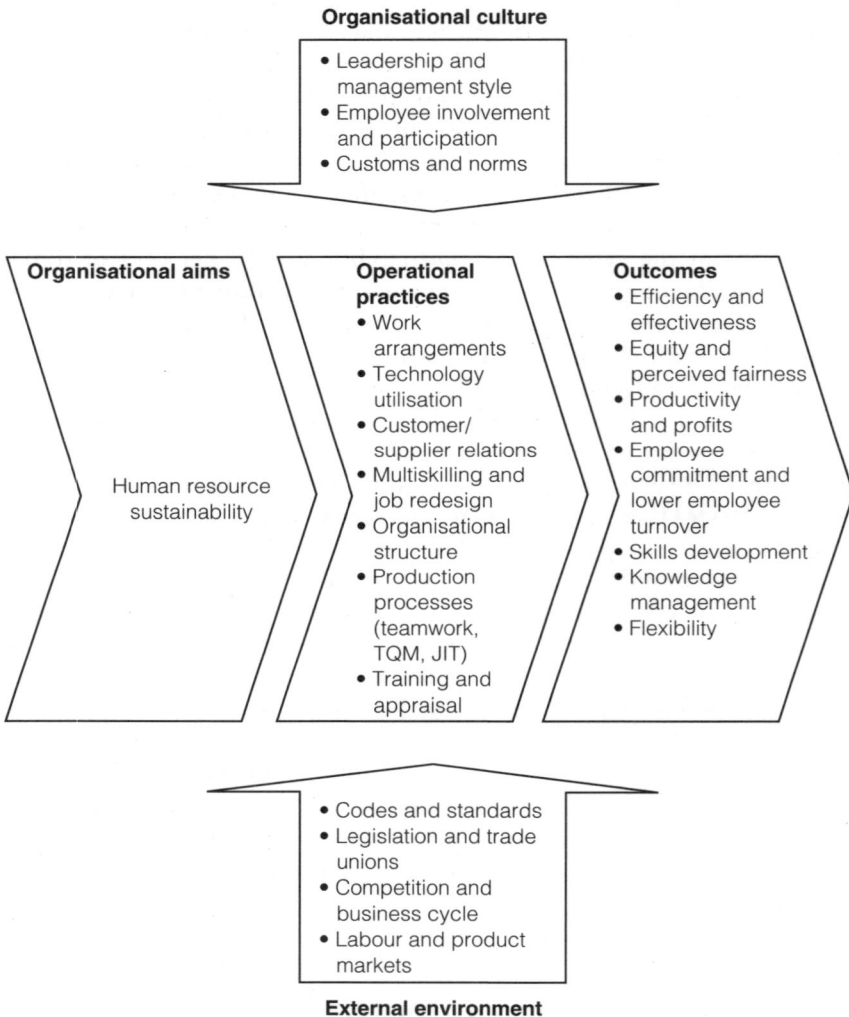

Organisational culture

- Leadership and management style
- Employee involvement and participation
- Customs and norms

Organisational aims

Human resource sustainability

Operational practices
- Work arrangements
- Technology utilisation
- Customer/ supplier relations
- Multiskilling and job redesign
- Organisational structure
- Production processes (teamwork, TQM, JIT)
- Training and appraisal

Outcomes
- Efficiency and effectiveness
- Equity and perceived fairness
- Productivity and profits
- Employee commitment and lower employee turnover
- Skills development
- Knowledge management
- Flexibility

- Codes and standards
- Legislation and trade unions
- Competition and business cycle
- Labour and product markets

External environment

into all aspects of the organisation's planning and implementation process (Gollan & Davis, 1997). It is important that an organisation 'continuously develops the organisational capabilities to identify and integrate within its vision and strategy the conceptual shifts needed to respond to dynamic markets and the operational capability to deliver' and enhance performance (Ford, 1999: 3). Increasingly the financial investors for superannuation and pension funds will realise that it is better to invest in companies where employers add value to their organisation by adding value to employees.

Figure 4.2 presents a model of an organisation pursuing a human resource sustainable approach. It emphasises the influence of organisational culture and the impact of the external environment on sustaining outcomes. The model shows that improved performance and productivity are predicated on the need for managers to use situationally attuned approaches to ensure that the potential of the organisation is contributing to desired organisational aims. Thus, there is no one best way for all organisations, only organic processes based on situational characteristics which satisfy the aims and objectives for the organisation and its employees in a sustainable way. As Roger Cowe (1999: 26) stated: 'The crucial issue is the value which underpins how companies go about their business, not whether they get everything "right".'

The lessons for human resource sustainability

If employers in advanced economies do not try to bridge the gap between the rhetoric of good people management and the reality, then the only likely outcome will be an organisation facing an exodus of bright and enthusiastic people. The lessons for organisations are that for true corporate sustainability a recognition and value must be placed on the internal human capability of the organisation.

In this process, the role of the human resource function is pivotal to the success of corporate sustainability policies. Dave Ulrich (1998) has suggested four ways in which human resources (HR) can deliver organisational excellence. First, by the HR function becoming a partner with senior and line managers in strategy implementation by forming the link between boardroom decisions and the marketplace. Second, by providing relevant expertise in the way work is organised and executed thus ensuring administrative efficiency. Third, representing employees' concerns to management while simultaneously giving employees the capacity to increase their contribution to organisational decision making. And fourth, the HR function should be an agent of change, shaping processes and culture that together improve and enhance an organisation's capacity for change (Ulrich, 1998: 124–5).

Importantly, this requires organisations to take a more holistic and integrated approach to people management. In particular managers need to reassess the role and level of the HR function, specifically its role in persuading organisations to adopt practices that support a sustainable approach (Hunt, 1999). This requires devolved decision making emphasising medium to long term sustainability rather than the short term horizons characteristic of more traditional, centralised corporate HR or personnel management approaches. The advocates of corporate level human sustainability issues and practices need to be political movers and leaders putting forward a HR agenda to support sustainability. At lower levels HR advocates need to be coordinators, mentors and integrators, linking and integrating human capabilities into organisational structures, technologies and practices of organisations (Hunt, 1999: 21). Ulrich has argued that:

> HR can be the architect of new cultures, but to do so, its purpose must to redefined. Virtually every imperative of the new mandate for HR requires such a redefinition. And for it to happen, senior managers must lead the way (Ulrich, 1998: 133).

The central challenge for the HR function will be to move organisations to adopt sustainable practices and structures towards different organisational strategies and create a climate whereby employees' potential can be released. As John Hunt has recently suggested:

> The key to the success of the function lies in the struggle to acquire more influence, something that is being carried out in a climate of downsizing and outsourcing. Even the change of name from personnel to HR is indicative that the way people view and perform this role is changing—with the new name communicating a desire to break with the past and to throw off an image that was limp and limiting . . . The future of the HR function may be far from certain . . . [however] . . . In situations of uncertainty, it is the confident who win through . . . I know of no organisation whose senior managers believe their company will operate, in the future, without any human beings. Whether ensuring the supply of those human beings resides in a function called HR or not is rather irrelevant (Hunt, 1999: 21).

Conclusion

Overall, the evidence presented in this chapter is that corporate sustainability is predicated on organisations recognising the needs of employees and implementing sustainable policies and practices to reinforce its values and principles. Only by acknowledging the importance of employee satisfaction and commitment through the development of integrated employee consultation, organisational change, work and life policies, workplace institutions and comprehensive career development programs, will the organisation achieve greater productivity and increased profits. The lessons are clear. It is up to organisations to ensure they are pursuing a comprehensive human resource sustainable approach for society's and their own survival.

References

American Management Association (AMA) 1996 *Survey: Corporate Downsizing, Job Elimination, and Job Creation*, AMA, Washington.

Australian Centre for Industrial Relations Research and Training (ACIRRT) 1999 *Australia at Work: Just Managing?*, Prentice Hall, Sydney.

Barber, L., Hayday, S. and Bevan, S. 1999 *From People to Profits*, The Institute for Employment Studies, London.

Bayliss, V. 1996 *Redefining Work*, Royal Society for the Arts, London.

Bevan, S. and Barber, L. 1999 'The benefits of service with a smile', *Financial Times*, 26 June.

Bilmes, L., Wetzker, K. and Xhonneux, P. 1997 'Value in human resources: A strong link between companies' investment in workers and stock market performance is revealed', *Financial Times*, 10 February.

Campling, J. and Gollan, P. 1999 *Bargained Out: Negotiating without Unions in Australia*, ACIRRT and Federation Press, Sydney.

Cascio, W. 1993 'Downsizing: What do we know? What have we learned?', *Academy of Management Executive*, vol. 7, no. 1.

Christy, D. 1998 'Downsizing to disaster', *The Guardian*, 5 November.

Cowe, R. 1999 'Ignore ethics at your peril', *The Guardian*, 24 April.

De Geus, A. 1997 'The living company', *Harvard Business Review*, March–April, vol. 75, no. 2, pp. 51–9.

De Lacy, A. 1999 'Understanding the knowledge worker', *HRMonthly*, February.

Department of Industrial Relations (DIR) 1995 *Annual Report: Enterprise Bargaining in Australia*, AGPS, Canberra.

Donkin, R. 1999 'Rewrite the rule book', *Financial Times*, 16 June, p. 19.

Dorfman, J. 1991 'Stocks of companies announcing layoffs fire up investors, but prices often wilt', *The Wall Street Journal*, 10 December.

Ford, J. 1999 'The Learning Enterprise: Market Driven Organisational Transformation in Lead Enterprises in Sweden', Working Paper, Bronte.

Freeman, R. 1996 'Growth and corporate behaviour', *CentrePiece*, Centre for Economic Performance, October.

Gallie, D., White, M., Cheng, Y. and Tomlinson, M. 1998 *Restructuring the Employment Relationship*, Oxford University Press, Oxford.

Gemini Consulting 1998 *Capitalising on the International Workplace Revolution*, Gemini Consulting Limited, London.

Gollan, P. 1998 *Having a Voice—Non-union Forms of Employee Representation in the United Kingdom and Australia*, British Universities Industrial Relations Association (BUIRA) Conference, Keele University, July.

Gollan, P. and Davis, E. 1997 'The implementation of HRM best practice: Beyond rhetoric', unpublished, Labour-Management Foundation, Macquarie Graduate School of Management, Sydney.

——1999 'High involvement management and organisational change: Beyond rhetoric', unpublished, Labour-Management Foundation, Macquarie Graduate School of Management, Sydney.

Gollan, P., Pickersgill, R. and Sullivan, G. 1996 *Future of Work: Likely Long Term Developments in the Restructuring of Australian Industrial Relations*, ACIRRT, Working Paper no. 43.

Guardian Weekly 1996 28 January.

Handy, C. 1997 *The Hungry Spirit: Beyond Capitalism—A Quest for Purpose in the Modern World*, Hutchinson, London.

Harvard Business Review 1999 'Editorial', May–June, p. 8.

Hunt, J. W. 1999 'Working in a rich human vein', *Financial Times*, 10 February, p. 21.

Kirby, J. 1999 'Downsizing gets the push', *Business Review Weekly*, 22 March, pp. 50–2.

Littler, G., Wiesner, R. and Vermeulen, L. 1997 'The effects of downsizing: Cross-cultural data from three countries', *Academy of Management Meeting*, Boston, MA.

Long, S. 1999 'College of Physicians warns Howard on health', *Australian Financial Review*, 8 April, p. 3.

Macken, J. 1999 'This is no time to be dwarf', *Australian Financial Review*, (accessed 26 May 199): http://www.afr.com.au/contant/990526/news/news10.html

Maitland, A. 1999 'A job that suits your lifestyle', *Financial Times*, 6 May.

Management Today 1995 Institute of Management (UK), November.

Morehead, A., Steele, M., Alexander, M., Stephen, K. and Duffin, L. 1997 *Change at Work: The 1995 Australian Workplace Industrial Relations Survey*, Longman, Melbourne.

OECD 1999 *OECD Employment Outlook*, OECD, Paris and Washington.

Patterson, M., West, M., Lawthom, R. and Nickell, S. 1997 *Impact of People Management Practices on Business Performance*, Issues in People Management no. 22, Institute of Personnel and Development, London.

Patterson, M. and West, M. 1998 'People power: The link between job satisfaction and productivity', *CentrePiece*, vol. 3, no. 3, Autumn, Centre for Economic Performance, London School of Economics.

Slavin, T. 1999 'Make a profit—do it for free', the *Observer*, 30 May.

Stewart, T. 1994 'Your company's most valuable asset: Intellectual capital', *Fortune*, 3 October.

The Economist 1996 'Fire and forget?', 20 April, pp. 57–8.

Thurow, L. C. 1993 *Head to Head: The Coming Economic Battle among Japan, Europe and America*, Morrow, New York.

Towers Perrin 1997 *The 1997 Towers Perrin Workplace Index: Great Expectations in the High-Performance Workplace*, New York.

Ulrich, D. 1998 'A new mandate for human resources', *Harvard Business Review*, January–February, pp. 124–34.

Universum International 1996 *Coopers and Lybrand Graduate Survey*, Stockholm.

Worrell, L. and Cooper, C. 1998 *The Quality of Working Life—The 1998 Survey of Managers' Changing Experiences*, Institute of Management, London.

5

Technologies and processes for human sustainability

Viv Read[1]

In virtually all successful science fiction movies, there is a common theme, an inadvertent and revealing contrast. Technology is breathtakingly elegant, precise and powerful. Improvements over modern technology are stupendous and glittering. But in this future, people relate to each other in exactly the same way they do now. The same duplicity, superficiality, hostility, strategising and competing. No improvement whatsoever. Titles are Star Wars, rather than Star Peace (Will Schutz, 1994).

The focus

The focus of this chapter is the 'people part' of an enterprise—and specifically the ways that technologies and processes can enhance work-places and work spaces, provide environments where people enjoy working and learning, and assist in building and sustaining meaningful relationships with all stakeholders.

Corporations are evolving and taking new forms. However, it would seem likely that corporations will be part of the foreseeable future. Underpinning the ideas explored in the chapter is a strong belief in the need for corporations to play an active role in all areas of society. In our view, governments have neither the resources nor the capacity for the learning, creativity, innovation and quick responsiveness required to address many of the issues facing the world.

Our intent is to provide stimulus for further dialogue and conversation. Ideally the chapter should be read in conjunction with Chapter 8 written by Alan Pears. In the process of preparing and reviewing material for this book, we discovered many parallels and interdependencies in the issues raised in these two chapters. The interaction between people and technology is a critical and fundamental relationship in developing sustainable organisations.

Key questions

In this chapter, we address some key questions:

- What constitutes human sustainability from the perspective of the executives and managers of an enterprise? From that of employees? From that of other stakeholders?
- How can organisations select technologies and processes that support alignment between the needs of the business, and its stakeholders?
- How can the application of different technologies and processes support sustainable employment relationships and working arrangements?
- How can technologies and processes enable employees to undertake work in ways which promote personal and organisational learning, and their psychological well-being?

Frameworks and definitions

These definitions are the same as those used by Alan Pears in Chapter 8:

- 'Technology' refers to the tools that are used to produce the goods and services of an enterprise—that is, the 'hardware' of an organisation. It includes, but is not exclusively concerned with, information and communication technologies.
- 'Processes' are the 'software' needed to support and enhance the tools and technologies and this includes policies and guidelines, ways of working together, organisation and work design.

Figure 5.1 outlines the interaction between various elements of an organisation, and the critical influence that values and assumptions play in the choice of a particular technology or process, whether the desired outcome has financial, human or ecological sustainability as its focus.

Technology and processes are tools that interact with other elements of the organisation and with each other in order to achieve desired outcomes. The interactions are complex, and are not value free. The tools, technologies and processes themselves have embedded values and assumptions about people, working relationships and the way in which the

Figure 5.1 Simplified framework of selection and use of tools in organisations

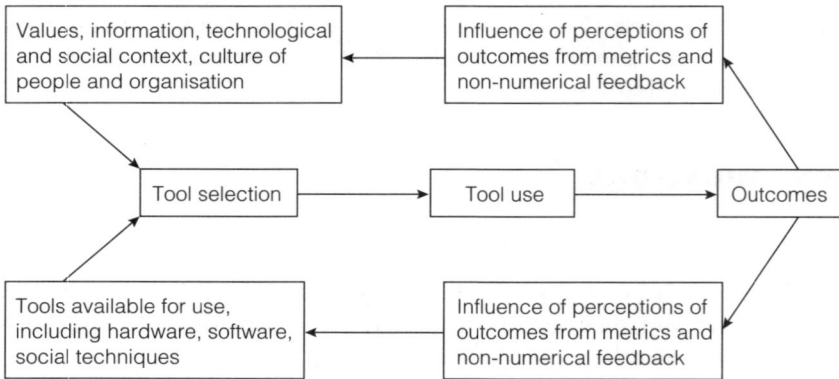

```
┌─────────────────────────────┐        ┌─────────────────────────────┐
│ Values, information,        │        │ Influence of perceptions of │
│ technological               │ ◄───── │ outcomes from metrics and   │
│ and social context, culture │        │ non-numerical feedback      │
│ of people and organisation  │        │                             │
└─────────────────────────────┘        └─────────────────────────────┘

        ┌──────────────┐        ┌──────────┐        ┌──────────┐
        │ Tool selection│ ────► │ Tool use │ ────► │ Outcomes │
        └──────────────┘        └──────────┘        └──────────┘

┌─────────────────────────────┐        ┌─────────────────────────────┐
│ Tools available for use,    │        │ Influence of perceptions of │
│ including hardware, software,│ ◄──── │ outcomes from metrics and   │
│ social techniques           │        │ non-numerical feedback      │
└─────────────────────────────┘        └─────────────────────────────┘
```

world should operate. Likewise, the values and assumptions of those establishing the outcomes and selecting what they believe to be appropriate tools also come into play—even if they are at times invisible or unconscious.

What is human sustainability?

From the perspective of the corporation . . .

The most obvious human sustainability imperative for enterprises is the alignment of the interests and needs of the business with those of their most important asset, their staff, so that business success can be achieved and maintained. The oft heard rhetoric of people being an important asset has become an imperative in the knowledge economy.

One of the great paradoxes of our time is that job security and loyalty have been weakened at the same time that organisations are more reliant than ever on their human and intellectual capital for business success. The impact of economic restructuring, and the advances in communication and information technology have fundamentally altered the employment relationship (see Chapter 4).

There are, however, other alignment challenges within the human sustainability arena for organisations that may not be so obvious. For example, there is the alignment with the needs and aspiration of shareholders, resulting in an increased emphasis on corporate governance and ethics. For example, shareholder expectations in relation to the transparency of decision making and access to information have changed significantly in the last decade in Australia.

At a global level, issues of corporate governance, including the rights of shareholders and the community to information, is the subject of a major OECD initiative, including ministerial level meetings. The 1999 OECD International Symposium on Intellectual Capital was addressed by Stuart Hornery, Chairman of the Lend Lease Corporation. In his view, we are moving 'towards a disclosure regime which is relevant, timely useful and reliable . . . inexorably towards real time reporting. The web page is where it will be at, and the annual report a matter of record' (OECD, 1999). Technology, therefore, has the capacity to transform the basis for investment decisions.

Contrasting cultures of capitalism impact also on the tools and strategies that are used. As Stace and Dunphy (1994: 24) point out, capitalism is practised differently in different parts of the world:

- Western Europe—stakeholder capitalism, balancing multi-party concerns and managing in a complex environment.
- US and other Western economies—shareholder capitalism, maximising share prices, with a focus on cost reduction and competitive strategies.
- Japan/Asia—collective capitalism, where the longer term, developmental and collective perspective results in a primary concern for developing an internationally competitive corporation.

There are also alignment needs for customers, suppliers and contractors. The challenge of alignment for staff, customers, shareholders and other stakeholders is not new, and has always been the role of management. However, traditionally, this was able to be achieved via command and control, in particular the control of information and knowledge.

Alignment will therefore result in the selection of very different tools and processes, depending on the desired outcomes. This also highlights why the transfer of tools and technologies across cultures (without addressing the embedded values and assumption at all levels of the process) is often ineffective and sometimes leads to costly problems in implementation.

From the perspective of the individual . . .

Human sustainability is essentially about psychological well-being, evidenced by a capacity for renewal, the nurturing of capability and an increasing capacity to cope with varied and unpredictable situations. Human sustainability has learning, growth, trust, freedom and choice as key elements. Outcomes include being able to take responsibility, make informed decisions based on information that is freely available, meeting the needs of self and others, and having relationships which contribute to identity and meaning for oneself and others.

Figure 5.2 Key elements of organisations

Key elements of the 'rational'
world of organisations

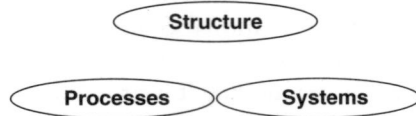

```
                                    ( Structure )

                  ( Processes )  ( Systems )
```

Key elements of the 'non-rational'
world of organisations

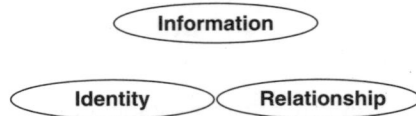

```
                                 ( Information )

                  ( Identity )  ( Relationship )
```

Source: Draws on the work of Margaret Wheatley, 1992. Acknowledgement: Phil Baas, Draft One
Communications, Melbourne, and Tim Dalmau, Dalmau & Associates, Brisbane.

For corporations, increasing interest in the psychological well-being
of its stakeholders, particularly staff, often derives from a better understanding of the costs incurred with high levels of staff turnover, conflict
and absenteeism.

The sustainable work environment: a framework

Within work environments, an environment that promotes human sustainability emerges as a result of the interplay between the factors shown
in Figure 5.2.

This diagram is the framework for the Queensland Public Service
Experiential Leadership Development Program. This model emphasises
the need to build structures, systems and processes that are based on the
'non- rational' elements at both the collective and individual level; that
is, systems and structures that take account of the questions and issues
relating to:

- identity (What do I stand for? What are we known for? What are
  the values that guide our actions as individuals or organisations?)
- information (attitudes to access, openness and transparency, the
  power, control and authority, who needs what, who has access, who
  can use it)
- the quality of the relationships (levels of openness, feedback, levels
  of influence).

The 'non-rational' world is the chief arena for developing work environments that promote human sustainability—and it is critical to note that the term is non-rational, not irrational! The stated need to pay attention to the 'non-rational' elements of identity, information and relationships—for individuals and the organisation—is not new. The socio-technical systems approach to work design, pioneered by the Tavistock Institute in the UK and Scandinavia in the 1950s and 1960s, emphasised the need for equal attention to be paid to both the social and technical systems. The fourteen principles used by Dr Deming in applying quality management also contained both aspects, and many of the more recent tools and processes, including re-engineering, likewise advocate the need to include consideration of the 'people aspects'.

There has, however, been a significant gap between acknowledging the need to be concerned about people, and having this concern manifested in practical and ongoing approaches to the development of firms that promote sustainability. The emergence and organisational legitimacy of personnel departments, and more recently employee relations and human resource departments, has generally been derived from a reluctance on the part of managers to identify these issues and a lack of capability in addressing them.

Even the language that has developed has contributed to these aspects of organisational life being seen as less important. For example, people management being based on 'soft' skills.

There is no quick technological fix to social and human issues in workplaces. For example, in 1973, when I was working as an industrial relations practitioner, the advent of containerisation on the Australian waterfront was heralded as a way to reduce the control that waterside workers exercised, based on the notion that their influence would be reduced if there were less of them. The impact was of course the opposite—a smaller number of people could, and did, have a greater impact. In Brisbane, after the introduction of this new technology, only one person needed to 'go slow' to significantly impact the productivity of the whole terminal. Disruption acquired a new ease and elegance, without losing any pay.

Alignment for human sustainability: manipulation or interdependence?

How can the needs of staff and stakeholders be aligned with the needs of the business? One view is that it occurs through an act of conscious manipulation. The values and assumptions that prevail within the enterprise, including those values held about people, directly inform the choice of initiative or strategy developed to encourage alignment. It could be likened to the political strategy of giving speeches based on the results of elector's fears and concerns.

Another view is that alignment occurs because organisations are driven to respond to the changes that are occurring in society and have not really adopted any of the core values and philosophies essential to long term human sustainability—that they are merely bowing to the inevitable rather than taking a lead. Those holding this view cite the apparent paradox of the numbers of people prepared to listen to business leaders such as Anita Roddick of The Body Shop, or Ricardo Semmler of Semco—without there being any upsurge in the implementation of different approaches.

For example, developing and promulgating visions and missions for organisations is regarded as a fundamental component of alignment—to enable stakeholders to know what an organisation's values are and what it stands for. However, there are certainly those who believe that this has been, in some organisations, a purely cynical process to manipulate alignment. The gap experienced by staff and customers between the rhetoric of espoused values and the policies, procedures and practices reinforces this view. Expressions such as 'we need buy-in', 'how will we get staff to sign off', 'developing ownership of the vision and values', while purporting to demonstrate a concern for alignment may simply obscure a deliberate and conscious choice of language rather than making real changes in the way things are done. Increasingly, the shift in the relationship between an organisation and its stakeholders enabled by technology is resulting in ongoing, dynamic and responsive processes being developed.

Management's alignment challenge

A sustainable corporation will need a willingness to change, a passion for developing the capacity and self-confidence of its inhabitants which are valued more than the physical assets. The organisation should be viewed not as a property but as a community, i.e., people are no longer considered to be human resources but are looked upon as citizens working toward a common purpose (Handy, 1997b: 28).

In the previous chapter, Paul Gollan identifies the impacts of some of the more recent approaches to strategic management. Government in-itiatives to support global competition, including floating the Australian dollar, the deregulation of markets, the removal of tariff barriers, and the mantra of competition and the level playing field provided impetus for restructuring of the economy on a massive scale, and led to the introduction of terms such as downsizing, re-engineering—and even right-sizing—into the language.

The dominant strategic management and economic rationalist approach is based almost exclusively on intervening at the rational level. Given the desired objective of planned and purposeful competition, this process often demands a high level of internal change, for example, mergers, acquisitions, divestments. While it may be argued that this was an appropriate response for the environment at the time, evidence is mounting that it does not create sustainable workplaces. In fact, few organisations realised the anticipated results that the approach promised, in large part due to the almost exclusive concern with the competitive environment and strategy. The approach says little about how to achieve strategic outcomes and many of the unintended consequences were often the result of social and ecological factors (for a more complete analysis see Dunphy & Griffiths, 1998: 109–34).

It is also predicated on the totally unrealistic assumption that all human behaviour is rational, and the people will respond appropriately to rational debate and discussion about what is needed to achieve economic and financial imperatives.

New concepts and language

Lead enterprises have already understood the limitations of the economic rationalist approach, and are adopting different metaphors and strategies to developing sustainable organisations. Leading writers and commentators (for example, Arie de Gues, Margaret Wheatley, Charles Handy and Peter Drucker) have influenced the transition of strategic management to incorporate processes designed to address long term corporate sustainability.

The emerging models and metaphors being used draw extensively on the increased understanding of ecological systems and include terms such as:

- interdependence
- integration
- open systems
- chaos theory
- quantum theory
- community
- learning
- relationships
- social responsibility.

This list should not be seen as exhaustive, however, the terms serve as the context for exploring human sustainability issues in greater depth. Many of the themes outlined here are explored in more detail in other chapters of this book.

The very notion of work is changing. It is shifting from a focus on tasks and activities, just 'doing things' to creating wealth and value for organisations, customers and ourselves, achieving these outcomes through knowledge. The 'workforce' is increasingly transitory. More people work as contractors, consultants, in part time roles. Many are choosing this, others have had full time work removed as an option. Some estimates are that within five years, more than 50 per cent of people involved in doing corporate work will not be core employees of the business. The values and expectations of the workforce are changing. Recent research demonstrates that the next generation of employees have different values, and therefore expectations of the workplace (see below). Both chaos and order exist. Increasingly, leadership is about establishing the intent, purpose and values of an organisation and the work to be performed—and then getting out of the way. People then behave in similar ways as the 'strange attractors' identified by scientists—if the purpose is clear, the bits will find each other and connect in the ways needed to achieve that purpose.

Boundaries are blurred—between organisations, between functions, between disciplines. Knowledge does not fit neatly into the compartments and structures that we have created to assist 'good management'. Customers are not prepared to interact with five or six different sections to achieve their desired outcome. They expect the organisation to provide that integration for them. It is a 'both/and' world, not an 'either/or' world. This is a world of infinite paradox—we want high tech *and* high touch; organisations demand stability *and* innovation; employers want flexibility *and* loyalty; employees want equity *and* individuality. There is no one 'right' answer—rather there are an infinite number of options and possibilities.

The focus must be on interdependence and relationships. If nothing else, we are already acutely aware that achieving outcomes requires people to be able to work together—in different and often fast changing combinations. Cyberspace project teams and multi-team membership are becoming more commonplace.

Places for work are now wherever the person is. Airports, homes, planes, cars, hotels, cafes and restaurants are all being reconfigured to support multiple usage. Some large hotels now have 'cyber' customer service staff—available 24 hours a day to assist guests with their communication connections. All airports provide opportunities for travellers to connect to communications networks and send messages. Cyberspace cafes increase in numbers. Some aircraft already allow Internet and phone connections.

Spaces for work have also undergone a revolution. There are multiple spaces—depending on the nature of the activity—rather than a personal space in which one person undertakes all activities. Spaces within office buildings can be shared, separate, quiet, open, configured for teams, designed for meeting with customers. The person becomes portable and mobile—moving to the most appropriate space for the particular activity.

The role of information and communication technology

While there is common agreement that technology has had an enormous impact, there are widely varying views on the likely outcomes. There are as many advocates for technology as a saviour, ensuring a new and glorious age of creativity and imagination, as there are purveyors of the view that the dark or shadow side of technology will create a divided society with an under class of employee.

Information and communication technology have certainly created a *shift in the power relationship* between employer and employee, between purchaser and supplier, between shareholder and corporation. The Internet is an anarchic organisation—where the traditional notions of access to and control of information are rendered obsolete. Information can be shared and made available without any reference to status or position.

Information: Collection and use

Sustainable organisations have realised the need to shift their focus/ mind set from technology as the driver and solution, to technology as the enabler, with people applying judgement to provide options. That is, technology enables access to information and knowledge—people are needed to apply judgement, discretion and initiative.

The focus of any business is shifting to developing and sustaining effective external relationships, as information about customers is more accessible. It has become easier to identify and/or predict customer needs rather than just reacting to them. It is the era of mass customisation, where customers—and employees—expect to be treated as individuals within the framework of the products and services on offer.

This results in a shift in the internal emphasis to the acquisition and sharing of knowledge, continuous learning and the elimination of demarcations. Employees are expected to be flexible and adaptable, and able to respond with increasing speed. And technology is seen as the deliverer of this capability.

However, as Rudy Ruggles (1998) points out, technology is only 25 per cent of the answer—the right processes and work organisation, and attention to people are the remaining 75 per cent of any effective knowledge management strategy.

To date, the emphasis has been on the storage and retrieval of data and information. This certainly is the absolute province of technology. The utilisation of the information, by translating it into knowledge, and ultimately wisdom, requires *people*. This necessity provides one of the greatest cross cultural learning challenges—having information technology (IT) people and people management specialists being able to understand each other, and work together.

Technology: The enabler, not the driver

Research undertaken by Cultural Imprints Pty Ltd (1994, 1996) demonstrated that Australians at least do not differentiate between the quality of the product or service and the quality of the relationship with the provider. We want high-tech and high-touch, as employees and customers. So, despite all of the high-tech solutions that might be available, it will be the nature and quality of the relationship which will be paramount.

In addition, knowledge is not beholden to hierarchy; in fact IT has the capacity to democratise knowledge. Whether this promise is realised is dependent on the values and assumptions that underpin the way in which systems are designed. Organisational design, and people management systems and processes, reflect the level of understanding about the ways in which people need to operate in order to achieve desired outcomes. They also reflect the values and assumptions that are made about people, particularly the level of trust.

It depends on your point of view . . .

Call centres are increasingly seen as a way of meeting the challenges of customer service in the era of speed and response—and availability 24 hours a day. The knowledge available to call centre operators, via sophisticated technology, means that in principle customers can get answers and decisions immediately. Call centres are seen as a source of employment, and geography no longer matters. In Australia, the governments of Tasmania and South Australia have invested heavily in the infrastructure to support call centres, to provide a source of employment given the demise of more traditional manufacturing and mining industries. These centres are seen as critical in the new customer relationship—doing business any time, anywhere. However, there is a potential downside.

The technology has sophisticated measuring and reporting capabilities, including the number of key strokes per minute, the number and duration of calls answered by an operator, time away from the console—and so on. For some operators in call centres, the experience is a more palatable version of the Tayloristic assembly line at the turn of the century, but nevertheless highly controlled, highly stressful, and totally lacking in the quality of working relationships. The phrase 'this call may be monitored for quality' which is used by some organisations seems to have more than a hint of 'big brother' and *1984* about it. Employees working in this environment tell of the level of pressure exerted on them, including huge electronic signs which indicate the number of 'calls waiting'. And so, while there may be customer service charters, and skills and training relating to customer relationships, the overwhelming value system remains one of lack of trust—and demands for quantity not quality. This can be exacerbated when the call centre is outsourced, and operators have minimal alignment with the organisation they are representing.

Telecommuting is another example where the application of the technology and the experience of telecommuters varies—not due to the technology, but to the values of the managers. Working from home, as a basis of providing flexibility to employers, and reduced costs to employees has long been advocated as making an important and valuable contribution to creating a better work environment. Additionally, there are those who see telecommuting has having a positive impact on the natural environment—reducing the numbers travelling, road congestion and so on. However, telecommuting and the use of mobile technology to maintain contact and productivity have also had significant negative effects on the quality of work life. Even Microsoft acknowledges the dilemma—even if their solution is yet another piece of software (see Box 5.1)!

Many managers, when asked about their concerns regarding telecommuting, rate as the most fundamental not being able to see whether or not the person is doing what they say they are—the classic concerns of control—and whether they as managers will retain their jobs given that these members of the workforce are managing themselves. In some organisations, policies regarding advance notice required for managers to visit people's homes have had to be developed—a mirror perhaps of union officials needing to have permission to visit a work site!

Box 5.1

8am 'In the ever decreasing space called peace and quiet, you contemplate the reason you came to work today. The past year has not been easy and this one is a repeat. And there's still New Year's Eve to look forward to. The company has taken to e-mail and now it is asking about e-commerce.'

Source: Advertisement for Microsoft Office 2000 in *Communiqué*, May 1999

What are employees seeking for their workplaces?

The Gallup organisation has undertaken extensive research over the past 25 years. An article by Harry Onsman identified the twelve core elements that attract and retain productive employees (Onsman, 1999). The twelve questions which the researchers believe are particularly important to the most productive and talented employees, although of little consequence to under-performing staff, were:

1 Do I know what is expected of me?
2 Do I have the materials and equipment that I need to do my work right?
3 At work, do I have the opportunity to do what I do best every day?
4 In the past seven days, have I received recognition or praise for good work?
5 Does my supervisor, or someone at work, care about me as a person?
6 Is there someone who encourages my development?
7 At work, do my opinions seem to count?
8 Does the mission of my company make me feel like my work is important?
9 Are my co-workers committed to doing quality work?
10 Do I have a best friend at work?
11 In the past six months have I talked with someone about my progress?
12 At work, have I had the opportunity to work and grow?

Most of these questions are directed to the quality of workplace relationships—and notice that pay did not make the list! In other words, while pay may be important for job satisfaction, it does not make the workplace a great place to be. High performing professional workers take it for granted that they will be well paid, or they will find another workplace.

The implications are clear. While issues such as pay and incentive schemes and other corporate-wide policies and strategies consume time and attention, the critical issue for the workplace in creating human sustainability rests with the experience of working relationships at the work group level.

The 1999 State of the Art and Practice survey, conducted by the Human Resource Planning Society (US), the Australian Human Resources Institute (AHRI) and others found that organisations were looking for 'missionaries—not mercenaries'. Yet, it could be argued, it is the recent practices of organisations in the search for competition and efficiency at all costs which have created the current cynicism, particularly in the generations following the baby boomers. For these generations their experience of the world means that they bring very different values and aspirations to work.

Why has loyalty declined?

Research undertaken by the Human Resource Institute (US) in 1997 identified the key factors that have contributed to the decline in loyalty among employees. The findings are hardly surprising; namely that restructuring (74 per cent), downsizing (63 per cent), re-engineering (48 per cent), and outsourcing (44 per cent) are the four most significant causes listed by participants in the survey. Some may wish to argue about what came first—the change in loyalty as a result of management behaviour or management behaviour changing due to changes in loyalty. It seems more important to acknowledge that the nature of the employment relationship, or psychological contract between employer and employed, has changed irrevocably.

Recent research from the Human Resource Institute (US), Hugh Mackay in Australia and Skandia Insurance (Sweden) demonstrates changes in values and assumptions in different generations of employees. These values emerge as a result of the way in which they have experienced the world as they have grown up. The boundaries for each of the generations under scrutiny vary, and should not be seen as absolute, and there are different titles given. For the purpose of our analysis it is the shifts over time that are important and that will have significant impact on developing human sustainability within organisations.

- Depression/war generation: These people have, to a significant extent, already left the workforce. They are, however, often involved in a wide range of volunteer work. Their formative years were dominated by the insecurities and uncertainties resulting from war, and the worldwide recession.

- Baby boomers: Born immediately post-Second World War, their numbers reflect the optimism of the time. They are strongly represented in the leadership structures of organisations.
- Generation X/options generation: This group have also been coined the 'me' generation. Hugh Mackay identifies the key behaviour of leaving as many options open as possible for as long as possible as a direct response to witnessing the impact of massive economic restructuring and downsizing. They have internalised the view that the only constant is change.
- Click and go: This title was coined by Leif Edvinsson of Skandia Insurance, with the subtitle 'born with a mouse in their hand'. Jay Jamrog, the US researcher, calls them the 'baby boomlets'. They are already making their presence felt in the world of communication technology.

The following tables draw on the work of all of the above.

Table 5.1 The generations

	Depression/war	Baby boomer	Generation 'X'/options generation	Click and go
Born	1927–45	1946—64	1965–83	1984–2002
Age in 2000	55–73	36–54	17–35	0–16
Age in 2010	65–83	46–64	27–45	8–26

Each generation has different values and expectations. Some of the differences are captured in the table below.

Table 5.2 Lifestyle characteristics

Depression/war	Baby boomer	Generation X	Click and go
Work hard	Work hard	Work hard if it	Good grades
Save money	Play hard	doesn't interfere	Make others pay
What is play?	Worry about money	with play	Save money
		Save money	
I Like it	Should I really like	I like it	Who are you
It's OK	it?	I don't care what	anyway?
	What will others	you think	You're old
	think?		
Buy a decent house	Buy the best house	Reclaim the inner	I like living with
	you can	city	my parents

These translate into very different values and expectations in the workplace.

Workplaces based on the values of the baby boomers do not necessarily attract and retain key staff from other generations. A recent survey

Table 5.3 Workplace characteristics

Depression	Baby boomer	Generation X	Click and go
Strong work ethic	Money/principles	Principles/satisfaction	There is no clear trend as yet
Independent but conventional	Care deeply what others think	Don't care what others think	Don't care what others think
Technically savvy	Technically challenged	Technically savvy	Technically sophisticated
Hoe to the end of the row	Work and family	Lifestyle first	Lifestyle first
Follow the leader	Lip service to mission	Care about mission	Must have a mission
Follow the leader	Want others to work with	Work best alone	Work best alone

Source: Jamrog, J. 1997 *The Generations at Work: Work Ethic, Loyalty and Attitudes*, Human Resource Planning Society Annual. Conference 'Business Issues: Get linked or get lost', 16–19 April, San Francisco

of Harvard graduates showed that the percentage that aspires to working for one of the Fortune 500 companies has plummeted. Large companies, successful in traditional terms, are not seen as sufficiently flexible, exciting and challenging (Jamrog, 1997).

Lead organisations are taking these shifts very seriously. Hewlett Packard employs social anthropologists in their research centre. Skandia Insurance and Financial Services (AFS) has a 'three generations policy'— any team concerned with developing new products and services or thinking about the future must have a minimum of three generations represented on it. IT companies in Silicon Valley are developing work environments significantly different to those we are used to, where 'Gen. X' employees come and go as they please, have all of the latest pieces of technology to use, the canteen consists of vending machines, and the focus is on delivering agreed outcomes. Individuals seek out assistance as and when they need to, to achieve their goals. Baby boomer managers are said to avoid the area!

The changing nature of employment relationships

Traditionally, employment contracts have been *relational*—based on an exchange of loyalty for job security and the possibility of promotion. More recently, the obsession with downsizing, restructuring, contracting and outsourcing has led to contracts which are *transactional*—short term financial relationships which result in low levels of emotional commitment.

What is emerging is the understanding that in this world, what is required is *relationship based contracts*, which have the following features:

- Shared vision, common purpose, learning relationships and common knowledge resources become the glue holding the enterprise together, and providing overall direction.
- Environments where people choose to add value to the large amounts of information available to them.
- Customisation of employment arrangements, where an individual has much greater scope to make decisions about the particular mix of money, time, immediate and deferred benefits wanted.
- Opportunities for continuous learning. The loyalty of people will be primarily to their knowledge networks, not any particular organisation or institution. Attracting and retaining key staff will require environments of challenge and learning which allow people to use and develop their knowledge networks.
- The boundaries of strategic purpose and intent provide space within which people have freedom to operate in their own preferred way.

A new era: the knowledge economy

If learning is the main characteristic of social and economic change, then human capital information and decision making systems—the determinants of learning—become central to efforts to cope with change. The need to rethink the way we make choices about the utilisation and acquisition of human capital arises from the profound upheavals taking place in the nature of technology, wealth creation and employment (OECD 1996).

Knowledge based organisations

Knowledge based organisations are organisations for whom intangible assets—skill knowledge and information—are more valuable than tangible assets (plant and equipment). The most often quoted example is Microsoft where the share price bears no relationship to the balance sheet. Organisations of this kind will increasingly dominate the economy.

Leif Edvinsson (1997), Vice president of Intellectual Capital for Skandia AFS, has three operating principles that underpin the development of that organisation's intellectual capital balance sheet:

- the value of intellectual assets exceeds by many times the value of assets that appear on a traditional balance sheet
- intellectual capital is the raw material from which financial results are made
- managers must distinguish between human capital and structural capital—while human capital is the source of creativity and inno-

vation, unless individual 'know how' is converted into products, processes and shared knowledge banks which become the property of the group, the quality and capability of individuals are not valuable.

In more recent times, it has been recognised that it is not just the so-called knowledge companies that need to pay attention to their intellectual capital—and to the ways in which value is created in the application of knowledge. A knowledge-based organisation can be established whenever the information being collected can be captured, shared and valued effectively. This means that mining and manufacturing companies can become knowledge-based, and use their intellectual capital to generate value.

Increasingly, there is attention directed to how it will be measured and reported. Stuart Hornery, Chairman of the Lend Lease Corporation, has said that 'the relevance of the balance sheet is less today than previously, and the importance of credible stories is increasing' (OECD, 1999).

Performance: measurement, management, reporting

> If the beginning of the next century will see the decisive breakthrough of the knowledge economy, it will be to a large extent the result of increasingly sophisticated ways of measuring human competence and other intangibles, and the harmonisation of these measures (OECD, 1999).

One of the ongoing and perplexing questions must surely be that if we know what we know, including how important people are, why don't we do things differently? If business leaders really believe that people are the most important asset, why is it that legislation is needed in areas such as equal employment opportunity, diversity and antidiscrimination? What are our business leaders responding to? And what, if anything, can be changed to shift the balance?

The weight of market forces in Australia and many other developed countries seems to have resulted in narrow measures of performance based on shareholder value, short term cost savings and competitive advantage. However, financial markets are starting to recognise the limitations of financial measures as an indicator of future performance, and new measures are emerging which focus on intangible assets, including customer capital, and structural capital. Stock exchanges, accountants, auditors, shareholders all have a strong interest in better indications of viability and sustainability than are offered by the traditional measure contained on a balance sheet. Practices, however, are slow to change.

Sustainable human resource management policies and practices

In his article, Arie de Gues (1997b) emphasises the shift that needs to take place in the values base of organisations that attempt to be sustainable. To aid human sustainability, people management strategies must:

- place commitment to people before assets
- respect innovation before devotion to policy
- understand that learning is a messy not an orderly process
- give people the space to develop ideas in an environment that gives some freedom from control.

This is supported by Peter Senge, the respected commentator and author on learning organisations.

> Top down leadership breeds fear, distrust, internal competition which is not commensurate with cooperation. In the future leadership will be distributed amongst diverse individuals and teams who share a responsibility for creating the organisation's future (Senge, 1997: 32).

Management should support this trend by supplying trust and respect, allowing flexible work hours and managing individual and team development and performance. Higher worker morale and loyalty will follow (this is the human sustainability challenge). In this type of organisation there will be a variety of conditions of employment, for example, employees, contractors, consultants, strategic partners.

Some of the shifts in workplace arrangements that are already evident include:

- Performance management systems are emerging that emphasise collective accountability for 'whole of organisation' performance replacing individual contracts; concern for outcomes is replacing a focus on inputs.
- 'Balanced scorecard' measures are being used to ensure that collective accountability and interdependence underpin working relationships and activities, and that expectations relating to the non-rational elements are explicit in the organisation's reporting systems and mechanisms.
- Cross functional teams are being created that include customers and suppliers working on real business issues and problems in real time—action learning/action research. Learning is provided 'just in time' as the team needs it rather than 'just in case'.
- There is a move toward communities of practice built around the core capabilities needed by the organisation. Communities of prac-

tice are groups of professionals focusing on a particular problem, issue or opportunity. They network informally to exchange ideas, skills and information to increase shared knowledge. They are fluid, flexible and cut through organisational boundaries.
- There is recognition that it is the quality of relationships which create the difficulties in contractual arrangements. Investing time in discussing the expectations for relationships and developing shared values can reduce litigation and contractual conflicts—resulting in values based contracts.

Delivering traditional human resource products and services

As with all aspects of an organisation, the human resource function is also being exhorted to be better, faster, and more responsive. The application of technology to many of the traditional roles and functions of human resource (HR) management practitioners is already extensive. As indicated above, the underlying paradigm is that managers and employees should be provided with the information and support necessary for them to make their own decisions, and to share in managing the employment relationship and working arrangements. If HR uses technology to increase the speed and quality of its people-related decision making, then HR can have a major impact on getting innovative products and services to the market with speed and efficiency.

'High-tech organisations' such as Intel and Sun Microsystems are exemplars of how technology can be used. The four emerging tenets of a high-tech HR strategy are:

- most HR work is no longer done face to face, but at a distance
- most traditional HR work is being shifted away from centralised HR managers to managers close to the employees and to employees themselves
- technology is the basic foundation of HR program design; it allows us to make more informed decisions, faster
- all HR programs must be continually improved (as a result they become difficult for competitors to copy)—attracting and retaining key talent is a competitive advantage (Sullivan, 1997; Jamrog, 1998).

The HR system is no longer just about processing information, but also about enabling the development of shared practices, and increasing the levels of autonomy and self-management of employees.

Employee services are increasingly available on intranets, and groupware. Already services include the following:

Table 5.4 Recruitment and selection

Online	Computer assisted
Video or text interviewing	Web page recruiting
Advertisements and job descriptions	Resume scanning and sorting
Application forms, applicant screening	Resume data bases
Internal job posting	Redeployment systems
Orientation	Internal labour market supply, forecasting,
Applicant skill testing	analysis
Search capability for managers seeking	Recruitment effectiveness tracking
applicants	

Table 5.5 Employee relations

Online	Computer assisted
Expert systems to advise managers	Trend analysis and identification of
Documentation of events/incidents	potential trouble spots
Performance appraisal systems	Affirmative action/EEO analysis and plans
360 degree feedback	
Instant and/or random employee/climate	
surveys	
Forums, bulletin boards	
Q and A sessions with CEO	
Exit interviews	

Table 5.6 Reward and recognition

Online	Computer assisted
Salary surveys	'At risk' calculations and measures
Paperless approval systems	Pay equity analysis
Kiosk systems—employees can self-select,	Job analysis forms and data analysis
adjust	
HR call centres	
Benefits surveys and benchmarking	
International/national comparisons	

Table 5.7 Skill and career development

Online	Computer assisted
Self-paced skill modules	Mentoring applications and placements
List servers and newsgroups as learning	Just in time course development and
forums	delivery
Learning needs assessment	
Video conferencing for information exchange	
Career development and advice	
Knowledge bank—articles, book summaries,	
speeches, graphics presentations etc.	
Groupware for team communication and	
learning	

By using IT developments, strategic human resource management can contribute to both ecological and human sustainability, in particular by:

■ managing remotely located people
■ customisation of the employment relationship
■ increasing self-sufficiency/self-management.

A warning . . .

Many of the systems and processes included in the new approach to human resource management are based on a value of increasing the capacity for individuals to exercise choice and self-management. This often assumes that employees already have the necessary skills, knowledge and confidence to do this. In fact, many do not.

When people do not have the capacity to cope with feelings of negativity, fear and helplessness, then systems which assume the ability to speak authentically and take responsibility for our own emotional health are irrelevant. Assuming that understanding and alignment is the responsibility of individuals rather than rethinking the organisation's demands and expectations may negate the intent for increased self-management.

Values and visions alone do not transform organisations. Too often, the gap perceived by employees between managerial rhetoric and organisational reality is so great that they become cynical and stressed. Designing elegant feedback systems and climate surveys will not be helpful—however quickly they may be administered and processed—if people do not have the skills to engage in direct, honest feedback, or a belief that feedback will be a learning rather than a punitive process.

There is a strong risk that the application of technologies obscures the fundamental and long held challenge—the quality of human re-flationships in work environments. It may well contribute to the people management process itself remaining, at its heart, a rational based approach, rather than addressing the real issues that will make meaning for people.

Ensuring sustainability

As the opening quotation from Will Schutz indicates, all of the glitter and glamour offered by new technology has the potential to obscure the real challenge for human sustainability—developing and sustaining effective relationships, and ensuring the psychological health and well-being of all stakeholders.

If we continue to manage and lead our organisations from the sole perspective of the 'rational' world of systems, structures, policies and procedures, the promises that the new technologies offer will not be realised. It would be history repeating itself, many previous transformational processes did not come to fruition—because of the lack of capability and commitment to developing and sustaining effective working relationships.

Alan Briskin (1998) suggests that the following questions be asked when considering issues of sustainability at an individual, organisational and societal level:

- *Individual emotional health and wellness:* Do I look forward to going to work, being at work, working with others? Do I bring enough of what makes me special to my work? Is there pride in what results from my work? Do I achieve some degree of balance between work and other areas of my life? Can I make choices about competing interests, and not feel guilty?
- *Organisational level questions*: How are power and authority distributed? How is compensation handled? Can we allow individuals and sub groups to act on behalf of the whole? Do our systems of compensation respect the different ways in which people contribute? Do we create a climate where our emotional lives and lives outside work matter?
- *At the societal level:* What is the net environmental impact of our business? What is the effect of our business on the community in which we operate? Would it matter to anyone other than ourselves if our product or service disappeared from the face of the earth?

Sustainable systems are living systems—whether human or ecological. They evolve in response to the questions that we are prepared to ask, the discussions and conversations we are prepared to have, the extent to which we really embrace inclusiveness and diversity. They cannot be copied from a notion of 'best practice models'; rather they must reflect the result of a collective exploration of identity, meaning and purpose.

While our environmental context is changing rapidly, providing additional and complex challenges in aligning people and business needs and outcomes, the foundation for human sustainability is the individual, team and organisational capability to develop and sustain effective working relationships. Given this base, the technology available can provide for mass customisation of meaningful workplace arrangements. Without this, employees may well choose to withhold their intellect, motivation and passion—and become mercenaries not missionaries.

Endnote

1 At the time of writing, Viv was National President of the Australian Human Resource Institute (AHRI). Acknowledgment is given to the work of staff at AHRI, particularly Jo Poxon, Information Central, and Richard Cranston and Diane Simic, Customer Service Centre, for their assistance in undertaking research for this chapter.

References

Briskin, A. 1998a *The Stirring of Soul in the Workplace*, Berret-Koehler, San Francisco.
——1998b 'Wrestling with Sustainability: Pitfalls abound for the Unwary', *At Work*, January–February.
Cultural Imprints Pty Ltd 1994 *Leaders in Australia: The Australian Cultural Imprint for Leadership*, Mimeograph, Warrandyte, Vic.
——1996 *Leadership in Australia*, Monograph, Australian Quality Council, Warrandyte, Vic.
De Geus, A. 1997a *The Living Company*, Nicholas Brearley, London.
——1997b 'The Living Company', *Harvard Business Review*, March–April, vol. 75, no. 2, pp. 51–9.
Drucker, P., Dyson. E., Handy, C. Saffo, P. and Senge, P., 1997 'Looking ahead; Implications of the present', *Harvard Business Review*, September–October, vol. 75, no. 5, pp. 18–32.
Dunphy, D. and Griffiths, A. 1998 *The Sustainable Corporation: Organisational Renewal in Australia*, Allen & Unwin, Sydney.
Edvinsson, L. 1998 'Skandia Corporate Story', Keynote presentation to Australian Human Resource Institute National Convention, Canberra.
Edvinsson, L. and Malone, M. 1997 *Intellectual Capital: Realizing your Company's True Value by finding its Hidden Brainpower*, Harper Business, New York.
Ellyard, P. 1998 *Ideas for the New Millennium*, Melbourne University Press, Melbourne.
Hahal, W. 1996 'The rise of the knowledge entrepreneur', *The Futurist*, November–December.
Handy, C. 1994 *The Empty Raincoat: Making Sense of the Future*, Hutchinson, London.
——1995 *Beyond Certainty*, Hutchinson, London.
——1997a *The Hungry Spirit*, Hutchinson, London.
Human Resource Institute (US) 1997 *Staffing Trends Survey*, Human Resource Institute, St Petersburg, Florida.

——1998 *HRI's 1998 Survey on Issues Impacting People Management Around the World*, Human Resource Institute, St Petersburg, Florida.

——1999 *The Generations at Work*, Human Resource Institute, St Petersburg, Florida or http://hri.eckerd.edu/10MFrames.htm

Jamrog, J. 1997 'The changing nature of work: People and HR', Presentation of HRI research to HRPS Convention, San Francisco.

——1998 'Future implications for organisations and HR executives' presentation of HRI research to HRPS Corporate Sponsors Conference, Scottsdale.

Johanson, U. 1996 'Increasing the transparency of investments in intangibles' Paper, OECD Conference 'Changing workplace strategies', Canada, December.

Long, S. 1998 'This woeful working life', *Australian Financial Review*, 7 November, p. 30.

Mackay, H. 1997 *Generations: Baby Boomers, Their Parents and Their Children*, Pan Macmillan, Sydney.

OECD 1996 'Measuring what People know: Human Capital Accounting for the Knowledge Economy', OECD, Paris.

——1999 International Symposium 'Measuring and Reporting Intellectual Capital: Experience, Issues and prospects', Amsterdam, 9–11 June.

Onsman, H. 1999 'The secret of a happy office', *Business Review Weekly*, 11 June.

Ruggles, R. 1998 'The state of the notion: Knowledge management in practice', *California Management Review*, Spring.

Stace, D. and Dunphy, D. 1994 *Beyond the Boundaries: Leading and Re-Creating the Successful Enterprise*, McGraw-Hill, Sydney.

Sullivan, J. 1998 'Hi Tech HR', *HRMonthly*, June.

Wheatley, M. 1992 *Leadership and the New Science*, Berett-Koehler, San Francisco.

Wheatley, M. and Keller Rogers, M. 1996 *A Simpler Way*, Berret-Koehler, San Francisco.

Wright, P., Takla, M. and Dyer, L. 1999 The 1999 State of the Art and Practice Report 'Execution: The Critical "What's Next" in Strategic Human Resource Management', The Human Resource Planning Society, www.hrps.org

6

Quality of work, home and community life

Jodie Benveniste

Introduction

> The essence of culture is not what is visible on the surface
> (Trompenaars and Hampden-Turner, 1997, p. 3).

We find ourselves at an interesting point in the history of the corporation. After 500 years of activity in the Western world and with the advent of post-industrialism and the information age, corporations face new challenges as the way people work and participate in the marketplace shifts focus and orientation. Many are heralding the rise of a knowledge and information economy as being as significant a change as the shift from agrarianism to industrialism. No longer ploughing fields, no longer turning out widgets, the industries of the future will increasingly be centred around providing services, either face-to-face or virtually. And service work is people-centred work. It is work that is powered by people *for* people. Economic might will no longer be associated with factories full of machinery. Instead wealth will flow primarily from brain power—the intellectual capital of the collective workforce.

Such changes require a new means of conceiving of and working with employees. The new questions to be answered are: How does an organisation harness the knowledge, skills and experience embodied in its workforce? How does the organisation attract and retain the right mix of people who can innovate, create and re-create so that the organisation remains competitive and relevant in a post-industrial landscape? These are the questions facing every organisation during the early years of the twenty-first century. These are the issues that every organisation must answer successfully in order to ensure its viability as a contributing member of society.

Central to such questions is the issue of what motivates people. What drives them to action? Why will people commit themselves to an organisation? In return for what? And more importantly, what will motivate them to perform to their optimum rather than simply turn up at work and do the minimum required? The answer was summarised some years ago by Emery and Thorsrud (1969) in their six psychological requirements of work. For work to be meaningful it must:

- be challenging
- provide the opportunity to learn
- allow for a certain degree of decision making
- provide social support and recognition
- be work that the individual can relate to their social life
- be work that the individual feels leads to a desirable future.

These six psychological requirements of work show clearly that people want work to be meaningful and relevant—not only in terms of their own lives, by providing individual challenges, but also in terms of the wider societal context in which they live. Work, in essence, needs to have a purpose beyond work. It must meet not only individual needs but also community and social needs.

Unfortunately, addressing community and social needs has, of late, taken a back seat to what has been deemed far more pertinent, addressing the economic needs of a nation. For the most part, developed nations have been driving ever harder toward economic outcomes at the expense of social outcomes. Such an emphasis on economics and more succinctly money, which is characteristic of modern-day capitalism, has its germination in the 1970s when the oil-producing countries banded together to raise the price of oil. It was then bolstered in the 1980s by Margaret Thatcher and Ronald Reagan coming to power, both strong proponents of the neo-liberal economist's view of allowing the market to run its course with limited state intervention. The rise of global capitalism and the corresponding pressure for global competition has increased this emphasis on financial gain, relegating social concerns to the status of a poor cousin. As George Soros states: 'It is no exaggeration to say that money rules people's lives to a greater extent than ever before' (1998: 116).

In fact, many decision makers have gone even further by denying social concerns any separate reality. Now economic concerns are often equated with social concerns—the maxim being that if one creates the right economic climate, then the right social climate will automatically follow with little need for further intervention. This is a modern version of Adam Smith's 'invisible hand' which guides the market—now it guides the entire economy. Organisations, in particular, have been feeling the pressure of economics and the drive for financial returns. Nobel prize winning economist, Milton Friedman, has been the fiercest proponent of the view that business has only one responsibility—that of economic performance. The emphasis, in particular, has been on shareholder returns, with a focus on high returns, normally gained through short term strategies and at the expense of longer term business goals.

But we are now discovering that economic wealth and growth are not sufficient to nourish the hearts and minds of a population. It is now evident that economic growth, long associated with improving the lot of society, is not necessarily an accurate indicator of 'a good life'. The assumption that the wealthier and more prosperous the society, the happier and more content the citizens will be, has been debunked. People, it has been discovered, do not become happier as their societies become wealthier just as lottery winners are no happier one year after gaining their riches (Eckersley, 1998). The pursuit of economic fortune, in itself, does not equate with 'a good life' because, after all, life is about more than simply watching one's bank balance. Richard Eckersley puts it this way:

> The belief that material progress equates with a better life is so
> ingrained in our culture that most commentators tend to overlook the
> importance of other factors—in particular, the personal, social and
> spiritual relationships that give our lives a moral texture and a sense
> of meaning—of self-worth, belonging, identity, purpose and hope
> (Eckersley 1998: 9).

Headley and Wearing (1992) confirm such a view. In their extensive research of what makes people happy, they discovered that the single attitude most strongly associated with life satisfaction is a sense of meaning and purpose. This perspective is reinforced by a majority of young Australians who wish for a society that places less emphasis on the individual, competition and material wealth and more on community and family, cooperation and the environment (Eckersley, 1998).

So how does any of the above relate to corporations and business in general? Why, in essence, should business be concerned with the way people live their lives? Why should corporations care about the social fabric? The reason is obvious on two fronts. First, without people organisations do not exist. They are simply empty shells, an organising structure without the might to operate or without the brain power to function. Second, without people, organisations have no reason for being. If people do not purchase their goods or services, they are merely constructs without purpose, entities devoid of a social function. Without people driving the bus and without people getting on the bus, organisations are nothing. People are therefore an integral aspect of any organisation. And this is becoming ever the more evident as the source of wealth creation shifts from the machine to the mind. In this new world, meeting individual and social needs becomes a business imperative rather than a side issue.

Meeting individual and social needs at work is about creating working environments people want to be a part of and company profiles that people want to be associated with. There are a number of factors involved in creating such an environment, which will require, for many organisations, fundamental cultural change. I have chosen to address five of these issues which I believe are crucial to such a re-positioning of corporations. They include the corporation as:

- community employer
- ensuring work/life balance
- pursuing and promoting diversity
- being an active member of the community
- being driven by values incorporating human and ecological sustainability.

Addressing the above concerns does require organisations to widen the corporate brief to include more than simply financial returns to shareholders. However, this chapter is based on the assumption and understanding that business needs to make money in order to stay in business. What is of interest, therefore, is that there exist corporations which are already looking ahead toward the new world of work and which have begun to take steps toward change—toward a new way of being in business that encapsulates many important aspects of human sustainability. Their examples provide compelling evidence to suggest that widening the corporate brief does not in fact endanger the bottom line, it strengthens it. The remainder of this chapter will explore each of the five areas of human sustainability listed above, providing both an economic and a social argument for change. In doing so, we will illustrate how we can conceive of our corporations in a different way—as places where we can contribute to a purpose beyond ourselves and as such be the kind of people we would like to be and build the kind of community of which we wish to be a part.

The corporation as community employer

Efficiency is not always the same as effectiveness (Charles Handy, 1997, p. 23)

Corporate downsizing has been the mark of organisational life in the 1980s and 1990s. As corporations have slashed away at their salary bill by laying off thousands, people and their knowledge, skills and experience have been sacrificed in the name of competition, with greater profits and shareholder returns the objective. In the US, 43 million jobs were eliminated between 1979 and 1995 (Cascio, 1997). In Australia's top twenty companies alone, more than 150 000 people were sacked between 1990 and 1997 (Kirkby, 1998). Downsizing, for many corporations, has become an automatic response to global competition, low productivity growth and technological change (Littler, Wiesner & Vermeulen, 1997). Few companies, in fact, attempt other means of decreasing the company's salary costs through such strategies as pay cuts, unpaid holidays, reduced work weeks or job sharing. For many corporations, downsizing is a first resort (Cascio, 1997). And downsizing is not only the domain of under-performing, unprofitable companies, profitable companies have also been lured down the path of downsizing toward promises of increased efficiencies and effectiveness.

So how successful is downsizing as a profit-generating and productivity-generating activity? Recent research from the US suggests that downsizing may not be as profitable as expected. A twelve-year longitudinal study of firms in the Standard & Poor's 500-stock index revealed that large companies that undertook major downsizing initiatives were generally no more profitable than those companies that did not downsize significantly. In fact, in some cases those companies that did downsize were less profitable than those that had retained their employee numbers at stable levels (Cascio, Young & Morris, 1997). Overall, it was concluded that profits increased in approximately 50 per cent of cases of downsizing while profits *decreased* in 20 per cent of cases. As for productivity, results have been mixed. In some cases of downsizing productivity has improved, whereas in other situations productivity has not exceeded that recorded by those companies that did not resort to large-scale retrenchments of staff. In a survey by the Society of Human Resource Management in the US, more than half of the 1468 companies who had undergone restructuring reported that productivity either stayed the same or decreased after downsizing (Cascio, 1993). Although conclusive data from an Australian context is yet to appear, US research makes it clear that downsizing does not necessarily improve either productivity or profitability and in many cases the organisation is worse off.

But downsizing is not only an economic issue. It is also a social issue. The psychological impact of downsizing on those who lose their jobs as well as on those who remain in the organisation is of critical importance when considering the social consequences of downsizing. First, to the so-called 'survivors' of downsizing. It was initially assumed that 'survivors', happy to still be employed, would work even harder in the wake of mass redundancies. These assumptions, however, have proved false. Research into so-called 'survivor syndrome' has revealed that decreased morale, commitment, job satisfaction, company loyalty and productivity are characteristic of organisations post-downsizing (Van Horn & Doris, 1996). In general, 'survivors' face a heftier workload in an environment marked by low morale and low organisational commitment. Those who lose their jobs as a result of downsizing also do not fare well. For those employees that are retrenched, research reveals that the majority suffer downward mobility, earning less in their next job than they had previously earned (Cascio, Young & Morris, 1997). Not only do these 'victims' of downsizing face a loss of income but loss of employment and ensuing unemployment are linked with psychological distress, loss of self-esteem, increased tension within families and a sense of powerlessness and resignation (Feather, 1990; Gallie & Marsh, 1993). The psychological and social consequences of downsizing affect both 'survivors' and 'victims' of downsizing such that one could well argue that all employees whether or not they retain their jobs are 'victims'.

Despite the pervasiveness of downsizing as a corporate strategy, there are many examples of companies that have chosen alternatives to downsizing and as a result have experienced increased productivity and profitability without contributing to the burgeoning levels of the unemployed. Two examples are Lincoln Electric and Eaton Corporation, both based in the US. Lincoln Electric took on a policy of no 'lay-offs' and instead offered to retrain factory workers in marketing and sales. As a result a new product, selling home welding kits to discount retailers, resulted in an increase in revenue of approximately $800 million. Eaton Corporation introduced a plant-wide profit sharing initiative, established worker-led teams to identify ways to improve operations and save money and shared financial data with all employees. As a result, sales and profits increased by 88 per cent and 85 per cent respectively over a calendar year.

Common values shared by such companies who have successfully restructured without resorting to downsizing include:

- viewing human resources as a source of sustained competitive advantage
- asking the question: 'How can we use the people we have most effectively?'
- seeing people as assets to be developed and from whom they can expect a long term return on investment (Cascio, 1997).

This stands in stark contrast to companies that view downsizing as the sole means of increasing profit and overall organisational performance. There is an alternative to downsizing and it comes in the form of thoughtful and considered cultural change.

The negative effects of downsizing are not the only reason why corporations should take seriously their role as employers in our society.

It is an economic fact that corporations rely on consumers to purchase their products and/or services to ensure their financial bottom line remains buoyant. Of particular interest to corporations, therefore, is ensuring that there are sufficient consumers capable of making such purchases. As unemployment rises, it may well become a bottom line issue for companies to take an interest in the numbers of people who are able to earn a living and therefore 'consume'. Henry Ford was in fact a pioneer when it came to making the link between employee financial viability and the financial viability of his own company. His policy of paying above award wages to all his employees was not an act of altruism but was rather a vested business decision. Ford understood that without consumers able to buy his cars, his company's future looked grim. The link between consumer ability to pay and levels of societal employment and unemployment is direct and relevant. Those corporations that fail to consider such a link face the prospect of a diminishing market.

Employment, quite clearly, plays a pivotal role in the psyche of a 'well' society. This is due to the fact that not only does employment offer a means by which to live (a living wage), it also provides society members with a sense of self-worth, self-efficacy as well as an opportunity to develop knowledge and skills. The pace at which corporations have leapt toward downsizing as a means of curing organisational ills does not reflect a commitment to creating a society in which people can work, live, consume and 'be'. The sustainable corporation, by contrast, is concerned with employing community members through the provision of meaningful work and is concerned about the impact of corporate activity on the levels of those disaffected in our society. Acknowledging that corporations can contribute to a healthy and prosperous community is the first step toward ensuring that corporations take seriously their role and responsibilities as employers in a modern society.

The corporation as a provider of work/life balance

> We don't have family coats of arms anymore, but we have the company logo (quoted by an employee in Hochschild, 1997, p. 21).

As corporations have cut away at their core workforce, retrenching thousands through downsizing initiatives and deploying others through outsourcing activities, employees have grown less trusting of their employers. As a result, the shape and nature of employee commitment and loyalty has changed from a position of life-time commitment to one of shifting loyalties dependent on what the corporation has to offer the employee. Such a shift provides a new challenge to the employer to provide staff with the types of conditions that foster loyalty. According to a survey conducted by Aon Consulting in the US, management's recognition of work/life balance issues correlates strongly with employee commitment. That is, those employers that recognise that employees have a life outside of work and that work affects the ability of people to establish a balance between their working and personal lives, are rewarded with stronger staff loyalty (Laabs, 1998).

Work/life issues or work/family issues came to the fore when women began to enter the male-dominated world of work in unprecedented numbers and faced work structures designed to accommodate the hard-working male breadwinner with the wife at home. Women, without a 'wife' of their own to take care of home life, were seizing responsibilities in the public world of work while relinquishing none of their responsibilities at home. Although work/family balance began as a women's issue it has advanced to include both women and men who desire a quality of life that includes both work and life—not one or the other. For those with families, work/life balance has become an issue of not only quality of life but of the rearing of the next generation. Many people want to be involved and committed parents as well as involved and committed employees—again, not one or the other.

There is now evidence to suggest that the economic and financial benefits of pursuing work/life balance as an organisational objective are substantial. Corporations that implement flexible workplace practices and make real attempts at accommodating their employee's private and public lives benefit from increased employee commitment, loyalty and trust in the organisation. This in turn can translate into improved productivity, lower turnover and higher customer retention rates (Flynn, 1997). First Tennessee Bank is one company that experienced clear financial gains as a result of family-friendly work initiatives. The bank discovered that managers who are supportive of work/life balance initiatives retain their employees twice as long as the bank average. This translated into better customer service and a 7 per cent increase in customer retention. The higher customer retention rates resulted in a 55 per cent profit gain amounting to $106 million between 1994 and 1995 (Flynn, 1997).

There are also individual examples of improved effectiveness and efficiencies for those companies which recognise that employees have knowledge, skills and experience developed outside of work which can make a direct contribution to the business. One sales employee in a US company had strong links with the alumni of one of the big ten universities. The company had had a poor record of attracting graduates from this university and was looking to improve its record and reputation on campus. Management decided to appoint this employee to a liaison position with the university, and although it took away time from other customers, the business value of hiring more sales representatives from the university outweighed the short term interruptions. As a result of the employee working in an area she was passionate about, her commitment to the company skyrocketed (Friedman, Christensen & DeGroot, 1998).

Those organisations that have responded proactively to the issue of work/family conflict have established initiatives such as work-based child care centres, subsidised child care at non-work based centres and introduced leave for care of sick children or other dependants such as elderly family members. The more progressive corporations have also been proactive in introducing more flexible workplace practices such as flexitime, telecommuting, job sharing and establishing part time positions where full time positions previously existed. Introducing such policies and practices is important in establishing work/life balance as a serious business concern but changing traditional managerial attitudes is also imperative.

Friedman, Christensen and DeGroot (1998) outline three management principles that reinforce a commitment to work/life balance:

- managers *clarify what is important* by openly discussing business priorities as well as identifying the employee's personal and work priorities
- they *recognise and support their employees as whole people*, understanding that knowledge, skills and experience can cross the personal/work divide
- they *experiment with the way work is done* to match business goals with employee's personal goals.

As Charles Handy acknowledges: 'the new workers want to bring their whole personalities to work with them, they want to feel at ease and at one with the aims and values of the organisation' (1997: 157). Treating work/life balance as a serious business issue is about acknowledging that employees are people not 'machines'—and that people require workplaces and work conditions that enable them to be full human beings.

Making a serious commitment to addressing work/life balance issues is not simply a matter of implementing a few flexible workplace practices. It is about changing attitudes and making fundamental cultural change. Many employers pay lip service to work/life balance while remaining grounded in a work culture which judges employee performance on subjective measures of the number of hours spent in the office as opposed to the output produced. Such pressures for 'face time' undermine corporate policies that encourage the taking up of more flexible ways of working. They also create a paradox in which employees are told on one level that it is okay to work more flexibly while on another level they are expected to work long and inflexible hours in order to gain recognition and reward.

Work/life issues have grown in significance with the realisation that the world of work and the world of family and home are *not* mutually exclusive. They are interrelated and interdependent. It is quite clear that human existence is not simply about work. Healthy societies need healthy families and balanced individuals—not only ones that devote themselves purely to work. As long as work/family and work/life initiatives remain an enigma, work/life balance will be sought but will be difficult to achieve and corporations will not benefit from the increased productivity and increased commitment that 'balanced' employees can provide. Flexible workplace practices and other work/life initiatives have the potential to allow all employees, not simply those with children, to experience some level of balance between what they gain from (and give to) work and what they gain from (and give to) their life outside of work. Becoming an employer of choice is about recognising the will of the new employee as well as recognising that people with life skills and wide experience enrich organisations.

The corporation as promoter of diversity

The organisation is, above all, social. It is people (Drucker, 1997, p. 5).

A focus on the individual and the specific talents that individuals bring to the organisation is at the core of 'valuing diversity'. Unlike work/family initiatives, which can be viewed as favouring only particular employees in an organisation (that is, those with children), diversity strategies are about acknowledging that people are different and that they thrive under different circumstances and conditions. What diversity shares in common with work/family strategies is an understanding that workplaces need to change in order to incorporate the variety of employees who now constitute the new workforce. The 'Workforce 2000' report tabled in the US in 1987 marked for many US corporations the realisation that the workforce no longer consists primarily of white male breadwinners but includes more females, minorities and immigrants than ever before (Gottfredson, 1992). An analysis of Australian demographics reveals a similar pattern—the workforce is growing more diverse (ABS, 1994). Such a workforce includes people who hold different attitudes, needs, desires and values and who display different work behaviours than those previously experienced. It is inevitable, therefore, that corporations in order to attract and retain the best and the brightest will be forced to employ more diversely and as a direct consequence, will become more diverse.

With the emergence of diversity, the management ethos of 'one size fits all' founded on the assumption of a homogeneous workforce has become increasingly irrelevant (DeLuca & McDowell, 1992). The system of scientific management developed by Frederick Taylor and perfected by Henry Ford in his manufacture of the Ford Model T saw the 'man as machine' metaphor applied to work structures and practices. As a result, organisational compliance was established through uniformity of practices, management hierarchies and pay for performance based on the outcomes of time and motion studies which 'scientifically' calculated optimum efficiency. If a worker met with expectations, 'he' received a full day's wage. Scientific management and Fordism are the epitomy of the homogeneous workforce following management directives about not only *what* work is done but *how* the work is completed.

Post-Fordism, in contrast, marked a move away from the machine metaphor of work to the metaphor of 'work as culture' whereby work practices involved more complexity and less rigidity (Cope & Kalantzis, 1997). Such changes were sparked by a number of factors including employee demand for more meaningful work, consumer demand for more differentiated products and the potentiality of new technologies to transform the way work is done. But the move to employ culture as the metaphor for work, although it heralded increased variance in how work was done, did not go as far as to accommodate a heterogeneous workforce. The main thrust of the emphasis on corporate culture was to ensure that employees fitted the culture as opposed to the culture fitting the employees. The reverse, however, now needs to become the maxim. As Gottfredson put it: 'No longer do organisations have the luxury of picking employees who fit the organisation, instead they must change the organisation to fit the available worker' (1992: 283).

There are a number of economic reasons why organisations should concern themselves with managing diversity. According to Cox and Blake (1991) valuing diversity can lead to more effective resource acquisition, cost reduction, creativity, problem solving and organisational flexibility—all of which can contribute significantly to the organisation's bottom line. Resource acquisition refers to attracting the best and the brightest from the diverse organisational 'gene-pool'. Quite simply, those companies that gain a reputation as providing great opportunities for all employees benefit from an increased capacity to attract the best people to their organisation. Such a diversity of employees also leads to increased opportunities for creative and innovative thinking, problem solving and decision making as heterogeneous work teams incorporate a wide range of different perspectives. Managing diversity is also linked to enhanced organisational flexibility as acceptance of differing cultural viewpoints leads to a general openness toward new ideas, new approaches and change.

Those companies that do not value diversity face serious cost issues as highlighted in *Workforce* magazine's article entitled, 'Don't make Texaco's $175 million mistake' (Caudron, 1997). The article reveals that in 1994, 1400 black professionals and middle managers brought down a class-action discrimination suit against Texaco for being denied promotions on the basis of their race. Taped evidence of Texaco's executives using racial slurs led to a landslide of negative publicity. As such, Texaco settled quickly, agreeing to pay more than $175 million to the 1400 disaffected employees. The threat of costly litigation and the negative publicity and public reaction that would ensue are compelling reasons why companies should consider diversity as a means of guarding against discrimination. But valuing diversity is also about much more than prevention of costly litigation—it is also about business success through valuing people.

Despite the increasing importance of workplace diversity as a business issue, few organisations view diversity as a business imperative (D'netto, 1997). This is not necessarily surprising given that promoting and managing diversity requires fundamental cultural change. But managing diversity is about more than simply recognising that the best employees will originate from diverse backgrounds, it is also about gaining a competitive market advantage from diversity. Competitive advantage derives from the realisation that not only is the workforce diversifying but the consumer market is also diversifying. No longer are mass market products targeted at the 'average consumer' able to sustain business objectives around profit and market share. Increasingly, consumers are demanding more customised products and services which cater to their particular needs. These niche markets provide corporations with great commercial opportunity if their products and services are able to 'speak' to consumers within those markets. Corporations that employ a diverse range of people are better able to understand niche markets and so can gain competitive advantage (Cox & Blake, 1991; Robinson & Denhant, 1997). Valuing diversity, therefore, is about recognising the changing demands of the consumer market and ensuring that your employees are equipped to meet such demands.

Although diversity can influence the bottom line, it is about much more than simply accounting. Corporations that promote and manage diversity have the potential to be at the forefront of elucidating a new model for 'how we should live'. Corporations that promote and manage diversity have the potential to create a microcosm of the kind of society we would like to be a part of. This is possible because managing diversity goes beyond affirmative action and beyond acknowledging cultural differences to promoting an organisational value that encourages everyone to be the best that they can be. Managing diversity in its broadest sense is not only about addressing imbalances in promotional ranks around gender and cultural differences, it is about everyone in the organisation contributing to organisational effectiveness by incorporating into basic business practice different viewpoints. Increased creativity and innovation in problem solving as well as greater organisational flexibility is available to corporations that take the issue of diversity seriously—because at its heart, managing diversity is about maximising organisational talent in all its different forms.

The corporation as community member

I act for others so I can live with myself (Eva Cox, 1995, p. 5).

Communities are what sustain people. It is through networks with others that we are at our most powerful. As Jung once remarked, 'I' needs 'we' to be truly 'I'. It is perhaps easier for us as private individuals rather than workforce members to conceive of ourselves as community members and to understand that our impact on others is influenced by the decisions we make in our daily lives. But corporations loom larger than individuals. Their impact on the community has the potential to create greater good, or conversely, greater harm. As such, corporations have a powerful role to play in contributing to community and, more generally, to 'the ties that bind us'.

That corporations are a social community in themselves as well as members of the wider social networks is gaining prominence as a means of conceiving of corporation's role in a modern society. Drucker quite plainly states that 'an organisation has full responsibility for its impact on community and society' (1993: 102). Others, like Greg Parston, the Chief Executive of the Office for Public Management, London, declare more boldly that 'socially responsible organisations will no longer be defined by their financial limits, their ownership, their products or their organisational charts but rather by their roles in society' (1997: 347). As Eva Cox pointed out in her 1995 Boyer Lecture series, 'It is our social relationships which constitute society, not our individuality' (1995: 70).

Recognition of the power and influence of social relationships in constituting the shape and nature of a society is encapsulated in the term 'social capital'. After all, the maxim 'It's not *what* you know, it's *who* you know', conveys a general truth. Social capital is defined as 'the processes between people which establish networks, norms and social trust and facilitate coordination and cooperation for mutual benefit (Cox, 1995: 15). In the past, the only capital most organisations concerned themselves with was 'financial capital'. However, more recently, corporations have begun to acknowledge that there exist other forms of capital which impact on organisational effectiveness such as 'human capital', 'intellectual capital' and even 'social capital'. It is now widely acknowledged that as we move into a knowledge economy, intellectual capital is all important, and will in fact distinguish those companies that thrive and prosper in the post-capitalist society from those that flounder. Knowledge or intellectual capital, however, is only useful if it can be harnessed and shared in and around the organisation. Left to reside inside people's heads, the worth of that knowledge in terms of providing the company with a competitive advantage, is limited. Nahapiet and Ghoshal (1998) argue convincingly that it is social capital, the trusting, binding relationships among work colleagues, that ensures the worth of the intellectual capital. Without strong networks of trusting relationships, without people working together to bring their collective knowledge to fruition, intellectual capital is near to worthless.

There is, therefore, a strong argument for organisations to view themselves as communities and to act like communities—not only inside the walls of the corporate offices, plants and outlets but also outside in the wider society. Corporations do not operate in a vacuum. The reason governments worldwide offer generous incentive schemes to lure businesses to their shores is because governments know that the presence of such businesses can provide community benefits—least of which are jobs. There are also well documented examples of the devastation that a company pulling out of a country can have on the community it leaves behind. The impacts can be enormous. Corporations, therefore, exist within a context—a context which they cannot ignore—and a context in which they have certain responsibilities.

Corporations that are aware of their links to community act as role models by leading the way in terms of social and ecological sustainability. They recycle, they are environmentally sensitive, they promote social cohesion and they value and support their employees. Corporations that understand that they are social beings sponsor community projects and offer employees the opportunity to initiate and partake in projects which not only foster a deepening sense of community but also directly benefit the community. The Body Shop has been a leading example of an organisation that is acutely aware of its place in and impact on community, so much so that it pays staff to do up to four hours a week of community work during normal business hours. It has also recently initiated the LOVE program, with LOVE an acronym for 'Learning is Of Value to Everyone'. The LOVE program pays each staff member up to $200 to pursue learning that is *not* obviously related to their job such as sports, arts, crafts and music classes. The emphasis is on learning as a way of life—not just on what you learn but the process of learning itself.

The Co-operative Bank in the UK has long been a pioneer in ethical business practices and in links with community. In their 1998 *Partnership Report*, the bank extended its key stakeholders to include not only shareholders, customers, staff and their families and suppliers but also local communities, national and international society and past and future generations. The bank aims to deliver 'value' to each of these stakeholder groups as defined by the group and not the bank. The bank's ethical investment policy reinforces this stakeholder approach by refusing to invest in companies that trade in arms, undertake animal testing, cause damage to the environment or violate human rights. Their commitment to the community also extends to an Affinity credit card scheme whereby the bank makes a donation to a partner organisation and further contributions based on the amount a customer spends on their card. Partner organisations currently include The Royal Society for the Protection of Birds, Oxfam, Amnesty International, Greenpeace and Save the Children.

Corporations that care about the community not only get involved in community projects, they also produce products and services that serve a community's needs, without damaging their prospects—and the community through a relation of interdependence rewards the corporation by loyally purchasing their products and services. There is now evidence to suggest that such socially responsible behaviour is rewarded through a significant positive effect on firm profitability (Allen, Blose & Kask, 1997). There are, it appears, bottom line benefits as well as feel-good benefits for corporations that pursue an ethical and social line. But beyond financial and economic concerns, corporations as social beings are, in essence, in business to provide goods and services that are of social value and which contribute to a social good. As Moss Kanter (1997) questions:

> Holders of financial capital are praised on ubiquitous lists of the world's richest companies and the world's richest people. Builders of human capital are not. How often do we see lists of companies that have created the most jobs or trained the most employees to build future capabilities?

The answer—not often enough. The corporation as a community member is about acknowledging and addressing the bigger picture that is life and creating a place for the organisation in its context—both socially and ecologically.

The corporation as driven by values incorporating human and ecological sustainability

> Vision directed thinking can change society (Ellyard, 1998, p. 42).

Consider for a moment the following scenario. How does it compare with the way you currently work and live?

You are a professional—well-educated and with skills that are in demand. You have been with your current employer for nearly seven years and, despite attractive offers from other employers, you are planning to stay where you are. And the reasons are plentiful. First, your workplace, when you need to be there, is within walking distance of your home or a short trip on the bus in case of rain. At least two days a week, however, you work from home, keeping in touch with the office and customers through an array of highly tuned communication devices. This allows for a sense of community in your neighbourhood which was lacking when the majority of people worked in the polluted and over-crowded central business district. Now you meet neighbours and colleagues for a coffee or a spot of lunch at your local cafe—and since this trend more cafes and local businesses have been opening and thriving.

Your children's primary school and child care centre are also within walking distance from your home and place of work. The primary school and the child care centre as well as the senior school, TAFE and university are integral members of the wider community that mixes with the local business community. Senior school, TAFE and university students are regulars at your workplace, involved in structured training and mentoring programs which allow the youth of the community to experience and contribute to a vibrant business culture. The local businesses frequently teach these young trainees the intricacies of quality customer service—and many seniors of the community help out at the local drop-in centre or the community library, passing on their knowledge and wisdom to the next generation.

The company you work for produces organic foodstuffs. Not so long ago, your company was one of the biggest promoters of chemically based farming methods. For years, environmentalists had been campaigning to stop such agricultural methods as they were polluting and damaging valuable ecosystems. Your company was also sinking most of its R&D

money into the burgeoning field of genetically engineered food and was seriously considering this as a future business strategy. Due to public and local community pressure and to conscience-raising among the senior executives and many of the employees, the company underwent a transformational culture and value shift. Led by the CEO, the company involved all employees in developing a new set of values and vision for the company which involved redefining its core business. Genetically engineered food and chemical based agriculture were rejected in favour of promoting organic produce that provided for a healthy community and a healthy natural environment. Since pursuing such a philosophy, profits are up and the company's share price has been steadily increasing. Ethical investment companies have strongly supported these moves.

The success of the organisation, you realise, is due largely to the fact that everyone who works there is committed to producing a quality product. Large pay cheques are not the prime motivator, although employees at all ranks are included in generous profit share plans and many are shareholders in the company. The structure of the organisation is flat and largely team based. Senior executives are accessible and information on company performance is shared with all staff. Although people work hard when they are at work, no one works later than 6 p.m., preferring instead to spend time with their families or to get involved in sporting groups or other community activities. In fact, the doors at the office don't open until 8 a.m. and no one is allowed entry before then.

Work/life balance and flexibility are two of the key values the company espouses. And these values are lived. Just over five years ago, with the birth of your first child, you took one year parental leave—with three months of that time paid for by your employer. During the other nine months, you received a government subsidy for being the primary care giver. During your parental leave you kept in regular contact with the office. On return from leave, you went back to your previous position on a part time basis and faced no pressure to return full time until you were ready. With sensible working hours being the norm and with grandparents and other carers living close by, your return to full time work was relatively smooth and trouble free. Occasionally, school plays and sick children take you away from work but an understanding employer means that you don't have to feel like you are choosing between your work and your children—both matter.

One of the reasons you love working for the company you do, is the diversity of people who constitute the organisation. You can remember when men in suits filled the boardroom and the executive lunch room with the only females present making coffee or taking minutes. Now people of both genders and of different nationalities and cultural backgrounds fill positions at all levels in the organisation. The increased diversity of the staff has led to increased cultural awareness and sensitivity that has fueled creativity and innovation as different perspectives merge to reveal new solutions to customer needs. The increased cultural awareness and sensitivity has also pervaded the wider community and is evident in the children your child mixes with when playing at the park and going to school or child care.

But one of the key reasons you are likely to stay with your company for yet another seven years is because you are proud to be one of its employees. Your company views itself as an integral member of the community. This position is reflected not only in the products it produces, but in its sponsorship of community projects and the way it allows employees to take time off to pursue activities that contribute to community well-being. As an example, two years ago, the company sponsored a group of underprivileged young adults to attend catering and business classes at the local TAFE. Following such instruction, the group formed their own business and tendered to provide services to the company canteen—and were successful.

There is also, beyond the sense of pride, the sense of a strong employer–employee contract whereby if you do right by the company, they will do right by you. A few years ago, when the country was in recession, the company was forced to consider laying off staff. While other organisations were downsizing, your company chose instead a temporary reduction in working hours and pay which was readjusted when the economy and company performance improved. This legacy has led to strong employee commitment and the feeling that people really are your company's greatest asset.

We paint in the above scenario an idealised view of the world where corporation and community are closely integrated and where employees of all ranks work side by side for common goals. This is also a world where work and life outside of work co-exist and whereby companies produce goods and services that serve the common good. The role of business in this scenario is about more than producing profits at all costs—but profits flow nonetheless. This is due largely to the fact that this company realises that if it is to remain viable it must produce the kind of products and services the community needs in ways that are sustainable. How far away from reality is this scenario? Is it in fact possible or is it simply a pipe dream, to be relegated to fiction and never to materialise?

The answer to such a question rests largely in our hands. Are we prepared to remain living in a society which is unsustainable (until we no longer can)? Or are we prepared to shift our expectations and envisage a new way of living and working and doing business that respects not only people but the ecological systems on which we all depend? This chapter is an argument for the latter—and there is evidence, slowly emerging, which reveals that such a future scenario is possible, that the economy and business systems will not collapse if companies pursue sustainability rather than profit and shareholder return alone. To the contrary, the evidence suggests that they will thrive. And this is largely the case because living the good life is about more than money in the pocket. It is about human relationships, connecting with community, breathing fresh clean air and striving for human potential. Corporations are made up of people and so require a purpose that looks beyond individual gain to community connections and involvement. Corporations driven by the values of sustainability—corporations who value employment, work/life balance, diversity, community and a healthy natural environment—can be the real substance of life. They can be places where people love to work and organisations that consumers love to support. As more and more corporations realise this potential, those that don't will surely face failure.

References

Allen, G., Blose, L. and Kask, S. 1997 Socially Responsible Firms: Return on Assets and Stock Price Returns, FMA Annual Meeting, 16 October.

Australian Bureau of Statistics (ABS) 1990–94 The Labour Force Australia, Cat. No. 6203.0, AGPS, Canberra.

Caudron, S. 1997 'Don't make Texaco's $175 million mistake', *Workforce*, March, pp. 58–66.

Cascio, W. 1993 'Downsizing: What do we know? What have we learned? *Academy of Management Executive*, vol. 7, no. 1, pp. 95–104.

——1997 'Responsible restructuring', public lecture.

Cascio, W., Young, C. and Morris, J. 1997 'Financial consequences of employment-change decisions in major U.S. corporations', *Academy of Management Journal*, vol. 40, no. 5, pp. 1175–89.

Cope, B. and Kalantzis, M. 1997 *Productive Diversity: A New Australian Model for Work and Management*, Pluto Press, Sydney.

Cox, E. 1995 *A Truly Civil Society*, ABC Books, Sydney.

Cox, T. and Blake, S. 1991 'Managing cultural diversity: Implications for organisational competitiveness', *Academy of Management Executive*, vol. 5, no. 3, pp. 45–56.

DeLuca, J. and McDowell, R. 1992 'Managing diversity: A strategic "grass-roots" approach' in S. Jackson & Associates (ed.), *Diversity in the*

Workplace: Human Resource Initiatives, Guilford Press, New York, pp. 227–47.

D'netto, B. 1997 'Managing workforce diversity in Australia', Monash University Faculty of Business Economics, Working Papers no. 05/97.

Drucker, P. 1993 *Post-capitalist Society*, Harper Business, New York.

——1997 'Toward the New Organization' in F. Hesselbein, M. Goldsmith and R. Beckhard (eds) *The Organization of the Future*, Drucker Foundation Future Series, Jossey-Bass, San Francisco.

Eckersley, R. 1998 'Perspectives on progress: Economic growth, quality of life and ecological sustainability', *Measuring Progress: Is Life Getting Better?*, CSIRO Publishing, Melbourne, pp. 3–34.

Ellyard, P. 1998 *Ideas for the New Millennium*, Melbourne University Press, Melbourne.

Emery, F. and Thorsrud, E. 1969 *Form and Content in Industrial Democracy: Experiences from Norway and other European Countries*, Tavistock, London.

Feather, N. T. 1990 *The Psychological Impact of Unemployment*, Springer-Verlag, New York.

Flynn, G. 1997 'Making a business case for balance', *Workforce*, March, pp. 68–74.

Friedman, S., Christensen, P. and DeGroot, J. 1998 'Work and life: The end of the zero-sum game', *Harvard Business Review*, November–December, pp. 119–29.

Gallie, D. and Marsh, C. 1993 'The experience of unemployment' in D. Gallie, C. Marsh and C. Vogler (eds), *Social Change and the Experience of Unemployment*, Oxford University Press, Oxford.

Gottfredson, L. 1992 'Dilemmas in developing diversity programs' in S. Jackson & Associates (ed.), *Diversity in the Workplace: Human Resource Initiatives*, Guilford Press, New York, pp. 279–305.

Handy, C. 1997 *The Hungry Spirit: Beyond Capitalism: A Quest for Purpose in the Modern World*, Hutchinson, London.

Headley, B. and Wearing, A. 1992 *Understanding Happiness: A Theory of Subjective Well-being*, Longman Cheshire, Melbourne.

Hochschild, A. 1997 *The Time Bind: When Work Becomes Home and Home Becomes Work*, Metropolitan Books, New York.

Kirkby, J. 1998 'The firing squad', *Business Review Weekly*, 2 March, pp. 44–8.

Laabs, J. 1998 'The new loyalty: Grasp it, earn it, keep it', *Workforce*, November, pp. 34–56.

Littler, C., Wiesner, R. and Vermeulen, L. 1997 'The effects of downsizing: Cross-cultural data from three countries', *Academy of Management Meeting*, Boston, MA.

Moss Kanter, R. 1997 'Restoring people to the heart of the organization of the future' in F. Hesselbein, M. Goldsmith and R. Beckhard (eds),

The Organization of the Future, Drucker Foundation Future Series, Jossey-Bass, San Francisco, pp. 139–50.

Nahapiet, J. and Ghoshal, S. 1998 'Social capital, intellectual capital, and the organisational advantage', *Academy of Management Review*, vol. 23, no. 2, pp. 242–66.

Parston, G. 1997 'Producing social results' in F. Hesselbein, M. Goldsmith and R. Beckhard (eds), *The Organization of the Future*, Drucker Foundation Future Series, Jossey-Bass, San Francisco, pp. 341–8.

Robinson, G. and Denhant, K. 1997 'Building a business case for diversity', *Academy of Management Executive*, vol. 11, no. 3, pp. 21–31.

Soros, G. 1998 *The Crisis of Global Capitalism: Open Society Endangered*, Pacific Affairs, New York.

Trompenaars, F. and Hampden-Turner, C. 1997 *Riding the Waves of Culture: Understanding Cultural Diversity in Business*, Nicholas Brealey Publishing, London.

Van Horn, C. and Doris, A. 1996 'Perceived communication barriers between management and support staff personnel undergoing organisational restructuring', *American Business Review*, June, vol. 14, pp. 95–107.

Part III
Towards ecological sustainability

7

Building corporate capabilities to promote ecological sustainability: a 'case study'

Philip Sutton

Introduction

Eliyahu Goldratt, a guru of business problem solving, believes that people learn best through stories (Goldratt, 1994). In that spirit, this chapter is devoted to a 'case study' showing how one particular firm, Paradyme Corporation, is building and deploying some key capabilities relevant to the commercially viable promotion of sustainability. The purpose of the 'case study' is to bring this process alive.

Paradoxically, it was found that this could be done most realistically by creating a hypothetical case study. There are two reasons for this. One is that the cut-and-thrust of real change can be illustrated in a less inhibited way when personal and corporate sensibilities do not need to be so carefully protected. And the other is that, in the Australian context at least, there is not as yet a large number of sustainability-promoting firms to be described[1]—especially where the purpose of the case study is to illustrate a bottom-up process for developing commitment to sustainability-promotion.

So the subject of the 'case study', Paradyme Corporation, is fictional. However its 'history', up to the point where the firm begins to explore the idea of becoming a 'sustainability-promoting firm', is based loosely on the history of a real, Australian-headquartered, multinational firm—Lend Lease.[2]

Many of the organisations mentioned in the Paradyme story are real but of course their relationship with Paradyme Corporation is entirely fictional and has been invented to illustrate issues related to sustainability-promotion.

Box 7.1

The five key actions of sustainability-promoting firms:

- declare the goal of helping society to be sustainable
- use the full product range as a major driver of society's move to sustainability
- promote society's 'sustainability take-off'[3]
- urge governments to be proactive in shaping the economy to promote the achievement of sustainability
- Promote large scale, urgent action

A number of additional fictional organisations have been added to the 'case study' where it would not be appropriate to use real firms. All fictional organisations are identified as such in an endnote at the point where they are first mentioned.

Sustainability promotion

Before moving on to the 'case study', a few words need to be said about the concept of 'sustainability-promotion'.

The objective of 'sustainability' is the maintenance or restoration of a desired state that has already existed. The concept can be applied in many spheres—ecological,[4] social and economic.

The promotion of sustainability is an active process of engaging society. Firms need to become involved in this process because, collectively, they are now so powerful that communities and governments often do not act sufficiently strongly to achieve sustainability if there is active or perceived opposition from the private sector. So sustainability-promoting firms[5] need to go beyond simply reducing their own negative environmental, social or economic impacts. They need to produce products that help society to become sustainable and they also need to use their influence to encourage society-wide action to achieve sustainability (Sutton, 1997c).

The five key actions of sustainability-promoting firms are spelled out in Box 7.1.

A framework for capabilities and competencies

To maximise organisational success, in both the short and the long term, firms need the capabilities to deliver results effectively in the here and

Figure 7.1 The seven key capabilities

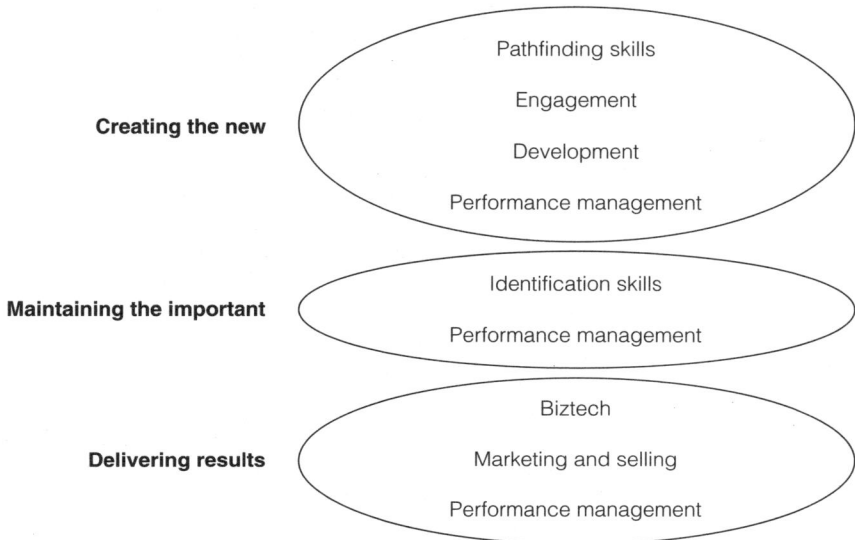

Creating the new

Pathfinding skills

Engagement

Development

Performance management

Maintaining the important

Identification skills

Performance management

Delivering results

Biztech

Marketing and selling

Performance management

Source: Developed from Turner & Crawford, 1998: 16, Fig. 1.3

now. They also need to be able to identify viable and desirable future directions. And in the face of the enthusiasm for the new, they still need to retain valuable attributes and resources (within the firm and in society/the environment). To achieve these three goals firms need special capabilities. The cluster of capabilities set out in Figure 7.1 is based on a modification of the framework developed by Turner and Crawford (1998).

These capabilities can be possessed by a limited number of key individuals (personal capabilities), they can be held by quite a few staff across the organisation (collective capabilities) or they can be embedded in the organisation by way of systems, databases, training programs, cultural traditions, structures etc. (corporate capabilities).

Competencies might need to be outsourced where firms do not have the scale to support the required level of performance or where the competence does not provide a crucial strategic advantage.

The focus of the 'case study'

This 'case study' focuses heavily on the use of the pathfinding capability that, in Paradyme's case, led to a decision to commit the firm to the promotion of sustainability and which helped it to decide on the core positioning strategies needed to deliver on this commitment. The reason

Table 7.1 The seven key capabilities

Creating the new	1 Pathfinding: Developing, crystallising and articulating new directions, strategies, purposes and values for the organisation
	2 Engagement: Getting people throughout the organisation informed, committed and motivated to act to achieve the organisation's purposes and future directions.
	3 Development: Developing all the resources (personal, physical, technological and systems) needed to achieve the organisation's future directions
	4 Performance management: Proactively managing the factors that drive the organisation's performance to ensure that it consistently and effectively achieves what is intended
Maintaining the important (the sustainability focus)	5 Identification: Deciding which of the organisation's, or society's, current attributes and resources should be retained and maintained
	4 Performance management: as above
Delivering results	6 Biztech: Commanding and understanding the technologies, processes and mechanisms through which the organisation produces and delivers its products and services to market
	7 Marketing and selling: Understanding the organisation's markets and how external events affect these markets and the organisation; identifying customers' needs and selling its goods and services to customers effectively
	4 Performance management: as above

Source: Modified form Turner & Crawford, 1998: 17, table

for adopting this focus in the 'case study' is that, managerially, it is much harder to make such a challenging commitment and to develop the key directional strategies than it is to tackle the technically complex task of implementing the strategies.

A comprehensive listing and description of the specialist capabilities and competencies needed if a firm is to promote ecological sustainability can be found at: http://www.green-innovations.asn.au/capabilities.htm

The 'case study': Paradyme Corporation

Corporate history: Deciding to be a sustainability-promoting firm

Paradyme is a public company headquartered in Melbourne, Australia. It was founded in 1949 by a Danish migrant, Bent Andersen. It now operates in Australia, New Zealand, the UK, the USA, Canada, the Netherlands, Scandinavia, Singapore, Malaysia, Hong Kong, India and South China.

In its earliest years Paradyme Corporation was an ordinary building contractor. But in the early 1960s the company reinvented itself as an innovative and progressive project management firm focusing on building development, with an integrated capacity for design, financing, engineering, construction, fit out and building management.

In 1984 the opportunity arose to take over Allstates Insurance[6] which, for several decades, had been a major supplier of finance for Paradyme developments and a major investor in Paradyme itself. This acquisition built on Paradyme's project management skills but brought to the fore its capacity for innovative but prudent application of finance. Initially the focus of this financial skill, in the expanded Paradyme, was real estate.

Paradyme opened its first overseas office in 1966 in New Zealand. This was followed in the 1970s by openings in Singapore, UK and the US and in the 1980s by openings in the Netherlands and Scandinavia. It was the 1990s however that saw Paradyme place great emphasis on the expansion of the scale of its operations overseas with substantial growth via acquisitions in Europe and North America and modest expansion in Asia, that is, Malaysia, Hong Kong, India and South China.

By the late 1990s Paradyme Corporation had grown to the point where it had an annual turnover of US$4.2 billion with US$43 billion in funds under management. It was now fully multinational, with a strong commitment to the localities in which it was operating.

The Paradyme culture and meta-strategies

Paradyme has developed a very strong and distinctive culture. Some of its elements can be traced back to the firm's founder and other elements have emerged as the corporation has gone through its periodic processes of reinvention.

Paradyme's founder, Bent Andersen, brought with him a number of personal and cultural characteristics from his native Denmark. He implanted in the early Paradyme a strong belief in collaboration and the value of each member of the team. He also valued creativity, reflection and the creation of quality products. For Andersen, arriving in Australia shortly after the horrors of the Second World War, it was a chance to help build a new world where people would be valued and where creativity and 'craftsmanship' could be appreciated and rewarded.

The experience, immediately following Paradyme's foundation in 1949, of being a building subcontractor with no responsibility for the whole project was deeply dissatisfying for Andersen. His ability to contribute to the creation of a project of high quality was sharply circumscribed by an Australian building industry culture that blocked integrated contributions from specialist subcontractors to the design and execution of a project. This dissatisfaction motivated the first reinvention of Paradyme—which in the late 1950s was transformed from a building subcontractor into a fully-fledged developer with its own access to finance.

This new structure gave Paradyme the freedom to craft quality projects and gave full reign to the project management skills of Andersen's team. The new structure and Andersen's combination of creativity and prudence enabled Paradyme Corporation to scrape through the 1960 credit squeeze that drove many other Australian firms into bankruptcy. It also emphasised the value of investment skills that would underpin the next major change in the corporation.

The Australian economic boom of the early 1970s gave the building unions the leverage they had long sought to push for better conditions. Paradyme's response was the opposite of that of the rest of the building industry. Andersen felt that the way to gain value and commitment from the workforce was for everyone to be treated fairly, rewarded adequately and trained well. So Andersen quickly concluded an agreement with the Builders Labourers Federation and was thus spared a great deal of industrial disruption, although this decision caused a rift with other building industry employers. The deal with the union not only improved the workers' conditions but also laid the ground for improved skills and productivity. Paradyme was now firmly locked into a mindset of seeing its workers as its key resource.

The property slump of the 1980s forced Paradyme to diversify and then to expand actively beyond the limits, and ups and downs, of the Australian economy. By buying Allstates Insurance, a large Australian financial institution, in 1984, Paradyme moved its centre of gravity from development to investment. Project management skills were still a vital strength but the new focus drove the organisation further in the direction of gaining its competitive advantage from knowledge resources rather than physical resources. After consolidating the organisation, following the takeover of Allstates Insurance, the final years of the 1980s were devoted to overseas expansion to reduce business-cycle risk and to expand the scale and scope of available business opportunities. It was also felt that a larger organisation was capable of supporting much more diversity in terms of skills, knowledge and viewpoints.

The massive overseas expansion of the 1990s forced the Paradyme organisation to think long and hard about what aspects of their culture and capabilities needed to be retained from its various units, both old and new, and implanted in the rest of the organisation. Paradyme management decided to systematise the consideration of cultural 'resources' and so now all acquisitions are formally assessed before and after purchase to identify what they might bring to the organisation as a whole.

So, the current Paradyme Corporation is an organisation that is:

- aiming to deliver superior value to both shareholders (via high margins) and customers by 'creating more value than they ever dreamed of'
- moving progressively up the value chain to target activities capable of supporting high margins and to avoid being trapped as a commodity producer
- building scale so that it can handle larger and more complex projects
- building strength through the acquisition and deployment of knowledge by having diverse and practical engagement in its markets and by 'growing' highly skilled and deeply knowledgeable staff
- investing heavily in its staff at work and in their private lives because it believes this is the ethical thing to do and because it encourages staff retention and hence knowledge retention
- never standing still, with, at any one time, one-third of its business in new areas of entrepreneurial endeavour and two-thirds of its business in mainstream but still growing areas
- capable of both creativity and effective delivery.

The practice of these values led to the emergence of an organisation that in 1998 took out second place in a contest organised by *Business Review Weekly* magazine for the most admired company in Australia as judged by leading business executives across the country.

The greening of Paradyme Corporation

Paradyme corporation first experienced environmentalism during the late 1960s and especially the early 1970s. There was a global burst of awareness of pollution, urban amenity, population and nature conservation issues. In Australia environmental activism had it own special character. The community at large felt it was time to benefit from the preceding decades of unprecedented economic growth. The new Labor government in 1972 gave expression to the desire for greater emphasis on cultural development and improvement in the cities, the physical environment in which most Australians lived. Left wing unions, especially the Builders Labourers Federation, took up the cause and applied 'green bans' to projects that were considered to be environmentally damaging. The OPEC oil price hikes of 1973 and 1979 created intense awareness of the need for energy conservation, adding further impetus to major anti-freeway campaigns during the 1970s.

Many of the great environmental clashes in Australia over the last thirty years that engulfed the resource industries left Paradyme untouched—for example, the conflicts over uranium and other mining, timber extraction from native forests, and wilderness preservation.

This burst of environmental awareness took most of Australian business by surprise, causing considerable alarm and fear among the affected firms. Paradyme however prospered in this environment of greater concern for a quality urban development, picking up work from relatively environmentally aware clients, such as state and local governments. Furthermore, Paradyme's shift of emphasis from developer to investor reduced its apparent impact on the environment.

This is not to say that Paradyme was controversy free. The company did become embroiled in urban development conflicts in the UK. However, because of the firm's general positioning, it was easier for society's concern for the environment to percolate its way into the organisation. Not surprisingly, Paradyme was one of the first Australian companies to appoint an environment officer within its construction division, the appointment being made in 1978.

Since its inception, Paradyme has had a strong commitment to quality and during the 1980s, in keeping with other progressive businesses, it adopted a systematic approach to quality inspired first of all by the Japanese quality approach and then by the methodology of ISO9000. On top of this came systems for ensuring financial probity and prudence, and further systems for driving down occupational health and safety risk which were implemented with a passion and effectiveness rivalling that of Du Pont.

It therefore came relatively easily to Paradyme Corporation to systematise the Construction Projects group's environmental management practices around the BS7750[7] standard in the early 1990s. By the late 1990s Paradyme's subsidiary companies in the construction area had all been fully accredited to either the European EMAS standard[8] or ISO14001, which were the two standards that took over from BS7750.

The Paradyme culture, however, placed more value on substance than policy and paperwork so, during the 1990s, the organisation's environmental commitment was better represented by a series of flagship green projects and by the internal staff-driven environmental improvement programs set up widely across the organisation. Paradyme deliberately sought out clients that demanded leading-edge environmental performance knowing that these projects would fund the learning required if high standards of environmental practice were to be a feature of all Paradyme construction projects.

Paradoxically Paradyme's experience of controversy in the UK in the late 1980s and early 1990s, where it undertook major car-based retail and commercial development projects in the English midlands, led to a rethink and the development of new skills in green development. This repositioning was rewarded in late 1996 when the City of Malmö in the Øresund region of southern Sweden awarded Paradyme and its team of leading European green designers the contract to develop a major 'sustainable' retail and business complex. The development was associated with the ultra-green Bo01 housing development.[9]

In 1993 in Sydney, Paradyme completed construction of the Darling Park tower, which, several years later, was to be rated by the Sustainable Energy Development Authority as one of Australia's very few 'four star' large buildings.

Paradyme was a member of a partnership that won the tender for the development of the athletes' village in the Sydney 2000 'green' Olympics. The design, assisted by leading world experts including the US-based Rocky Mountain Institute, involved rooftop photovoltaics, advanced water conservation systems and a host of other environmental features.

Paradyme was also active in the Australian government's Greenhouse Challenge Program and the Australian Construction Wastewise Program, which aimed to reduce waste going to landfill by 50 per cent by the year 2000. As a contribution to the latter program, Paradyme, in its Latrobe Street, Melbourne redevelopment, was able to achieve a record 96 per cent recycling of the materials in the demolished building.

So, by the late 1990s Paradyme Corporation could sum up its environmental policy as follows:

- 'our projects should aim for a positive impact on the environment'
- 'Paradyme aims to achieve leadership in sustainable business practices to benefit our stakeholders and the community generally'
- 'our experience has shown that the best environmental solution is the best business solution'.

The initial impetus: Paradyme's environmental management system

It is a truism of management theory that any major corporate change must have strong support from top management if it is to be driven forward in the face of organisational inertia and competing priorities. And this is true for Paradyme too. The major environmental repositioning that this 'case study' reports owes its success in significant measure to the commitment of Paradyme's Board and CEO to embed a commitment to sustainability-promotion across the whole organisation. However, if we are to have a complete picture of the change process, we must look at what caused the board and the CEO to make this

Figure 7.2 The Paradyme organisation chart

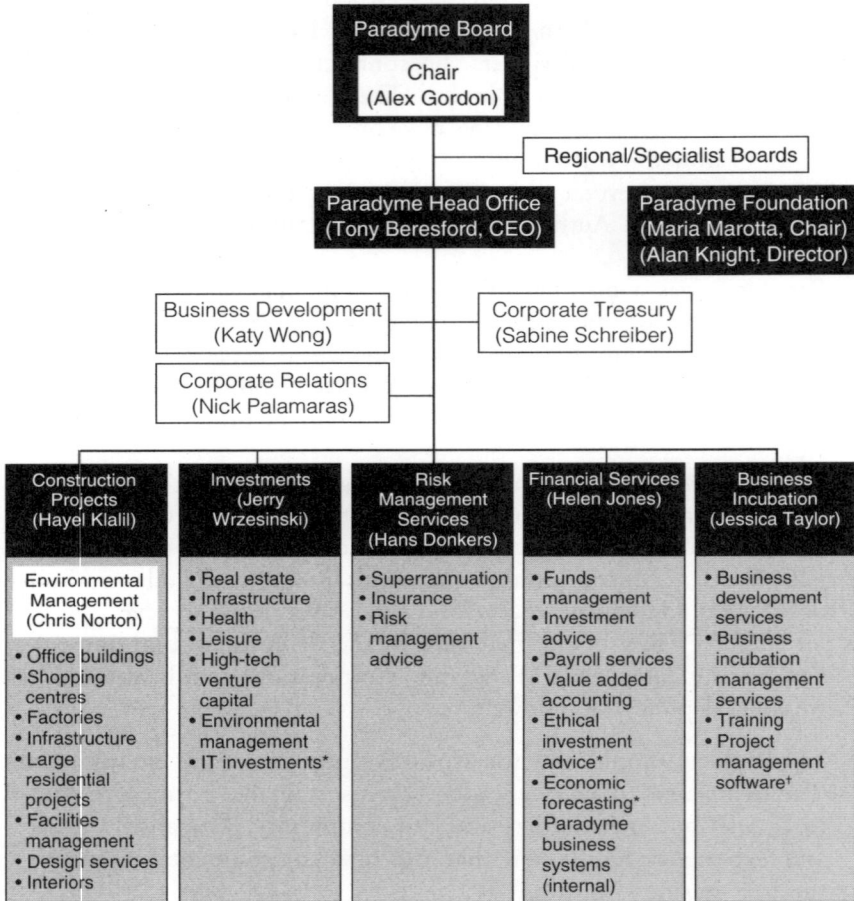

```
                    ┌─────────────────────┐
                    │   Paradyme Board    │
                    │  ┌───────────────┐  │
                    │  │     Chair     │  │
                    │  │ (Alex Gordon) │  │
                    │  └───────────────┘  │
                    └─────────────────────┘
```

Paradyme Board
Chair
(Alex Gordon)

Regional/Specialist Boards

Paradyme Head Office
(Tony Beresford, CEO)

Paradyme Foundation
(Maria Marotta, Chair)
(Alan Knight, Director)

Business Development
(Katy Wong)

Corporate Treasury
(Sabine Schreiber)

Corporate Relations
(Nick Palamaras)

Construction Projects (Hayel Klalil)	Investments (Jerry Wrzesinski)	Risk Management Services (Hans Donkers)	Financial Services (Helen Jones)	Business Incubation (Jessica Taylor)
Environmental Management (Chris Norton) • Office buildings • Shopping centres • Factories • Infrastructure • Large residential projects • Facilities management • Design services • Interiors	• Real estate • Infrastructure • Health • Leisure • High-tech venture capital • Environmental management • IT investments*	• Superannuation • Insurance • Risk management advice	• Funds management • Investment advice • Payroll services • Value added accounting • Ethical investment advice* • Economic forecasting* • Paradyme business systems (internal)	• Business development services • Business incubation management services • Training • Project management software†

Source: Ingrid Sjöberg, Swedish interior design unit
  + New ventures, co-managed by staff from Business Incubation
  * New venture, co-managed by staff representative of all five major business clusters

commitment. The key steps leading to the initial top level decision, made in early 1998, were as follows.

Paradyme's corporate environmental management system (EMS) was due for review in late 1998 as part of its routine recertification process. But several years before this, feedback from a number of the bodies responsible for certifying Paradyme's units around the world indicated that Paradyme's EMS was beginning to show its age. When it was first implemented, most of the EMS consultants who were involved in the task had gained their experience directly or indirectly from the manufacturing sector and they automatically assumed that Paradyme's EMS was most relevant to its 'area of highest impact', that is, its Construction Projects group. However, in the years that followed, the development of an EMS in the office-based services sector demonstrated that these systems were apparently relevant to more than construction and manufacturing. The fact that by 1997 the Paradyme EMS applied to only about a third of the business transacted by Paradyme no longer seemed automatically justifiable.

Tony Beresford, Paradyme's CEO, was aware of this imbalance in the application of the EMS. But for some time he had been reluctant to update the EMS structure because he felt that the EMS would not deliver much added value outside of the Construction Projects group and, indeed, could waste staff time on paper work and pointless procedures. Hans Donkers, the Managing Director of Paradyme's Risk Management group that dealt with superannuation and insurance, only a year earlier had carried out a major business re-engineering project that had delivered major savings by simplifying procedures and eliminating unproductive paperwork. It didn't make sense to Beresford to reverse these gains for a minor environmental benefit. In any case, without even needing to operate in a formal EMS structure, staff environment committees in the finance and investment groups of Paradyme were doing good work reducing the environmental impact of their offices.

In May 1997, Beresford personally made his feelings known to Paradyme's Environmental Manager, Chris Norton. Beresford said that while he wanted Paradyme to be genuinely environmentally responsible he would not support a more complete application of the EMS unless there was a clear net benefit.

Although Norton's EMS experience was largely in the construction area he was well aware that Paradyme's greatest impacts were actually generated, indirectly, by the organisation's investment decisions. However, the investment area generated a high proportion of the organisation's total profit stream and everyone was careful not to harm the goose that was laying the golden eggs. So Norton had, for some time, left the issue in the 'too-hard basket'.

This internal dilemma seemed to reflect the tension in the wider community generated by the perceived clash between economic growth and environmental protection and resource conservation. But, whatever the difficulties, it was increasingly clear to Norton that, if Paradyme's reputation for environmental care was to continue to be justified, something had to be done to extend and upgrade the EMS.

Norton decided that he needed a new 'angle' to make the EMS relevant to the finance groups of the organisation. He decided that, before trying to formulate any firm proposals, he should set up an exploratory process in the organisation to try to unearth some new approaches. If this process produced any useful results he would then approach the CEO with a plan for a major EMS upgrade. If nothing significant was forthcoming he would maintain the EMS in roughly its present configuration, making only those changes that were necessary to satisfy the EMS auditors.

Towards the end of May 1997 Norton discussed his tentative plan with Jessica Taylor, head of the small but influential Business Incubation group of Paradyme. Taylor had a personal interest in environmental issues and she had good access to senior management because of the business development focus of her work. Taylor suggested that Norton present the Paradyme staff with a challenge: How could the EMS create significant value-added for the business? This approach would pick up on the CEO's concerns and, if successful, should make it easier to get approval to significantly upgrade the EMS.

Whether or not the EMS would eventually prove itself capable of stimulating the creation of significant value-added for the organisation, Taylor's tactic certainly helped to get a wide ranging review process started. On 12 June 1997 Chris Norton was given approval to launch an organisation-wide search for ways in which the EMS could add significant value to the business in all of its major groups. An internal email list and web page was set up on the intranet to facilitate this search process throughout the global Paradyme organisation. Norton personally contacted colleagues working in counties that were environmentally the most advanced (for example, Holland, Denmark, Sweden and the other Scandinavian and Germanic countries) and countries that were host to leading environmental programs (for example, USA, UK, Japan) to see if they knew of examples where firms had used their EMS in the creative way they were looking for. Armed with the results of the somewhat random internal search process, Norton commissioned three EMS experts to carry out some quick reviews of leading-edge practices in Europe, North America and Asia.

At the same time as the organisation-wide search was going on Norton undertook a personal, unpublicised project to identify factors that might be inhibiting a more proactive environmental stance by Paradyme and factors that might drive it forward.

The search: The initial findings

By the end of October 1997, the internal search process and the consultancies revealed the following situation. As expected:

1.1 EMSs were rare among small and medium-sized businesses—even where they had high direct environmental impacts

1.2 EMSs were relatively common among the small group of (large) companies with high direct environmental impacts, and were relatively rare among companies which had small direct impacts but large indirect[10] impacts

1.3 most EMSs were still focused on helping companies reduce their negative impacts rather than gearing the firms up to help society achieve sustainability

1.4 legal compliance and risk and cost reduction were the main EMS focuses, with the creation of competitive advantage a relatively infrequent focus.

Some interesting but less predictable findings of the survey were that:

2.1 Germany was the country with the largest number of certified EMSs—under the EMAS standard—largely with a manufacturing and pollution/waste focus

2.2 local councils and a small number of service sector companies were beginning to put EMSs in place

2.3 a small but significant number of Asian companies selling products into Europe, and to a lesser extent into North America and Japan, were putting EMSs into place to ensure continued access to these markets

2.4 the most far reaching programs for the greening of businesses and products (for example, Factor 10[11]/MIPS,[12] the Natural Step, zero emissions[13]/sustainability stretch goals, cleaner production, industrial ecology, whole system design,[14] ecodesign/design for the environment, the triple bottom line,[15] ecological foot printing,[16] innovation in technology and product innovation,[17] sustainable industrialisation[18]) generally had not been developed as part of an EMS and in most cases the process of integrating these concepts into ISO14001 and EMAS conforming systems had only begun recently

2.5 it was the far-reaching programs or methods mentioned above, rather than EMS systems per se, that were being used by firms to drive much of the product innovation and value adding that was in fact occurring

2.6 some case studies showed that firms[19] that adopted radical leading-edge environmental programs had done well financially and in terms of market share and growth;[20] But it was not clear to what extent it was the environmental program per se that made this possible and to what extent it was the result of general good management.

Drawing on his own experience and from the experience of employees and consultants working for Paradyme, as expressed to him in private conversations, Norton identified the following common reasons why Paradyme did not routinely take a strongly green position across the whole organisation:

3.1 many of the people in the investment-oriented groups felt they could not maximise returns for Paradyme if they limited their attention solely to 'green' investment opportunities

3.2 only a few clients (across the organisation) came to Paradyme demanding ultra-green outcomes

3.3 people in the Construction Projects group of the organisation felt that trying to make projects very green increased costs and made the job more difficult

3.4 many of Paradyme's competitors cut corners on the environment putting limits on how far Paradyme could go

3.5 some people felt that Paradyme couldn't afford to look extremely green as this would undermine its image as a commercially competent organisation and would threaten its ability to attract business and its standing with shareholders

3.6 in many countries in which Paradyme operated, community and government pressure to be green was not very compelling

3.7 some people felt that the organisation did not give enough support to those who were trying to target sustainability.

Personal experience and anecdotal evidence suggested that the motivators for taking a green approach included:

4.1 a professional commitment to deliver a quality product

4.2 personal preferences and strong cultural expectations in some countries

4.3 an organisational expectation that Paradyme would deliver unexpectedly high value for clients

4.4 the routine use of 'stakeholder-sensitive' design methods

4.5 a consciously 'progressive' management culture

4.6 the operation of the environment management system in the Construction Projects group

4.7 a strong commitment by top management to risk management, backed up by a well developed formal management system

4.8 from time to time, the requirements of clients.

At the end of October 1997 Norton sent these findings for comment to the managers of Paradyme's five business groups and the head office units. He also posted a copy of the findings on the EMS review intranet website. In the note introducing the initial findings he foreshadowed his intention to hold a workshop early in the new year to examine how Paradyme could generate significant value-added from a revamped EMS.

Responding to the findings

The most significant responses that Norton received were those of Jessica Taylor, Managing Director of Paradyme's Business Incubation group and Ingrid Sjöberg, an employee of Paradyme's interior design unit in Sweden.

Taylor offered the services of her training unit to organise the proposed workshop. Also she had noted the reference in Chris Norton's findings to the leading-edge environmental methods (item 2.4 above). She felt that participants in the workshop should be given some basic grounding in these methods prior to it being held in order to increase the chance of getting highest-common-denominator results out of the workshop. She said she would get her training unit to organise this pre-workshop education if Norton was interested. Taylor also offered to get her business development unit to find out more about possible linkages between leading-edge environmental management and superior business performance that Norton had noted in item 2.6 of his findings.

Ingrid Sjöberg raised different issues. Sjöberg indicated that she was very worried by the idea that commercial value-adding should be the main driver of the review of the EMS. She said that Paradyme had a responsibility to show moral leadership and that the company should commit itself to sustainability first, and then work out the practical implications afterwards. Norton said that, while he sympathised with Sjöberg's views, he was sure he couldn't get corporate support for such an approach. Sjöberg said she was convinced that a commitment to sustainability would help Paradyme in the longer term and would help it avoid 'hitting the wall'.[21] Sjöberg urged Norton to involve Paradyme employees generally in the EMS review process. She felt that there was a real risk that any strategy developed purely by senior management would not be sufficiently far-reaching and would not be very motivating for employees.

Norton contacted Paradyme's Scandinavian management and was told that Sjöberg was a competent person whose passion for environmental issues had helped Paradyme build up a very successful design practice in the region. A little later Norton invited Sjöberg to be involved in the forthcoming EMS workshop and asked her to suggest how Paradyme might develop the EMS using a moral commitment as a major driver while also achieving good commercial results. Sjöberg said she would see what she could do.

Two weeks later, in late November 1997, Sjöberg got back in touch

Figure 7.3 The six paradigm shifts for sustainability promotion

Unaware	Rejecting	Reducing own negatives • risk reduction • cost reduction • process • life-cycle	Ethical-market driven	Product innovation for sustainability	Catalysing for sustainability	Making it happen *fast enough* and on a *big enough scale-* so that sustainability is achieved as soon as possible
From: 'oblivious'			...to: 'aware'			
	From: 'defensive'			...to: 'opportunity-seeking'		
		From: 'reducing the firm's own negatives'		...to: 'helping society to take action to be sustainable'		
		From: 'purely self-interested'			...to: 'altruistic & self-interested'	
		From: 'taking limited responsibility'			...to: 'taking full responsibility'	
			From: 'reactive and slow incremental change'			...to: 'proactive & urgent leap-frogging'

with material gleaned from the web. She was particularly interested in some ideas she had downloaded from the Environmental Creativity[22] web site. Environmental Creativity had identified six paradigm shifts necessary for firms to become 'sustainability promoting' (see Figure 7.3):

- from oblivious to aware
- from defensive to opportunity-seeking
- from reducing the firm's own negative impacts to helping society take action to become sustainable
- from purely self-interested to altruistic and self-interested
- from taking limited responsibility to taking full responsibility
- from reactive and slow incremental change to proactive urgent leapfrogging.

Sjöberg said she thought that the first four transitions were well under way in Paradyme but that it had yet to initiate the critical fifth and sixth paradigm shifts.

She also passed on some material on the enhanced greenhouse effect that Environmental Creativity used to illustrate the scale and speed of change needed to achieve sustainability. According to this information, over the last 160 000 years the highest level of CO_2 in the atmosphere was about 300 parts per million by volume (ppmv) (Jouzel et al., 1987). However, in 1997 atmospheric CO_2 levels reached 364 ppmv (Brown, 1998). At this level the globe is already experiencing a strong warming trend that has virtually locked in the destruction of the world's coral reefs, including the Australian Great Barrier Reef (Hoegh-Guldberg, 1999). Some atmospheric scientists think that if atmospheric CO_2 goes beyond one-and-a-half to two times the pre-industrial levels, then sea ice will largely cease to form at the poles and the thermohaline circulation of the oceans would stop. This in turn would cause the oceans to be starved of oxygen below the 200 metre surface layer (Strong, 1999; Hirst, 1999).[23] If, to avoid this and other problems associated with the greenhouse effect, society aimed, on the basis of the precautionary principle, for a target of 350 ppmv or less for atmospheric CO_2, then human-caused greenhouse gas emissions would need to be cut by 100 per cent (Enting, Wigley & Heimann, 1994), not the grossly inadequate 5.2 per cent negotiated at the 1997 Kyoto conference.

The implications of this information were so dire that Norton at first thought that they must be alarmist propaganda. However, a quick check of the references showed that the information was scientifically well founded—which left Norton feeling rather depressed. However, this was offset, to some extent, a few days later when Sjöberg sent Norton an email suggesting that he have a look at some material on the hypercar that she had also found on the Environmental Creativity web site.[24] The material showed that the Rocky Mountain Institute, a radical public interest organisation in the US, had been able to design a car that reduced energy use by an astounding 75 per cent to 90 per cent, depending on the precise design. Not only this, but since the early 1990s when they started working on the project, the Institute had managed to position the world's major car companies so that virtually all of them were now committed to one version or another of the new technology. Sjöberg said that this case illustrated her point that a commitment to major change had to come first before radical new solutions could be generated.

Norton now felt torn. Jessica Taylor and Ingrid Sjöberg appeared to be offering diametrically opposed approaches to the development of the EMS (that is, build it on a commitment to commercial value-adding or build it on a moral commitment to 'save the world') and yet both strategies made sense when considered separately. Norton was not at all sure what to do. However, the breakthrough he needed came in a conversation with his wife. She said that if both arguments made sense then why not act on both strategies at once. When Norton got back to Taylor to get her reaction, she said that the combined strategy made perfect sense to her. She said the practical usefulness of using a 'this and that' rather than an 'either/or' approach had been spelled out years ago in influential management books such as *The Art of Japanese Management* (Pascale & Athos, 1981) and *Built to Last* (Colllins & Porras, 1997).

So at last Norton felt ready to move forward. He accepted both Jessica Taylor's offer for her people to organise the workshop and the pre-workshop education and he decided to incorporate Ingrid Sjöberg's ideas as well. He also accepted Taylor's offer to undertake some research into possible linkages between leading-edge environmental management and superior business performance.

Preparing for the workshops

Now things started to move fast. Norton and Taylor agreed on an organising team made up of themselves, Alan Hall from the training unit, Katy Wong, Manager of the corporate Business Development unit and Ingrid Sjöberg.

Given the size and geographical spread of Paradyme it was decided that a single workshop couldn't do the job. So Alan Hall devised a suite of workshops. Each of Paradyme's five business groups would 'meet' separately for a half day by videoconference and then there would be a final two-day in-person intensive workshop to pull things together.

Each initial videoconferenced workshop would involve sixteen people from a particular group and one person each from the other groups. The videoconference groups would prepare a report to brief the participants in the final workshop. The final workshop would involve one person from each of the five initial workshops as well as members of the organising committee. The people chosen to represent Paradyme's five groups would be selected so that they collectively represented a slice through the organisation's hierarchy—from the bottom to just below the general managers of the groups.

As part of a 'drip feed' education process, the selected individuals were encouraged to access, during February and March 1998, written material, short courses, speakers, and video and audio tapes introducing the leading-edge environmental management concepts mentioned in item 2.4 of the interim findings (above). Short articles and case studies were also distributed by email and were put up on the intranet EMS web site. In addition to this, at Ingrid Sjöberg's suggestion, concepts developed by Paul McIntyre of the Australian organisation Environmental Creativity and other material assembled by the group were made available too. The concepts and material included the 5-in-1 customer (see

Figure 7.4 The 5-in-1 customer

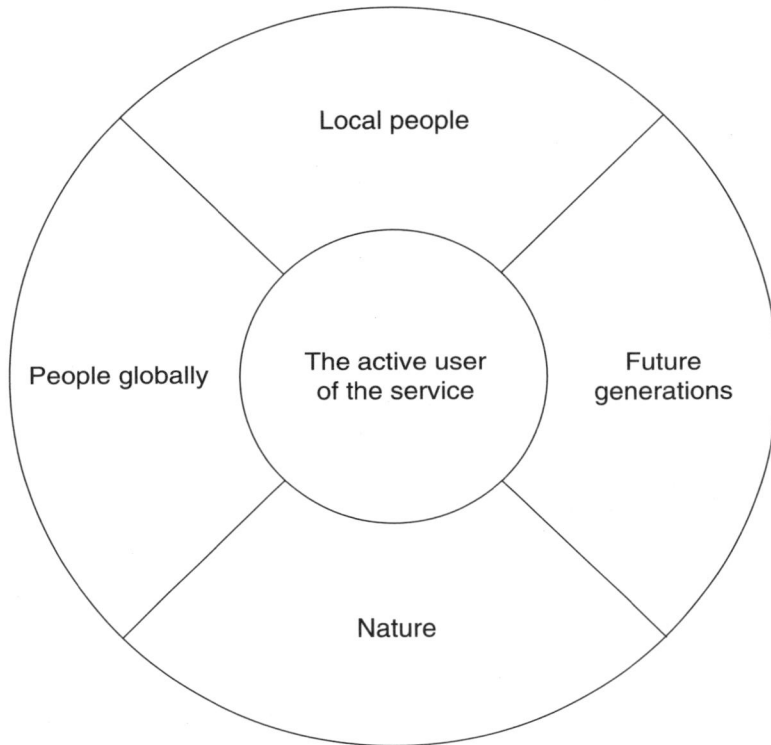

Figure 7.4) and sustainability-promoting firm concepts (see Box 7.1); information on the desirable speed and scale of change needed to achieve ecological sustainability; and sustainability-oriented system conditions, stretch goals and generic strategies (see Table 7.2)).

In late March 1998, Jessica Taylor circulated the research report prepared by her business development unit on the links between leading-edge environmental performance and financial performance. The findings were that:

- For most firms the link was coincidental, that is, well run firms produced good financial returns and they tended also to have progressive approaches to the environment.
- Some firms had been burnt by trying to be too green ahead of the market. Sometimes this was caused by poor market research or poor judgement, and sometimes it was caused by doing what 'ought' to be done rather than what the customers wanted.

Table 7.2 Strategic directions for achieving ecological sustainability

Policy: Society should be ecologically sustainable		
Objectives: (9 system conditions)	**Actions:** (15 generic strategies)	**Targets:** (9 stretch goals)
Ecological sustainability must not be undermined by systematic:	Society should aim for:	Society should take action to:
1 increases in concentrations in nature of substances that come from the earth's crust	1 'zero' extinctions	1 contain human activity (for nature)—don't encroach, boost land efficiency
2 Increases in concentrations in nature of substances produced by society	2 'zero' climate damage*	2 tread lightly (for nature)
3 increases in the manipulation or harvesting of nature	3 'zero' soil degradation	3 restore habitat (for nature)
4 failure to restore the ecological basis for biodiversity and ecological productivity	4 'zero' waste	4 dematerialise
Society must make it easy to achieve system conditions 1–4 by ensuring that:	5 'zero' pollution	5 create a closed-cycle economy
5 society has the capability and resilience to solve its major problems	6 a 90% improvement in resource use efficiency (Factor 10')**	6 use renewable resources
6 material flows into and out of society do not increase systematically	7 'zero' net greenhouse gas emissions	7 design for no toxicity
7 society's aggregate use of resources and land is ultra-frugal	8 'zero' encroachment on nature	8 protect people from environmental threats
8 the human population does not increase systematically	9 75% of land for nature	9 strive for a sustainable population
9 the speed and scale of responses are adequate		10 green up business
		11 green up lifestyles
		12 green up culture
		13 encourage 'sustainability take-off' in the economy/society
		14 boost social and economic capability
		15 achieve results at a desirable speed and scale

*   Given the huge injection of greenhouse gases into the atmosphere over the last half century and the enormous lead times for correction, this stretch goal becomes a long term recovery target rather than a preventive goal

**   See the International Factor 10 Club (1997)

■ Some firms had been able to maintain their image for quality and community responsiveness by being (as Woody Allen once said), '15 minutes ahead of the market' by offering products, without any noticeable cost penalty, that were environmentally better. This had enabled them to maintain and sometimes improve customer loyalty.

■ In a few cases, firms had gained very significant strategic advantage by taking a strong green stand. For example: (a) Electrolux when it avoided a commitment to HCFC refrigerants and leapfrogged straight to non-cumulative refrigerants such as R134a and pentane; (b) the Dishlex division of Southcorp that rebuilt its competitive position in the Australian whitegoods market by developing an environmentally friendly dishwasher; and (c) Kafus that was able to enter the medium density fibreboard market in the US and grow massively by employing a new technology to utilise wood scrap from the building industry rather than timber from native forests. In these and similar examples the firms had been able to take advantage of breakpoints in the market caused by changed environmental aware-ness or by changed government policy settings.

The key issue for Paradyme arising from this research was that it needed to refine its capacity to tell which beneficial strategies it should follow in specific cases and when it had to avoid adopting an inappropriate 'green' strategy.

The workshops

The initial workshops, held in April 1998, focused on the following questions:

1 How have environmental issues come up already in the work of your group of Paradyme?
2 How big and how fast would the changes in the society and economy have to be in order to achieve ecological sustainability?
3 What discontinuities/crisis points/breakpoints/avalanches[25] in society and the economy are required for a successful transition to sus-tainability?
4 How could your group, or Paradyme as a whole, help society to achieve ecological sustainability?
5 What challenges/threats do environmental issues pose for your group and for Paradyme as a whole? (Are we acting in a responsible way? Are there any blockages to responsible behaviour?)
6 What opportunities do environmental issues open up for your group and for Paradyme as a whole?

7 How might a formal environmental management system help your group to create significant value-added for Paradyme?

The answers to these seven questions for each Paradyme group were then made available to the ten people who met face to face for two days in the last week of May 1998. This group went through the same questions as they applied to Paradyme as a whole, but they devoted a significant proportion of their two days to the last two questions.

The key outcomes from the workshops

The initial workshops resulted in five reports and their key findings were as follows:

All of Paradyme's groups had been engaging with environmental issues for some time. For the Construction Projects group any failure to apply current best practice increased project risks. On the other hand Paradyme's best practice performance helped add unexpected value for many clients and for some potential clients gave additional reasons to employ the organisation. On balance, the Construction Projects group saw environmental issues more as a source of opportunities than as a threat. This was why the Construction Projects group was more and more often seeking out environmentally demanding clients—initially to provide a learning experience and more recently because they had developed above-average competence in this area. However, the construction staff noted that what they were building was much further away than they had previously realised from what was needed to be truly sustainable. The Investments group had been dealing with environment as a useful niche area but it felt, overall, that environmental concerns were a significant constraint on their ability to maximise investment opportunities. Environment and sustainability issues were not a dominant concern for the Risk Management group. However, the specialist risk management advice unit had been factoring in environmental matters (especially contaminated sites) for some time and it had recently begun to look at the implications of climate change. The Financial Services group's main involvement with environmental issues was through its ethical investment advice unit and in relation to the discussions it was having with the Investments group and the Business Incubation group about forming an ethical investment fund.

The Business Incubation group had little structural connection with environmental issues. The strong environmental interest of the group's manager had meant that the group tended to be the catalyst across the organisation for undertaking office-based environmental improvements. But until the activity related to the EMS review had come up this group had not been looking at the business opportunities that environment might open up. There was now, however, a strong feeling among the group's workshop participants that this was about to change.

The success of the drip feed education program prior to the workshops was evident when people addressed the question of the size and the speed of the changes needed to achieve sustainability. Across the board, the urgency and massive scale of the required change was recognised. About half the participants, however, felt that society would not be able to make the necessary response.

The empowering effect of the education program about leading-edge environmental methods was most evident in the Construction Projects group as these methods in many cases had a strong physical orientation. But it was also clear that the Construction Projects group staff had a stronger mental image of what a sustainable society might look like. Also, one of the leisure sector specialists from the Investments group suggested that Paradyme could target the financing of the production of the goods and services people needed to live green lifestyles. However, exactly what this meant was not elaborated on.

The main discontinuities identified were:

■ the need to completely eliminate the use of fossil fuels as soon as possible because of the greenhouse effect and also because of the imminent peaking of world oil production (the feasibility of a fossil fuel phase-out prompted a lot of debate)
■ the need to eliminate persistent biologically active chemicals from the environment
■ the need to protect the remaining biodiversity around the world
■ the impact of an increased total population
■ the possibility of falling birth rates.

A great many ideas were developed by each workshop group about how the business groups and Paradyme as a whole could help society to be sustainable. A synthesis of these ideas is reported below in the discussion of the final workshop.

Whether or not economic growth would slow down and whether it should slow down was the subject of a heated, but inconclusive, debate in the Investments group's workshop.

Despite the emergent view that large scale environmental change was needed, all the groups felt that environmental issues did not pose any great threat to Paradyme. A participant in the Construction Projects workshop said that 'Paradyme is just lucky to be an urban firm and not in the resources sector'. The perception that Paradyme did not face a threat was a reflection, on the one hand, of Paradyme's general willingness to be as green as the market allowed, and on the other, of the widely held view that society was unlikely to demand fast and far reaching change.

The Construction Projects group was the most consistently optimistic about the opportunities that environmental issues opened up 'provided society wants to go that way'. The Investments group was fairly evenly divided. The Risk Management Services and Financial Services groups thought that environmental issues would not make much difference to them. And the Business Incubation group was not yet clear what the opportunities were but they were generally keen to explore the possibilities.

Uniformly across the five groups, people were sceptical that the EMS had much to offer in the way of creating significant value-added for the firm. One participant summed up the general attitude when he said 'it's just a quality system by another name, to stop us back-sliding'.

The result from the final intensive workshop had a very different flavour. The final workshop participants[26] moved quickly through questions 1 to 3 above, their views not differing significantly from those of the participants in the initial workshops. When they came to question 4, Taylor suggested that they reword it to read: 'How can Paradyme make an excellent financial return from helping society achieve sustainability?' Wong then asked the group how they thought Paradyme's special capabilities and positioning could shape its contribution. After some inconclusive discussion, Ligteringen from the Construction Projects group said that Paradyme had started as a builder. Although it was obviously now essentially an investment company, its heart still lay, in effect, with the building of cities. So why couldn't its mission be to help society create sustainable cities?

Hall, who was acting as facilitator, asked the others what they felt about this idea. Tytherleigh from the Investments group led off immediately by pointing out that by far the bulk of Paradyme's profits came from his group but he said that the strength of the Investments group was Paradyme's deep, practical knowledge across the organisation of the areas in which it invested. He then went through the current specialised investment areas to test their fit with the 'sustainable cities' focus. He felt that the proposed focus sat quite well with the current areas of specialisation. At this point Wong broke in saying that, for her, the strength of the sustainable cities theme was that it not only played to Paradyme's strengths in construction, investment, project, relationships and complexity management, but it also provided the rationale they needed for Paradyme's next big leap in scale. Her guess was that to fully benefit from a sustainable cities focus Paradyme would need to increase its scale by at least a factor of ten, which would bring turnover about the US$40 billion mark. This was in the ballpark already being discussed by the CEO and the board.

The workshop group was about to move on to brainstorming the ways in which Paradyme might 'make an excellent financial return from helping society achieve sustainability' when Sjöberg urged the group to think first about whether Paradyme should make a conscious commitment to being a sustainability-promoting firm. In particular she wanted participants to consider what such a commitment would mean in terms of the six paradigm shifts (see Figure 7.3) that Environmental Creativity felt was essential if a firm was to be sustainability-promoting.

Everyone was happy with the idea that Paradyme make an in-principle commitment to being sustainability-promoting and they felt that the first four paradigm shifts were already well under way. It was the fifth and sixth paradigm shifts, resulting in firms taking 'full' responsibility for the achievement of sustainability in the light of the need for large scale fast change, that stirred the most discussion.

Sjöberg said that, to date, most environmentally responsible firms identified a circumscribed area in which they could contribute by, for example, reducing the negative impact of their products or production processes, by offering products that made it easier for their clients to be environmentally responsible or by contributing to environmental awareness. But very few shaped their actions to make sure that, at the end of the day, when everybody's efforts were added together, the total effort was guaranteed to deliver sustainability.

She said that to her knowledge Interface[27] came closest to what she had in mind. One of Interface's environmental programs was called 'redesigning commerce' and it seemed to be aimed at moving the whole marketplace and not just the bit that Interface happened to work in. Annette James, from Risk Management, wanted to know what adopting the full responsibility paradigm meant in practice. She felt that even a large firm like Paradyme had limited resources and couldn't do everything. Sjöberg agreed but suggested that Paradyme could devise strategic, catalytic actions that would help mobilise other firms and governments.

The group agreed to build in this idea of taking 'full responsibility' through catalytic action when they did their brainstorming to identify new business areas arising out of the sustainable cities focus. The brainstorming took up most of the remainder of the workshop and the results are set out in Table 7.3.

Many of these ideas would only be demanded currently by the greenest of clients—to be found most frequently in the leading-edge 'green' countries. Many of the ideas were more realistically second or even third generation services that would be in demand in the future as society deepened its commitment to achieving sustainability. However, the final workshop group felt that their list of sustainability-oriented

Table 7.3 Brainstorm list of sustainability-driven new business opportunities

Building Projects
- Ultra-high efficiency buildings built for a 'dematerialised', closed-cycle economy based on renewable energy
- 100%-recycled building systems
- Industrial—ecology industry parks
- Urban villages/car 'free' urban developments
- Suburban serviced offices as multi-company nodes for companies promoting telecommuting
- Waste warehousing facilities as replacements for tips/dumps
- Waste recycling facilities
- Urban refurbishment/restructuring to achieve leapfrog improvements in environmental performance
- High-tech multi-company repair centres
- Multi-company filling facilities for reusable packaging
- A 'take-back' service for Paradyme buildings and facilities at the end of their life

Investments
- Sustainable cities R&D fund
- Sustainable cities venture capital fund
- Sustainable cities low-risk fund
- Skewing existing investment programs towards 'sustainable city' investments

Risk Management Services
- Risk-prevention strategic planning for sustainability issues
- Sustainability-oriented scenario development service

Financial Services
- Sustainability accounting/sustainability management systems consulting
- Adapting current programs to build on the sustainable cities theme

Business Incubation
- Corporate, government sector and NGO sustainability training/education programs
- Urban sustainability collaborative learning programs
- Sustainability design consultancy and training service

Other
- Sustainability-oriented urban planning service
- Sustainability-oriented urban economic development and industry policy service
- Sustainable industrialisation strategies for newly industrialising countries
- Industrial, commercial and domestic asset maintenance management service (including associated client financing)

business opportunities demonstrated the rich range of possibilities offered by a 'sustainable cities' orientation.

The final issue addressed was the role of the EMS in generating significant value-added for Paradyme. The issue that had taken so long to work up to was, in the end, resolved in a surprisingly short time. Norton pointed out that EMSs are system-based performance management mechanisms and to date they have almost always been directed at exercising control. He felt however that Paradyme would get best value out of its EMS if it were used first and foremost to systematically drive the application of creativity to the creation of business opportunities. Wong said she thought the EMS should be structured to bring environmental concerns into the heart of the business development process. However, James said that her experience in Risk Management suggested that the control aspect of an EMS was crucial.

MacDonald, from Business Incubation, said that both purposes were essential, but that the current Paradyme EMS was unbalanced. In addition, he suggested that every major management unit should have its own mini-EMS and that a Paradyme-wide EMS policy council could be formed. The policy council could be chaired for a year or two by whichever unit had strength in an area where the corporate EMS needed to be enhanced. So if the current priority was linking the EMS to business development then perhaps the corporate Business Development unit should take on the facilitation role for a while. Adding to this, Norton suggested that his EMS unit, located in the Construction Project group, could report to the chair of the EMS policy council. There was general agreement with these ideas.

Approaching the point of decision

Chris Norton and Jessica Taylor presented the initial and final workshop reports in a face to face briefing with the CEO on 12 June 1998. Beresford was clearly interested in the findings but he said he would think about their implications and would discuss the matter with his senior management team (SMT) before any decisions were made.

The EMS issue was discussed at the next SMT meeting in August 1998. Jerry Wrzesinski, general manager of the Investments group, led off by saying he was more comfortable with the extension of the EMS to the whole corporation now that the emphasis was on business development and value-adding. He said he could see the attraction of the sustainable cities focus but he was opposed to locking things in until his group had assessed the scope for business opportunities with the new focus. He also felt that a policy change of this magnitude should be considered by the main board and by the relevant specialist boards. The 'sustainable cities' focus was given a strong endorsement by Hayel Khalil, general manager of the Construction Projects group, and also by Katy Wong and Jessica Taylor.

Tony Beresford said he had been convinced that if the EMS was used to promote creativity, especially directed at business development, then he was happy with its extension across the whole organisation. He said that he was quite excited about the sustainable cities focus, but he still felt a bit uncertain about whether it was a strong enough concept to carry the whole organisation. Wrzesinski, in agreeing, said that people are 'on about more than just sustainability' and that Paradyme risked painting itself into a limited corner with a sustainability focus. Khalil then suggested that maybe they should focus on facilitating 'sustainable and progressive cities' which he felt was simply an amplification of what they were already on about.

Beresford then offered a possible resolution of the issue. He suggested that:

- the EMS be extended to the whole organisation with a strong emphasis on promoting creativity in the environmental area
- each major management unit have its own mini-EMS and that as recommended by the final workshop group that a Paradyme-wide policy council be established and that Katy Wong, as manager of corporate Business Development, should chair it for the next two years
- the EMS processes should be used to explore the merits of a business focus on 'sustainable and progressive cities'
- separate from the EMS, the business and organisational implications and opportunities presented by (a) a formal commitment to being sustainability-promoting and (b) a 'sustainable and progressive cities' focus should be investigated thoroughly with the intention of making a policy decision within twelve months
- the main board and relevant specialist boards be consulted and the views of the markets and other stakeholders be ascertained
- a strategic positioning policy be presented to the main board for consideration and decision in about twelve months time.

This approached was adopted by the SMT.

Commitment

In November 1998 the revision of the EMS began, leading to a new version being rolled out across the whole organisation. Then, in September 1999, the main board decided that Paradyme should declare itself to be a sustainability-promoting firm and that it should undertake its next phase of development driven by a focus on 'delivering sustainable and progressive cities'.

Engagement with the new direction

From earlier experience with major organisational repositioning, the Paradyme SMT knew that it was essential to actively engage the whole staff in the process.

Figure 7.5 The EMS implementation and continual improvement cycle

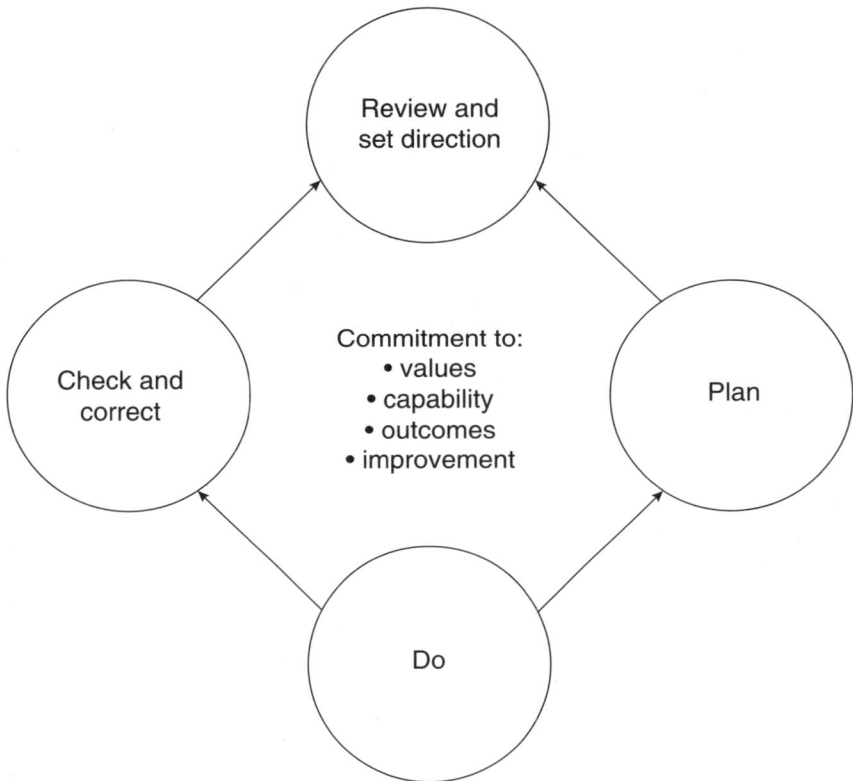

The first stage of the engagement process began in November 1998 when the roll out of the EMS across the whole organisation began. During the ensuing twelve months all Paradyme staff, including the senior management, went through a sustainability training program. Tony Beresford and the other senior managers gave high profile support to the EMS upgrade and roll out. Beresford made a considerable effort to attend key EMS sessions around the organisation and in each of its major geographical regions. He and the other senior managers made it clear that the EMS was expected to contribute directly to improvement in Paradyme's business performance as well as it being justified by ethical concerns for the welfare of people and the rest of life on the planet.

The training unit in the Business Incubation group ran the EMS training around the world, supplemented by local training organisations in each region. One of the key concepts, introduced to all staff as a new

Paradyme policy through the training program, was the notion of the 5-in-1 customer (see Figure 7.4). This was seen as a way to drive the sustainability ethic into everything that Paradyme did.

A seed-funding budget of US$30 million was assigned to support action on employee suggestions to implement the focus on 'delivering sustainable and progressive cities'. Senior management emphasised that it expected most sustainability initiatives would come up through the normal budgeting and corporate planning process since delivering sustainable and progressive cities was now the core focus of the organisation.

To highlight and reinforce the substantive change, the physical manifestations of Paradyme's corporate image were redesigned. And a media campaign was launched in each country in which Paradyme operated to generate public awareness about the corporation's new direction.

Development and performance management

The development phase began in early 2000 with senior management and special task forces examining in detail the competencies that Paradyme would need for its new focus. There were a number of strands in this process. Generic competencies[28] that were missing or were not widespread in the organisation were identified. Training programs were devised and recruitment policies were modified. The EMS was expanded and revised so that it became the core system infrastructure for driving performance management for the entire 'sustainable and progressive cities' focus, that is, it was gradually transformed to become the performance management system for all aspects of the corporation.

Katy Wong, as head of the corporate Business Development group, spearheaded a Paradyme-wide search for new business opportunities arising from the new theme. New options were generated through individual staff initiatives and through structured programs to spark ideas. Options were screened and task groups put to work to develop the most promising ideas.

Careful attention was paid to developing the specific capabilities and competencies needed for the specific initiatives. Internal development was promoted with the active support of the Business Incubation group. Also, strategic partnerships and acquisitions were carefully examined as potential sources for missing competencies and capabilities. Each of Paradyme's five main groups were encouraged to begin building the needed capabilities and competencies, and the group management teams actively encouraged their business units to do the same.

As decisions were made to launch new ventures, inspired by the focus of 'delivering sustainable and progressive cities', the pathfinding, maintaining, engaging and developing steps (see Figure 7.1) were repeated at the level of the venture.

Learning from Paradyme

So, Paradyme Corporation became a sustainability-promoting firm. What can be learned from its experience?

The focus of the 'case study' was the way a moderately large Australian multinational company:

- deployed an existing pathfinding capability to revise its approach to the management of environmental issues
- undertook a major consequential repositioning of its core business
- began to build the competencies needed to successfully pursue its new strategic directions.

Because every firm is different, we need to clearly distinguish where Paradyme's history is so idiosyncratic that it has little wider relevance and where it can provide useful insights for others.

Paradyme differs significantly from most other firms by being large, multinational and not being a commodity producer. The fact that Paradyme aims for competitiveness through boosting value creation, rather than through reducing up-front costs, marks it out as being very different from many other large firms, especially in Australia. Paradyme is also unusual because it is a developer that sees environmental concerns leading to more opportunities than threats. The firm is also atypical in that it relishes complexity. Precisely because most other firms find complexity hard to handle, Paradyme is able to take advantage of the opportunity their weakness has created.

Paradyme's business and environmental positioning is summarised, and located within the spectrum of possibilities, in Figure 7.6.

Interestingly, some of Paradyme's atypical characteristics mean that it is pioneering some of the management approaches that are likely to become much more widespread in the future as society's commitment to sustainability increases.

For example, while it is true that the major organisational changes required for firms to be sustainability-promoting will not occur effectively without strong senior management support, there are simply not enough senior managers with the level of personal commitment needed to initiate the change in enough firms. So, for most firms the only way the change will get under way is through a bottom-up approach that ultimately engages top management. Even where senior management is inclined to make a commitment to promote sustainability, support

Figure 7.6 Paradyme's current business and environmental positioning

Environmental stance:	The business strategy that defines the firm's culture:				
	Cost leader	Fast follower	Quality leader	Pioneer	Social activist
Adopter			Specific environmental technologies		
Adaptor					
Originator			Systems integration		
Catalyst					
Firms typical of each strategy:	Woolworths, Hyundai	AMD,[29] Acer	Toyota, Elextrolux	3M	Body Shop

coming up from below reduces the risk that the change of direction will not 'take'.

While Paradyme, in engaging in bottom-up strategic change to promote sustainability, is doing what will need to become commonplace, its ability to pioneer this approach was due to it having an unusually deeply embedded pathfinding capability. But once enough firms have taken pioneering steps to use a bottom-up approach, they will create models that can become widely accessible to and more frequently adopted by 'follower' businesses.

Paradyme is also pioneering the six paradigm shifts that must occur for firms to be sustainability-promoting. The first paradigm shift from 'oblivious' to 'aware' is facilitated whenever a firm like Paradyme, especially because it is large and has the confidence of the mainstream business community, demonstrates that it sees the environment as an ongoing serious strategic issue.

The second paradigm shift from 'defensive' to 'opportunity seeking' has a very interesting implication for environmental management. When firms are in defensive mode (that is, preoccupied with managing their negative impacts), their environmental management system is focused on control to prevent mistakes or keep a lid on the issues. However, as the Paradyme case illustrates, once a firm starts to look for opportunities, its environmental management has to place its main emphasis on the encouragement of sustainability-directed creativity.[30] However, to date, most people experienced in the development of environmental management systems have worked with firms that are operating in defensive mode and so their perception of how an environmental management system should be structured is rather skewed.

The Paradyme experience shows that the third paradigm shift from 'reducing the firm's own negative environmental impacts' to 'helping society take action to achieve sustainability' causes firms to treat environmental issues in an entirely new way. Rather than operating on a standard list of environmental issues—related to either cost saving, legal compliance or the management of community outrage—firms need to develop a sophisticated understanding of what a sustainable society might look like so that they can produce products that help society to achieve sustainability and so they can deploy their influence in ways that encourage society to aim for sustainability. A new knowledge base and new design and management skills are needed.

One useful way to focus a firm on meeting society's need for sustainability is to use an expanded customer concept, such as the 5-in-1 customer notion, to encourage staff to think at all times about how best to integrate the needs of people, nature and the firm.

The fourth paradigm shift, from being motivated solely by the firm's self-interest to being motivated by both self-interest and altruism, requires firms to explicitly develop commercial, technical and managerial strategies for 'doing well by doing good'. Collins and Porras (1997) in their influential book *Built to Last* show how some of the world's most successful companies have done just that.

The Paradyme experience also shows that it is easier to get internal agreement for firms to act altruistically if the self-interest of the firm is being looked after at the same time, for example, the decision to extend Paradyme's environmental management system to the whole organisation, for society's sake, was facilitated by deciding to use the environmental management system as a mechanism to add value commercially by helping to generate business opportunities.

In the 'case study', Paradyme had not yet begun the fifth and sixth paradigm shifts. However, they did explore what these shifts might mean for the firm's operations.

The fifth paradigm shift, to adopt 'full responsibility for ensuring the achievement of sustainability', implies that, given the limited resources that firms can devote to the pursuit of the public good, they must develop well-honed skills in establishing social change. Being able to deploy the catalyst skill to get the marketplace reshaped to favour sustainability resolves the apparent tension between offering sustainability-promoting products and commercial success. At any particular time there is a limit to how green products can be if the firm is to make a profit. If the products are not green enough then, rather than risk its profitability, the firm needs to do what it can to get the market changed—so that products that society needs will be commercially viable.

The Paradyme experience suggests that innovative firms are the ones most likely to voluntarily make the sixth paradigm shift from 'reactive and slow incremental change' to 'proactive urgent leapfrogging' in relation to sustainability.[31] Paradyme decided to actively explore the needed pace and scale of change issue so that it could identify potential breakpoints in the marketplace that it could exploit. Fast follower firms would need to consciously keep an eye on society's needs and the actions of pioneer companies to ensure that they are ready to move quickly once a major change begins.

Drawing this all together, the Paradyme experience has much to offer other large, innovative, knowledge-based firms in market segments where there are no strong, intrinsic conflicts between the core business and the needs of a society that is seeking to be sustainable. Other classes of firms may find that methods and knowledge-bases developed by companies like Paradyme are useful once developed.

What can business consultants learn from Paradyme? First, that some firms have the capacity to go a long way further than the pack and that such firms should not be held back by applying methods that are appropriate to less innovative and knowledge intensive firms. Second, pioneers like Paradyme are proving grounds for new ideas and knowledge-bases and once these have been developed they may well be transferable to adaptor and follower firms.

There are some important lessons from the Paradyme story for advocacy groups and public sector policy managers. It is common, especially in countries like Australia, to focus attention on the firms that cause the greatest amount of environmental harm and wastage. While there is clearly a lot that these firms can and should do they often face difficult transitions to a sustainability-compatible profile. On the other hand, companies like Paradyme, which can be the great winners from the transition to an ecologically sustainable economy, tend to get over-looked. This is unfortunate because these firms have the capacity to contribute very significantly to the effort of pioneering a sustainable society. They have the resources and skills to develop new methods and knowledge-bases, they often have the strategic leverage to trigger transformations in sectors of the economy and, together, they can be significant advocates for sustainability-promoting public policy.

Conclusion

This 'case study' has begun the task of fleshing out how firms can use key capabilities to become sustainability-promoting and how they can go about developing the specific competencies required if they are to be commercially viable sustainability-promoting firms. The basic capabilities needed by sustainability-promoting firms are no different from those required by any other firms (see Figure 7.1). However, the special challenge for sustainability-oriented firms is to be able to find viable strategies for 'doing well while doing good'. A whole constellation of new skills and competencies are required to make this possible in the sustainability area. While a good many of the needed competencies are known, there is still a great deal of work to be done to make them routinely available to all firms.

Endnotes

1 ACTEW Corporation, headquartered in Canberra, is an honourable exception, as is Interface Inc. which is based in the US but operates globally, including in Australia. Very useful case study information can be found on Interface in Anderson (1998) and chapter 6 of Nattrass & Altomare (1999). See the firms' web sites as well:
ACTEW Corporation: http://www.actew.com.au/about/default.htm
Interface Inc.: http://www.interfaceinc.com/
2 For information on Lend Lease go to: http://www.lendlease.com.au/
3 'Sustainability take-off' describes a condition where concern for sustainability is embedded in the culture, where action to achieve sustainability is continuous over decades, where sustainability programs do not get significantly wound back during economic downturns (or better still they are advanced in ways that are appropriate to that stage of the business cycle), where changes in government do not significantly set back sustainability-promotion, where public policy is driven by a vision of a preferred sustainable future and where the leading sections of the business community are sustainability-promoting. A discussion of the related concept of

ecological take-off can be found at: http://www.green-innovations.asn.au/takeoff2.htm

4 This chapter defines ecological sustainability as a state in which key biological or physical attributes of the environment are maintained and, where relevant, restored. These attributes include for example (a) the restoration of the *very* low extinction rates that occurred before technology-using humans started to have their impact, (b) the maintenance of life support systems (nutrient flows, hydrological cycles, climate conditions, ocean circulation, screening of ultraviolet light etc. and (c) the substitution of renewable resources for fossil resources, etc. Sustainability is *not* defined as the integration or 'balanced' treatment of economic social and environmental issues per se, even though the integrated treatment of these issues is necessary if sustainability is to be achieved. Nor is sustainability considered to be synonymous with 'ethical progress'. The objective of sustainability is the maintenance or restoration of a state that has existed, whereas the central purpose of progress is change to a new state that has not yet existed.

5 This chapter does not refer to 'sustainable firms' because, in the context of ecological issues, there is no such thing. Sustainable organisations are ones that are able to persist through time despite changing circumstances (Kelly & Allison, 1999: 234). Probably the world's oldest organised religions have the best claim to being called 'sustainable organisations' in this sense. Environmental or ecological sustainability is a whole-system issue, so you cannot meaningfully refer to a *component* of the larger system, such as a product or a firm, as being ecologically sustainable in itself. Not only that, most firms are still a very long way from ideal environmental performance so to refer to them as 'sustainable' is simply to attribute to them more than they deserve. However from the day that the commitment is genuinely made, a firm can legitimately call itself 'sustainability-promoting'.

6 Allstates Insurance is fictional. However, the purchase of Allstates parallels Lend Lease's real-life takeover in 1985 of MLC, a major Australian financial institution.

7 BS 7750, developed by the British Standards Association, was the first standard for environmental management systems. It drew heavily on the methodology of the quality management standard pioneered by the British Standards Association, BS5750, which was later internationalised as ISO9000.

8 The EMAS standard is the European environmental management standard. It is quite similar to the ISO14001 environmental management standard but has more stringent requirements for reporting to the public on environmental performance.

9 The Bo01 development is a real one and details can be found at: http://www.bo01.com/eng/index.html

10 'Indirect' impacts are caused by a firm's supply chain, by the users of the firm's products and by their products when discarded.

11 Associated with the Factor 10 Club and the German Wuppertal Institute.

12 Material inputs per service unit—a concept developed by the Wuppertal Institute.

13 Associated with Du Pont's ' the goal is zero' program and, in a more holistic application, with the Zero Emissions Research Initiative [ZERI].

14 Associated with the US-based Rocky Mountain Institute and applied, for example, to buildings and the creation of the hypercar.

15 Associated with the UK-based consultancy SustainAbility.

16 Associated with Mathis Wackernagel and Rees (1996).

17 Associated with the Netherlands National Program on Sustainable Technology Development.

18 Associated with David Wallace (1996).

19 Such as Interface, Electrolux, IKEA, Scandic Hotels and Collins Pine Co.

20 Nattrass & Altomare (1999) and Anderson (1998).

21 This is an expression used by the Natural Step organisation to refer to running into environmental constraints that cause problems for a business.

22 Environmental Creativity is a fictional organisation. Materials and concepts identified in this chapter as being developed by Environmental Creativity or its fictional principal, Paul McIntyre, are in real life the work of the author of this chapter. A fuller exposition of these ideas can be found at: http://www.green-innovations.asn.au/

23 The thermohaline circulation works as follows: Each northern and southern winter sea ice forms at one of the poles. As the ice forms it expels salt causing the sea to become denser. The dense water sinks setting up a flow in the oceans so powerful that cold oxygen-rich surface water is drawn down and flows from the poles to the equator. By this stage the water has warmed and become dilute and it flows back to the poles on the surface where it is recharged with oxygen. The computer models of the Division of Atmospheric Research of the Australian public research corporation, the CSIRO, indicate that increases in atmospheric CO_2 that are 1.5 to 2 times the pre-industrial level may cause sea ice formation to largely cease with the result that the thermohaline circulation is shut off.

24 The hypercar story is discussed in real life in Chapter 2 of Hawken, Lovins and Lovins (1999) and there is a wealth of information about

the hypercar on the Rocky Mountain Institute web site at: http://www.rmi.org/ The change strategy behind the success of the hypercar is described in the Green Innovations paper 'Tapping the sustainability market'—see http://www.green-innovations.asn.au/tapsmrkt.htm

25 Crisis points are explored in Grove (1988), breakpoints in Strebel (1992) and avalanches in Kelly & Allison (1999).

26 The participants were: (a) from the initial workshops: Bernhard Ligteringen (Construction Projects), Geoff Tytherleigh (Investments), Annette James (Risk Management), Vandana Gupta (Financial Services) and Andrew MacDonald (Business Incubation), and (b) the organising team: Chris Norton (Environmental Manager), Jessica Taylor (Manager of the Business Incubation group), Alan Hall from the Training unit, Katy Wong (Manager of the corporate Business Development unit) and Ingrid Sjöberg (Interior Design unit, Sweden).

27 See end note 1.

28 See the catalogue of specialist capabilities and competencies required by sustainability-promoting firms at: http://www.green-innovations.asn.au/capabilities.htm

29 AMD manufactures computer microprocessors and is Intel's main rival.

30 There is an interesting exception to this defensive/control versus opportunity-seeking/creativity dichotomy. Firms pursuing major stretch goals, such as 'zero waste' for the firm, are still essentially acting defensively but they do need to apply a significant amount of creativity to pursue these goals effectively.

31 And also the fourth and fifth paradigm shifts (see Figure 7.3).

References

Anderson, R. 1998 *Mid-course correction: Toward a Sustainable Enterprise: The Interface model*, The Peregrinzilla Press, Atlanta, USA.

Arnold, M. and Day, R. 1999 'The business case for sustainable development', *Greener Management International*, vol. 23, UK.

Blanchard, K. and Waghorn, T. 1997 *Mission Possible: Becoming a World Class Organisation while there's Still Time*, McGraw-Hill, New York.

Brown, L. et al. 1998 'World is economically richer and environmentally poorer' (Vital Signs 1998 Press Release, 9 May 1999): http://www.worldwatch.org/

Campbell, C. J. and Laherrere J. H. 1998 'The end of cheap oil', *Scientific American*, March, vol. 278, no. 3, pp. 60–5.

Claxton, G. 1997 *Hare Brain, Tortoise Mind: Why Intelligence Increases when you Think Less*, Fourth Estate, London.

Collins, J. and Porras, J. 1997 *Built to Last: Successful Habits of Visionary Companies*, Century Business, London.

De Gues, A. 1997 *The Living Company: Growth, Learning and Longevity in Business*, Nicholas Brearley, London.

Ellyard, P. 1998 *Ideas for the New Millennium*, Melbourne University Press, Melbourne.

Enting, I., Wigley, T. and Heimann, M. 1994 *Technical Paper No. 31: Future Emissions and Concentrations of Carbon Dioxide: Key Ocean/Atmosphere/Land Analyses*, CSIRO Division of Atmospheric Research, Melbourne.

Goldratt, E. 1990 *Theory of Constraints*, North River Press, Croton-on-Hudson, New York.

——1994 *It's Not Luck*, Gower, Aldershot, Hampshire.

——1997 *Critical Chain*, The North River Press, Great Barrington, MA.

Grove, A. 1998 *Only the Paranoid survive: How to Exploit the Crisis Points that Challenge Every Company and Career*, Harper Collin Business, London.

Hawken, P., Lovins, A. and Lovins, H. 1999 *Natural Capitalism: The Next Industrial Revolution*, Earthscan Publications, London.

Hirst, A. 1999 'The southern ocean response to global warming in the CSIRO coupled ocean-atmosphere model', *Environmental Modelling and Software*, vol. 14, pp. 227–41.

Hoegh-Guldberg, O. 1999 'Climate change, coral bleaching and the future of the world's coral reefs', Greenpeace scientific report, from the Greenpeace Australia web site: http://www.greenpeace.org.au/

Holmberg, J. 1999 'Backcasting: A natural step when making sustainable development operational for companies', *Greener Management International*, vol. 23, UK.

International Energy Agency 1998 'World energy prospects to 2020—oil supply prospects', IEA paper for the G8 Energy Ministers' Meeting in Moscow, 31 March.

International Factor 10 Club 1997 Statement to government and business leaders, Wuppertal Institute for Climate, Environment and Energy, Wuppertal, Germany.

Jouzel, J., Lorius, C., Petit, J., Genthon, C., Barkov, N., Kotlyakov, V. and Petrov, V. 1987 'Vostok ice core: a continuous isotope temperature record over the last climatic cycle (160,000 years)', *Nature*, vol. 329, pp. 403–8.

Kelly, S. and Allison, M. 1999 *The Complexity Advantage: How the Science of Complexity Can Help Your Business Achieve Peak Performance*, Business Week Books (McGraw-Hill), New York.

McLaren, D., Bullock, D. and Nusrat, Y. 1998 *Tomorrow's World: Britain's Share in a Sustainable Future*, Earthscan, London.

Meadows, D., Meadows, D. and Randers, J. 1992 *Beyond the Limits: Global Collapse or a Sustainable Future*, Earthscan, London.

Moore, J. 1996 *The Death of Competition: Leadership and Strategy in the Age of Business Ecosystems*, Harper Business, New York.

Nattrass, B. and Altomare, M. 1999 *The Natural Step for Business: Wealth, Ecology and the Evolutionary Corporation*, New Society Publishers, Gabriola Island, British Columbia, Canada.

Pascale, R. and Athos, A. 1981 *The Art of Japanese Management*, Penguin Books, Harmondsworth, UK.

Peters, T. and Robert Waterman, R. 1982 *In Search of Excellence: Lessons from America's Best-run Companies*, Harper & Row Publishers, New York.

Sachs, W., Loske, R. and Linz, M. 1998 *Greening the North: A Post-industrial Blueprint for Ecology and Equity*, Zed Books, London.

Strebel, P. 1992 *Breakpoints: How Managers Exploit Radical Business Change*, Harvard Business School Press, Boston, MA.

Strong, G. 1999 'Putting our greenhouse in order', the *Age*, 26 June.

Sutton, P. 1997a 'Tapping the sustainability market', *Greener Management International*, vol. 18, UK.

——1997b 'Targeting sustainability: the positive application of ISO 14001' in C. Sheldon (ed.), *ISO 14001 and Beyond: Environmental Management Systems in the Real World*, Greenleaf Publishing, Sheffield, UK.

——1997c 'The sustainability-promoting firm: An essential player in the politics of sustainability', *Proceedings of the Ecopolitics XI Conference, Melbourne University 4–5 Oct.*: Melbourne, Australia: see http://www.green-innovations.asn.au/spf.htm

——1998 'Ecological sustainability' at: http://www.green-innovations.asn.au/ecolsust.htm

——1999 'The sustainability-promoting firm', *Greener Management International*, vol. 23, UK.

Sutton, P. and Preece, K. 1998 'Putting the green into greener purchasing: protecting nature consciously' in T. Russel (ed.), *Greener Purchasing: Opportunities and Innovations*, Greenleaf Publishing, Sheffield, UK.

Turner, D. and Crawford, M. 1998 *Change Power: Capabilities that Drive Corporate Renewal*, Business & Professional Publishing, Warriewood, Australia.

Wackernagel, M. and Rees, W. 1996 *Our Ecological Footprint: Reducing Human Impact on the Earth*, New Society Publishers, Philadelphia.

Wallace, D. 1996 *Sustainable Industrialisation*, Earthscan, London.

von Weizsäcker, E., Lovins, A. and Lovins, H. 1997 *Factor 4: Doubling Wealth, Halving Resource Use*, Allen & Unwin, St Leonards, NSW.

8

Technologies and processes for ecological sustainability

Alan Pears

Overview

In this chapter, we review the roles of technology and processes within organisations that are working towards environmental sustainability. This discussion parallels that of Viv Read in Chapter 5 on technology and processes, which deals with similar issues from a human sustainability perspective.

Technology provides the tools for organisations to function, and the products of technology are often the output, or the basis of services from which profits are made. Technology is the *hardware* of an organisation. Processes such as buying, selling, negotiating and forecasting are the essence of organisations. Processes are the *software* of organisations.

Technology and processes interact with other elements of the organisation and each other to determine the environmental impact of the organisation and its products and/or services, as shown in Figure 8.1. These interactions are complex, and often occur at a subconscious level for individuals, and an informal level in organisational terms.

Technology and environmental improvement in organisations

Technology is both a filter and an enabler. The technologies around us shape the way we experience our environment, and help to define what we believe to be possible. In these ways, technologies act as filters between people (and hence organisations) and their world. A person who

Figure 8.1 Simplified framework of selection and use of tools in organisations

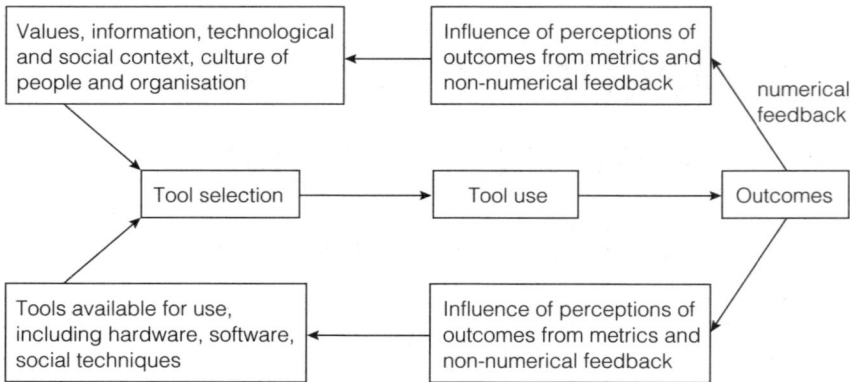

```
┌────────────────────────────┐        ┌────────────────────────────┐
│ Values, information,       │        │ Influence of perceptions of│
│ technological              │◄─────── │ outcomes from metrics and  │──┐ numerical
│ and social context, culture│        │ non-numerical feedback     │  │ feedback
│ of people and organisation │        │                            │  │
└────────────────────────────┘        └────────────────────────────┘  │
        │                                                              │
        ▼                                                              ▼
  ┌───────────────┐          ┌───────────┐              ┌───────────┐
  │ Tool selection│─────────►│ Tool use  │─────────────►│ Outcomes  │
  └───────────────┘          └───────────┘              └───────────┘
        ▲                                                      │
        │                                                      │
┌────────────────────────────┐        ┌────────────────────────────┐
│ Tools available for use,   │        │ Influence of perceptions of│
│ including hardware,         │◄─────── │ outcomes from metrics and  │◄─┘
│ software, social techniques│        │ non-numerical feedback     │
└────────────────────────────┘        └────────────────────────────┘
```

grew up in a car-based society in which public transport services were poor sees future possibilities through a different filter from a person who grew up with comprehensive public transport. Technology also amplifies human capabilities: for example, a spanner amplifies muscular strength, while a computer amplifies brainpower. Both enable humans to carry out tasks that might otherwise be impossible.

By their nature, technologies (or hardware) only take on significance within a human and organisational context. If a technology cannot be meshed with the people and cultures within organisations, it is of little value in that context at that time, regardless of its objective technical potential. This is simply because this potential will not be utilised. To capture the potential, processes must be pursued. This involves making the human, organisational or societal contexts more amenable to the characteristics of the technology, and/or developing the technology's characteristics to match the requirements of users. Thus the processes that mediate between technologies, people and organisations are of critical importance.

An example of the importance of these processes is the adoption of electronic mail within organisations. In principle, electronic mail has the technological potential to drastically reduce paper consumption—a substantial cost overhead and major environmental impact for many organisations. However, many staff simply print out most of the mail messages they receive, thus negating the environmental and financial benefits. Failures in staff training and updating of standard procedures are key issues here. In contrast, the explosive growth of the fax machine (which was not foreseen by many experts) seems to have been due to its use of electronic communication technology to provide speed, combined with its delivery of a hard copy output, which was culturally familiar to office workers and managers.

Each technology also fits within a technological context. If the technological systems around it do not support its use, it may fail, regardless of its positive attributes (Rosenberg, 1995). For example, the disc brake was developed in the 1920s. But it had to await the increasing focus on braking performance, improved materials and advanced hydraulic systems of the 1950s before it could begin to replace the drum brake. The computer and telecommunications industries are now very aware of the importance of agreed standards for interfaces between technological systems: they can make or break a product or technology. Improvement in energy efficiency often involves optimised control of systems, which depends on the availability of cheap sensors, computing power and sophisticated controls.

Adoption of many environmentally sustainable technologies can therefore be blocked by the limitations of either the technologies themselves, the systems required to ensure their utilisation, or the cultures of the groups applying them. For example, in some cases renewable energy technologies have not developed to the point where they can supply energy that is competitively priced and available at the times when it is needed. In other cases, they are cost-effective and practical, but inappropriate financial evaluation methods, lack of familiarity of technical staff with renewable energy systems or other process failures work against their use. There is an element of the chicken-and-egg, too: wider adoption of renewable energy technologies would reduce their cost, increase the likelihood that relevant employees would be more familiar with their application, and lead to establishment of systems that facilitate their wider use.

So, for technology to fulfil its potential capacity to contribute to an organisation's environmental sustainability it cannot be viewed in isolation. It must be treated as part of a complex and ever-changing system. And it is not sufficient to invest resources in technologies themselves: resources are also required to create processes that will mesh the new technologies with their technological and social contexts.

Environmental improvement processes in organisations

Often, processes aimed at achieving environmental sustainability are treated as separate from many of the core processes involved in operation of the organisation. This is a fundamental error. It virtually guarantees that environmental improvement will be costly, as opportunities for savings through integration of environmental objectives with other organisational objectives will be lost. And it makes it difficult to gain staff commitment, as environmental responsibilities become an additional burden on top of what are often already crippling workloads.

At the same time as they isolate environmental improvement from core business, many managers attempt to achieve environmental objectives without allocating appropriate resources. If environmental performance is a core business objective, why is its management often delegated to a junior staff member, to a person who already has a heavy workload, or to a voluntary committee? This virtually guarantees failure.

From 'end of pipe' responses to 'win–win' strategies

This isolationist approach to environmental improvement is typified by the 'end of pipe' solutions widely adopted as responses to pollution. That is, once pollution has been created, efforts are made to capture and treat it. The smart solution, of course, is to redesign systems to avoid generating pollution in the first place. This is similar to the approach now being widely applied to quality control. Instead of inspecting and fixing or discarding faulty products at the end of the production line, quality assurance systems are now used to avoid faults. This approach has been demonstrated to improve productivity and quality, while cutting costs. But it requires new cultures, new systems and new procedures. The organisation that looks for 'win–win' environmental opportunities and incorporates environmental values into its culture is in a much stronger position to make environmental performance profitable (Pears, 1998a).

Many efforts to implement systematised approaches to improving environmental performance, such as compliance with ISO14000, have mixed outcomes. Often, there is insufficient emphasis on prioritisation and benchmarking of performance against best practice (or best feasible practice). Instead, the vague principle of 'continuous improvement' is promoted. Not that application of 'continuous improvement' is *necessarily* a bad thing. It is a significant improvement over ignoring environmental performance, as it introduces the principles of monitoring and measuring environmental performance. Likewise, establishment of formal environmental policies, manuals and guidelines are also worthwhile steps forward. But measures such as these do not go far enough. They often reinforce the image of environmental performance as an additional, isolated issue that gets in the way of effective management of core business. 'Continuous improvement' may also obscure the potential for radical improvement. Efforts to deliver 2 per cent improvement in environmental performance each year will tend to focus attention on fine-tuning of existing equipment and systems.

A transformational approach based on a broader analysis may result in a dramatic improvement in environmental performance and profitability, but may often require significant investment that cannot be funded from recurrent expenditures. Such opportunities have been documented by von Weizsäcker, Lovins and Lovins (1997) in their book *Factor 4*, and by others advocating 'stretch goals' of Factor 10 improvements in environmental performance (that is, 90 per cent reduction in environmental impact per unit of activity).

Environmental auditing: essential tool or dead end?

Another process issue that can undermine effective environmental performance is over-emphasis on auditing. In principle, environmental auditing is a good idea. It provides documentation of existing performance, and can highlight major issues and clarify priorities. But the resources involved in comprehensively auditing an organisation's performance and identifying areas of waste can be so great that the process of auditing leaves few resources to actually implement change. For example, a number of Australian schools attempted to carry out energy audits using a pilot energy auditing kit developed in Victoria in 1993. The tasks of counting lights, equipment and appliances were so large that only one school completed them and their estimate of energy use based on the audit was three times larger than their actual consumption as documented in energy bills. Staff and students were so demoralised that little progress was made on implementing energy saving measures! In response to this outcome, a revised energy saving kit was developed. This provided information as to the likely main areas of energy use in schools. It used limited auditing and strategic diagnostic measurement and observation activities to pinpoint energy wastage and demonstrate the potential for savings (SECV, 1993). This new, more focused approach met with a much improved response.

The first environmental audits of an organisation are likely to identify a serious lack of data on which analysis can be based. This should not be seen as a negative, for it can pinpoint the data collection and reporting processes that need to be established to monitor ongoing environmental performance. Initial audits can also identify a number of the more obvious opportunities for environmental improvement, which can become the focus of the early phases of an environmental improvement process. Organisations should be encouraged to undertake analyses that are within their capabilities, and which lead to action plans that are within the resource capacity of the organisation to implement. Otherwise these initial studies may be the last.

An environmental audit is not a 'quick fix'. It is just one element of a comprehensive approach to environmental improvement. Ongoing auditing is necessary to identify opportunities that will emerge as business activity evolves, knowledge improves, and the range of financially viable environmentally-acceptable products and services expands. This requires allocation of resources on an ongoing basis. This is not a problem for an organisation committed to environmental improvement, but it can be a problem for managers who think environmental performance can be achieved by a once-off burst of activity.

The reality is, environmental improvement that is both effective and financially viable requires review and re-engineering of core processes within an organisation, as discussed later in this chapter. While this may sound draconian, it does not necessarily mean the organisation's operations must be drastically altered. It means managers and staff have to be prepared to look beyond their usual assumptions. For example, a business that buys-in most of its operational equipment may simply specify new purchasing criteria for that equipment. As a result, staff work practices may not have to change at all! The examples at the end of this chapter illustrate the range of issues that may be addressed.

Technology, processes and organisations

Technological evolution

Technologies undergo continuous evolution, with occasional leaps forward or steps sideways into new technologies. Their evolution is often dependent on a synthesis of developments in a number of previously unrelated areas. Indeed, the capacity of technologies to contribute in new ways to environmental sustainability is much more dependent on the evolution of complementary technologies than many people realise. New developments in one area can 'piggy-back' on developments in other areas. For example, movement sensors for controlling lights to save energy use technologies similar to those for security systems.

There is a widespread failure to recognise the technological progress that has been made already, and to underestimate the potential for further improvement. For example, if power station conversion efficiencies had not improved from the 10 per cent of 1910 to 35 per cent and better today, we would be using three or four times as much fossil fuel for electricity generation as we do today—with much greater environmental impacts and higher operating costs. And in the mid-1980s, running a typical two-door family refrigerator using, at that time, 1300 kilowatt-hours (kWh) per year would have required more than 10 square metres of solar cells costing $12 000. To run the best high efficiency refrigerator of similar capacity today (which uses around 200 kWh per year) would require less than 2 square metres of cells, costing around $1500. Similarly, almost every manufacturing process (when carried out at best practice) generates much less pollution today than it did a decade ago. And the knowledge gained in achieving these gains provides a basis for further ongoing improvement—as long as sufficient resources are committed.

A serious challenge for organisations pursuing sustainability is to recognise the scope for dramatic improvements in utilisation of energy and materials, and to apply this potential to reduction of environmental impacts. Unfortunately, technical specialists closely involved in particular areas often reinforce the view that there is limited scope to improve the efficiency of use of energy and materials and reduce environmental impacts. For example, technical staff in the Australian appliance industry in the mid-1980s were adamant that the scope for improvement in the energy efficiency of refrigerators was limited to about 15 per cent. After the introduction of mandatory appliance energy labelling, it took less than a year to exceed this level of improvement and a decade later many models save 50 per cent. Best technology products (in limited production) save up to 80 per cent compared with mid-1980s performance.

This technological pessimism may be due to a variety of factors. Sometimes technologists in one field become insular, and are unaware of developments in other fields that may be applicable in their own. Others are so focused on delivering incremental improvements that they miss the big opportunities. Still others are protecting their status within the organisation by blocking 'alien' ideas from outside their own intellectual tradition. Others prefer the security of trouble-free operation rather than the risk of innovation, given the high visible cost of system breakdowns. Managers need to recognise the limitations of their technical experts, and put in place constructive response strategies. These might include staff development programs, seminars run by independent experts, reports prepared by a range of people with expertise in non-traditional areas, and so on.

Status of technology issues in organisations

In many organisations, attitudes to technology verge on schizophrenia. On one hand, managers and policy advisers are often sceptical of the potential contribution of technological development to contribute to organisational (or societal) success. This is reflected in their inclination to isolate technical experts and issues from core decision making processes in the organisation. This often leads to a denial of resources for development and adoption of technology, which slows progress towards sustainability. Yet, in other ways, they are naively optimistic about the capacity of technology to deal with broader or longer term challenges. By contrast, this can lead to poorly considered, lemming-like scrambles to drive the rapid introduction of new technologies with little consideration for the human, social and environmental implications, their cost-effectiveness and their effects on the long term strategic positioning of the corporation. For example, some industries have resisted whole hearted involvement in recycling because they have focused on the short term economics instead of the bigger picture. This has led to government intervention and loss of community trust, which have limited the scope for pursuit of the most cost-effective solutions and led to unnecessary financial costs.

The recent focus on marketisation, deregulation and competitive frameworks has exacerbated both these tendencies, by leading to increased emphasis on short term financial success. Cost-cutting measures aimed at making organisations more competitive often result in heavy pruning of technical and specialist expertise, justified by the argument that it can be 'bought in' when required. The focus on capturing market share also distracts from long term strategies. While these actions may lead to short term success, and may even lead to short term increases in the rate of take-up of near-commercial technology, they risk undermining long term development of technical functions and the maximisation of the potential contribution of technology to the sustainability and profitability of the firm's operations. R&D is often a casualty in this process—a failure often exacerbated by government cutbacks in R&D incentives.

Our frequent inability to manage technology issues is also illustrated by the common failure to integrate them into management frameworks and processes. This reflects many complex factors, among which are the ignorance of technology issues among non-technologists, and poor communication between technologists and non-technologists. In many organisations, technologists seem to either have too much status and power (for example, in the electricity industry until the past few years) or too little to maintain effective dialogue with financial and marketing groups, who dominate many organisations. Either situation creates an imbalance in the optimal integration of technology with corporate strategic development.

An illustration of the subservience of technology and technologists to financial and project management objectives can be seen in the design and development of new office buildings. Each technical expert generally works independently, within a tightly defined framework established by project managers and developers. Professional fees are often based on a percentage of the capital value of the system being designed. The negotiation is generally focused on containing costs, so the first casualty of cost-cutting is time for analysis and optimisation of the design. There is also no incentive for a building developer to optimise long term performance, while there is an incentive to minimise capital cost. As a result, the outcomes are often appallingly energy-wasteful and unnecessarily costly on a life cycle basis. The lack of integration between specialists in the planning stage also often leads to costly system faults, imbalances and failures as the system goes into operation.

Using the conventional approach, there is limited scope to optimise the overall building system. For example, rarely does the heating and cooling engineer explain to the architect the implications of design features such as large west windows for the capital cost and operating cost of the heating and cooling system (see Pears, 1998b). One estimate suggests that after 1 per cent of the project budget for a new building has been spent, 70 per cent of its life cycle costs have been locked-in by design decisions (Romm, 1994).

If technology is to fulfil its potential to facilitate environmentally sustainable solutions, planners and managers must develop a better understanding of its productive utilisation. Industries must create incentive systems that reward decision makers for the time and imagination needed to create long term systemic solutions.

Technology, processes and people

Organisations often fail to adequately consider the human and societal implications of their technology strategies. In most developed countries, including Australia, the workforce is becoming split into three distinct groups: those who are working ever longer hours and feeling less secure, those who see themselves as winners in the emerging work paradigm, and those who have no place in employment and are increasingly marginalised. Technology is being used to displace employment across all sectors, with the objective of cutting costs and improving productivity. Not only does this exacerbate social problems, but it is often poor business. In Melbourne, we have recently seen the replacement of station staff and tram conductors with automated ticket vending machines. Problems of fare evasion, violence and vandalism have led to the employment of large numbers of security staff and ticket inspectors. This has had a serious impact on the attitudes of travellers: instead of a positive interaction with staff, involving financial transactions and information transfer, staff are now playing a policing role in which most interactions are interpersonally hostile.

Often, negative outcomes from the implementation of technology are due to the cultures of the organisations and their management. Failure to adequately trial a technology, and failure to cost and consider all of its implications are common symptoms. These are failures of management processes rather than failures of technology—although there are also plenty of examples where grand promises based on assumed technological breakthroughs have not been delivered.

Technologies that contribute to environmental improvement offer potential for increased employment and improved quality of work, but this is not guaranteed. Conscious effort is required to deliver these benefits.

In principle, environmental improvement involves reducing material resource use through application of high value activities such as improved design and control, or increased labour such as recycling or maintenance and repair programs. As the resource sector (mining and resource processing) is a small employer and is very capital intensive, there is often economic benefit and increased employment from such change.

Environmental improvement measures often impact employment differentially over time. Clean up projects and 'end of pipe' solutions may involve significant employment increases, although the quality of work involved may not be particularly attractive. As environmental improvement becomes integrated into organisational systems, the number of additional jobs may decline, while the job quality improves. For example, electronic mail has the potential to reduce the labour and cost involved in information management. Similarly, early recycling programs have been very labour intensive, but automated sorting and economies of scale are likely to reduce the labour intensity of recycling in the future. Rapid overall growth in the scale of these activities, however, means that total employment levels are likely to rise, and it would be difficult to envisage a situation where environmental systems declined to the low level of labour intensity of resource industries. As an example, mining in Australia now directly employs less than 90 000 people out of a labour force of 8.5 million.

In the long term, environmentally sound businesses will require more sophisticated analytical and decision making tools, and they will offer products and services with higher value-added content. More labour will be required to ensure systems continue to operate at optimum levels, while resource recovery and recycling and harvesting of renewable energy resources are inherently more employment intensive than large scale resource extraction and processing.

The key issue here is that while adoption of environmental improvement technologies has potential to create more employment and to enhance the quality of work, these outcomes are not guaranteed. Conscious analysis and policies are needed to ensure that these outcomes are realised. At the same time, the all too common reluctance of management to employ more people, or to see their employees as resources rather than costs, means that efforts to implement environmental improvement strategies are often deprived of the human resources they need for success.

Technology, risk and opportunity for organisations pursuing sustainability

A major fear of managers and others contemplating the pursuit of environmental sustainability is that their efforts will backfire. Some decision makers believe that any effort to improve environmental performance, or to tell the community about such improvement, could actually increase the risk of criticism from environmentalists (who may be stereotyped as having impossibly idealistic goals). Such criticism could have potentially negative outcomes for the organisation. If environmental measures involve significant investment in new technology and organisational systems, these fears intensify and decision makers try to take actions to protect the viability of the business, for example, by engaging in public relations campaigns.

The term 'green-wash' is increasingly used as a criticism of the use of public relations strategies to create a veneer of environmental respectability for activities which are considered by some to have net negative environmental impacts. For example, efforts by car companies to support tree planting programs are considered by many environmentalists to be an attempt to avoid addressing the fundamental environmental impact of cars. Similarly, greenhouse offset programs (tree planting to absorb the carbon dioxide from burning oil) being developed by an oil shale mining company in Queensland, Australia, are seen by many as an attempt to obscure the severe environmental consequences of an enormous fossil fuel mining operation in an environmentally-sensitive region.

The risks are exacerbated by a number of factors:

- Many managers have partial perspectives on the environmental impacts of their organisation's activities. What managers genuinely believe to be significant efforts to improve environmental performance may be, in the broader context, modest achievements.
- Many people within organisations fear that the changes required to achieve improved environmental performance will be dramatic, and will make their lives difficult or impossible, or even force them out of their present employment.

- Within both environmental groups and the broader community, many people judge environmental performance on a limited range of criteria (with different groups often applying different criteria!). They may also have limited knowledge of the detail of an organisation's environmental impacts, so they may make unrealistic judgements.
- Lack of trust of business, views based on past performance, and preconceptions colour many outsiders' assessments of organisational performance on environmental issues.
- Our understanding of the environmental impacts of many activities and products is evolving. This makes good performance a moving target. After all, when the car was introduced, it was seen as an excellent way of reducing the pollution from horse droppings. And urban sprawl is the end result of people's attempts to avoid the pollution of inner urban areas, and to gain improved access to the environmental assets of areas outside heavily-developed urban regions. These seemed like good ideas at the time!
- Achieving an improvement in environmental performance may create competition or encourage external pressures for further improvement. This should really be seen as a positive outcome, but for many it is something to be feared or avoided.

This situation leads to a necessity for organisations to invest significant effort into understanding both the realities of the environmental impacts of their business and the perceptions of the public and interest groups. In some cases, information programs can clarify issues and correct misconceptions but, in others, it makes more sense for an organisation to work within the limits of the commonly held views. Either they can redefine their business within this framework, or they can develop a sufficient level of trust and knowledge within the community to gradually develop a path based on a consensus perspective. Whatever the approach taken, business must continue to monitor community perceptions and research its environmental impacts, so that its planning and development can respond to changes in perceptions and understanding of environmental issues.

The outcome of such analysis may lead to recognition of the awkward reality that an organisation's activities have an overall negative impact on the environment. This may be traumatic, but it's probably better to begin to address this sooner rather than later! The good news is that this outcome is likely to be relatively rare. Most business activity has the potential to fit within an environmentally sustainable framework. And many new business opportunities will emerge from a focus on environmental sustainability.

Practical progress toward environmental sustainability

In this section, we look briefly at the processes and tools which can assist an organisation to move towards environmental sustainability. This discussion is far from comprehensive, but the questions posed provide a useful starting point. Examples are included later in this chapter, which may help with the interpretation of principles and application to practical situations.

How does my business impact on the environment?

This broad question can only be answered by examination of the various stages of the organisation's production process or sequence of operations. There is a need to examine:

- the provision of inputs to an organisation (including products and services)
- the ongoing operations of the organisation
- the impacts of the products or services provided when they are being used
- the impacts of customers or clients when buying and using the products and services
- the impacts associated with end of product life (disposal, recovery, etc.).

Initially, rough estimates of the significance of impacts of each of the above phases can be made. These estimates can be improved over time. In many cases, information will have to be sought from others such as suppliers, or broad assumptions made. Usually, an important outcome of this process is that a much better understanding is gained of the information needed, and the systems necessary to collect it.

Issues such as these are often considered in a life cycle analysis of particular products. Such an analysis evaluates the environmental impacts of each step in the manufacture, use and disposal of a product. However, here we are interested in the impacts of the organisation as a whole, rather than specific products. Life cycle analysis of a particular product is still very useful, as it does assist in identification of many direct and indirect environmental impacts associated with business activity.

In principle, how—and to what extent—could I influence the environmental impacts of each of these stages?

Remember, this is an 'in principle' question, not one related to costs or to the immediate availability of technologies. For example, where I am a large buyer of equipment which I re-sell, I may be able to encourage or require my supplier to shift to sustainable materials and processes. Alternatively, I may be able to switch to a supplier who already achieves high environmental standards. Or I may be able to actively inform potential suppliers that, if they meet certain standards of environmental performance (and other essential performance criteria), I would switch to them. For example, an audit of a fast food restaurant found that only 10 per cent of the energy used by a coffee maker ended up as hot coffee. The rest was wasted as heat lost from the poorly insulated hot water tank in the unit, and from the uninsulated coffee jug. The same audit showed that the restaurant's refrigerators used four times as much energy as the most efficient domestic refrigerators of the same capacity. These are classic opportunities for the development of performance specifications to be used as a basis for future equipment purchases.

It is likely that you will find that you have control over some things, substantial scope to influence others, and limited scope to influence some issues. You may also find that your capacity to influence some outcomes is dependent on the provision of suitable infrastructure, market frameworks, or even regulations, by other organisations or government. The scope for control or influence may also vary with time frame. In the short term, the scope for change may be limited but, in the longer term, there is often greater potential for change. In some cases, there may be 'once off' opportunities associated with a planned upgrade of equipment or relocation of offices or manufacturing plants.

Can I imagine a scenario in which my business (including its inputs and outputs) could be environmentally sustainable

This is the *big* question. For many businesses, it will be surprisingly easy. For example, for a sales-based business the scenario might be:

- my suppliers provide all my business inputs from sustainable sources
- my business is energy-efficient and the energy it uses is from renewable sources
- it is feasible for my customers to use sustainable options to reach me and interact with me
- I transport my products using sustainable transport
- the inputs required during operation of the products are from sustainable sources
- the products I sell (and their packaging and associated materials) are managed in a sustainable manner when they no longer perform their intended function

■ I contribute funds to projects, such as recycling, tree-planting and land rehabilitation, that offset the environmental impacts I cannot avoid.

For some businesses, such as those processing non-renewable resources, it may be difficult to map out an environmentally-sustainable scenario. This is an important warning: perhaps you should consider diversifying sooner, rather than later. Major resource companies like BP and Shell are already redefining their operations to position themselves for a sustainable future by investing heavily in renewable energy technologies.

In many cases, it will be clear that environmental sustainability cannot be achieved by one organisation in isolation. The reality is that many of the environmental impacts are associated with the activities of others, and the infrastructure, market frameworks and regulatory arrangements put in place by society. Recognition of this means you are ready to begin to identify priorities for action.

What priorities should I set?

To set priorities, you need information on issues such as:

■ What are the major environmental impacts of my business and its products/services, both directly and indirectly?

■ What are the environmental priorities of key groups that relate to my organisation, such as my suppliers, customers, neighbours and local community, lobby groups, etc.?

■ Which impacts can I control, which can I influence to a significant extent, and which do I have little influence over?

■ What are the costs and benefits of action in each area of impact (including impact on production costs, marketing benefits, etc.)?

■ What once-off opportunities for step improvements can I foresee?

■ What additional information do I need to improve the quality of my environmental decision making, and what systems will deliver this?

■ What are the trends in the cost and performance of environmentally-preferable technologies and services?

Based on a first round of information (with gaps and uncertainties), a preliminary strategy for environmental improvement can be mapped out and implemented. Of course, such a strategy should be flexible. New information and evolving understanding of issues will lead to frequent revision. Also, the availability, cost and performance of environmentally-preferable products and services are changing rapidly. What was not viable a year ago may be attractive today. Unfortunately, few consultants and advisers have the resources to keep up to date on all the latest developments. Even if they know about them, they may self-censor because they don't think you would be interested, or they are nervous about recommending new options until they are well proved. Because of time pressures or lack of depth of knowledge, consultants may rely on advice from established equipment suppliers. Since these people are often at risk of losing market share to new competitors, they may be unreasonably critical of new developments. High quality, independent advice is difficult to come by. You will find that you may have to pursue information yourself. Many 'old engineers' tales' spread throughout professions, unnecessarily undermining the acceptance of innovations.

What actions can I take quickly to get 'runs on the board'?

In most organisations there is a tension between long term development and short term output. If substantial resources are allocated to evaluating environmental impacts, the patience of management (and the resources of the organisation) may be exhausted before there are tangible outcomes. So it is necessary to identify a range of actions that can quickly deliver outcomes valued by the organisation. These might include:

- solving a public relations crisis
- identifying areas of non-compliance with environmental regulations and addressing them, thus avoiding potential fines and embarrassment
- cutting operating costs through reducing waste of materials and/or energy.

It is strategically important to pursue these actions, and to effectively promote the benefits that have been gained to management, staff and, where appropriate, government and community. Careful documentation, clear reporting and good public relations strategies are essential. And a large proportion of financial savings achieved should be allocated for re-investment in future environmental action. For example, in one Australian government organisation an environmental review identified energy savings exceeding $50 000 per annum (out of a total energy budget of just over $200 000) through relatively high rate of return actions. These savings were used to fund employment of an environmental coordinator's position. This re-investment of savings facilitated pursuit of further environmental improvement.

What strategies do I need for ongoing success?

For ongoing success, the core processes and systems of a business must incorporate environmental criteria. Recording and reporting of environmental impacts is a basic step. Ensuring that organisational decisions factor in potential environmental impacts may involve a variety of strategies such as:

- clear enunciation of corporate environmental objectives by senior management
- strong emphasis on environmental performance within public reporting and corporate publicity
- setting of visible examples by senior management—where senior managers drive fuel-guzzlers and insist that reports be submitted on non-recycled paper printed single-sided, it is difficult for staff to believe the organisation is serious about larger environmental issues
- making environmental outcomes a major criterion for staff and business unit performance measurement and associated rewards
- allocation of clearly identified staff and financial resources for environmental monitoring and improvement
- introduction of processes and systems that use environmental criteria.

Another strategy includes the use of life cycle financial costing for decisions, instead of up front cost. While it may not be possible to consider the full life cycle, even consideration of three or four years' operating costs can dramatically change decisions. Consideration of operating costs locked in by a purchase is, of course, better business. It reduces the risk of being trapped into a high operational cost system. Increasingly, marketing businesses are transferring costs from the purchase price to ongoing costs in efforts to increase sales (for example, many inkjet printers now cost less to buy than three or four replacement cartridges), and the traditional purchasing focus on up front prices plays into the hands of such strategies.

And, finally, the introduction of internal 'environmental taxes' that raise revenue from environmentally damaging activity which can then be invested in actions that reduce environmental impacts is another strategy. This creates an incentive for each business unit to reduce environmental impacts to cut costs, and creates a pool of funds for which business units can bid to finance further reduction of impacts. This also provides practice for staff to operate within emissions trading markets which are likely to appear over the next few years.

What government actions are likely to assist or obstruct my progress towards environmental sustainability?

Many organisations fail to act in environmentally sustainable ways because regulations, market frameworks, lack of supportive infrastructure or other factors mean they would be disadvantaged relative to their less environmentally aware competitors. Also, it may be difficult to capture the financial benefits. For example, the developer of an environmentally-sound building may find it difficult to sell it at a premium that covers the costs and risks involved, even though the future occupants may save money on operating costs and reduced absenteeism.

Governments define 'the rules of the game' for business. In most countries, governments have repeatedly fallen into the trap of creating inadequate regulatory frameworks and toothless regulators that allow businesses to ignore the environmental consequences of their actions. Where regulation exists, governments have often been reluctant to actively enforce environmental protection legislation. Such practices make it more difficult for businesses that genuinely wish to pursue socially and environmentally responsible practices.

Organisations that are striving for environmental excellence *need* governments to set high standards of environmental performance. However, most executives spend more time complaining about government regulation than lobbying for more rigorous measures. When the author was developing Australia's appliance energy labelling scheme in the mid 1980s—against intense opposition from Australian manufacturers—it was something of a shock to be asked by the general manager of a European appliance brand: 'Why are you taking so long to introduce this labelling scheme? In Europe, we have labelling schemes for all sorts of environmental issues, and we don't understand what the problem is.' The Australian car industry's long fight against car fuel efficiency labelling suggests that things haven't changed much.

There is no doubt that development of practical and efficient systems for assessing environmental performance and ensuring standards are maintained is a challenging task for governments. The constructive thing to do is work with them, not ignore or oppose them. The evidence is that the Australian community places high value on environmental performance. Credible criteria and measurement systems developed with and monitored by governments and independent authorities such as Standards Australia are essential if good performance is to be rewarded. This has been recognised, for example, by the Sustainable Energy Industry Association (Australia), which has actively supported the introduction of mandatory commercial building energy performance standards and appliance standards. This association has reached the conclusion that the market failures in these areas are so pervasive that the only remaining option to achieve adoption of ccost-effective energy-saving features is through regulatory mechanisms.

Technology and implementation of environmental improvement

In this section we consider two hypothetical examples of businesses that wish to move towards environmental sustainability, one a service business and the other a manufacturer of appliances.

A service business

This business provides general consulting and advisory services to a wide range of business and individual clients around Australia. It does not sell products.

As a first step, the managers in this business made some attempts to identify its environmental impacts. Areas considered included:

- wastes, including paper, plastics, organic materials
- water use
- CFCs
- impacts on sites
- energy use
- transport
- toxic materials.

It was quickly recognised that this organisation did not produce large quantities of toxic materials. So one useful way of gaining an overview of many of its impacts was to consider the greenhouse gas emissions associated with activities. By including estimates of the energy embodied in buildings and materials, and the emissions from energy use, transport and CFCs, a common basis for comparison was established. This initial analysis did not address water use and some other issues such as contribution to urban road congestion and air pollution, but it was a good start. Figure 8.2 shows the outcome of this initial study. It should be noted that some of the estimates were very rough. This highlighted where there was a need for improved data collection and further analysis, but the initial analysis was sufficient for setting some priorities.

Some preliminary conclusions drawn from the initial analysis were:

- energy use in operating equipment and buildings comprised almost half of total emissions
- air travel was almost a quarter of emissions
- resource use, particularly paper for publications and reports, was almost 15 per cent of emissions.

Figure 8.2 Approximate carbon dioxide emissions for activities

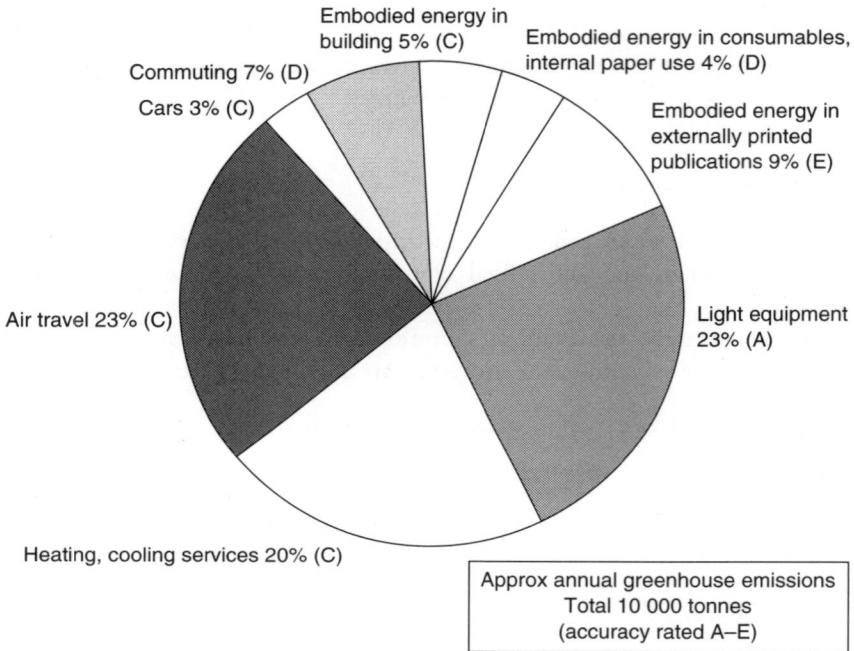

Embodied energy in building 5% (C)

Embodied energy in consumables, internal paper use 4% (D)

Commuting 7% (D)

Cars 3% (C)

Embodied energy in externally printed publications 9% (E)

Air travel 23% (C)

Light equipment 23% (A)

Heating, cooling services 20% (C)

Approx annual greenhouse emissions
Total 10 000 tonnes
(accuracy rated A–E)

Some other interesting issues also surfaced, including:

- air travel was a significant business expense, and time spent travelling was a significant factor affecting staff productivity—so options such as videoconferencing and even establishment of regional offices could be seen to offer multiple benefits
- energy use in buildings and by equipment had never been seriously evaluated, but it was recognised that modern technologies offered scope for significant cost-effective energy efficiency improvements— renegotiation of leases could be used as a strategy to force landlords (who controlled heating and cooling energy use and influenced lighting) to improve their performance in this area without much effort on the part of this business
- emerging technologies for electronic communication and use of the Internet offered potential to cut paper consumption—and costs
- there was scope to reduce emissions or offset emissions through actions such as signing *Greenpower* contracts for electricity supply (where, for an additional surcharge, an electricity supplier agrees to deliver a specified percentage of electricity from renewable energy

sources into the electricity system) and supporting re-afforestation projects via schemes such as *Greenfleet* (where an annual fee per car is paid towards planting of forests on marginal land).

A review of the organisation's clients showed that a number of them were resource-processing organisations with very large environmental impacts. One staff member suggested that they might be able to develop a new service, helping those companies to monitor and address their environmental impacts through the accounting software the business leased to them.

Now comes the difficult part—implementation. Will this business allocate sufficient staff resources with sufficient status? Will attention be focused on revising systems, frameworks and decision processes? Will staff be trained? Will senior managers be prepared to replace their fuel-guzzlers with fuel-efficient cars—or even consider catching the train to work or working from home sometimes? It is too early to answer these questions.

An appliance manufacturer

This appliance manufacturer produces a range of products, but the initial focus was on evaluation of its clothes washing machine production, as this was an area where significant changes in the manufacturing plant were under consideration.

A life cycle analysis of their appliance was undertaken (the life cycle analysis used in this example was prepared by Deni Greene (1992) for the Australian Consumers Association, and it compared three different washing machines). Figure 8.3 shows the results of the life cycle analysis for a range of emissions. Note that the profiles for a range of environmental impacts are similar in this case. This suggests comprehensive analysis of all impacts may not always be necessary, at least in the early stages of progress towards environmental sustainability. An action that reduces environmental impacts of one type often reduces other environmental impacts, too.

The results of the life cycle analysis were something of a shock to the company, for it discovered that its manufacturing impacts were not the main problem. The major environmental impacts were in the operation of the appliance, the detergent used during operation, and the production of the materials used. The ways the company could influence emissions were then identified, including:

■   a strong focus on product design to minimise material use, use recycled materials and re-use components, facilitate recovery and recycling of components and materials at the end of product life,

Figure 8.3 Units of polluted air produced during the life cycle of a washing machine (Greene, 1992)

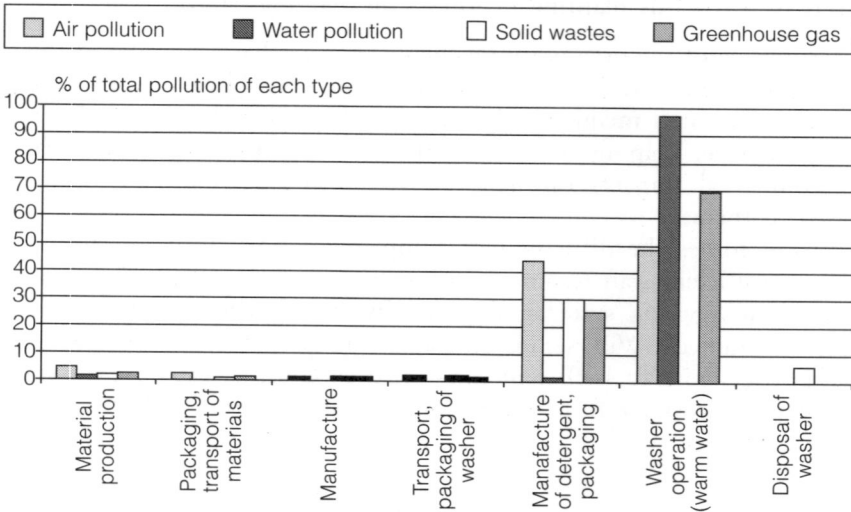

optimise energy efficiency and water efficiency, minimise the quantities of detergent required and make the appliance suitable for use with less environmentally-damaging cleaning agents

- a reduction in the use of disposable packaging by component suppliers
- a review of transport practices, including (in the long term) consideration of relocation of manufacturing and warehousing to reduce transport energy use and costs
- a focus on environmental performance in the manufacturing plant—even though this was not the major environmental impact, this was an area where the business could potentially cut operating costs by reducing waste, and was important from a public relations perspective
- education campaigns to help customers play their part in reducing the environmental impacts of using washing machines—this was a public relations and marketing opportunity
- lobbying of government to enhance public education and labelling campaigns that would support sale of improved product
- identifying suppliers of lower environmental impact materials and components, or working with existing suppliers to reduce their impacts
- working with their preferred detergent supplier to reduce the environmental impact of the product.

This analysis identified the need for a wide-ranging and ongoing environmental improvement program. Review of the annual environmental reports of a number of European companies (such as Miele (1996) and BSH Bosch (1998)) showed that the company had some ground to make up.

Will this company commit sufficient resources to R&D, design, market research and marketing to redefine its products? Will it be able to encourage its customers to place value on improved environmental performance? Again, it is too early to answer these questions.

Conclusion

Technology has an important role to play in progress towards environmental sustainability. But it plays its role in an organisational, social and cultural context. It is only when an integrated strategy is developed and implemented that an organisation can expect to make rapid progress towards environmental sustainability in ways that enhance organisational performance. There are many traps for beginners, but many rewards for those prepared to commit to action.

A technology strategy should be an integral part of an organisation's overall business strategy and its transition towards sustainable business practices. But such a strategy does not have to be developed in its entirety before action is possible—the important thing is to begin the process and develop the strategy on the basis of the organisation's emerging experience. We are all learning, and those who learn from their own and others' experience will gain strategic advantage. Those who sit on the sidelines, observing and waiting for certainty, risk serious disadvantage.

References

Bosch und Siemens Hausgerate (BSH) GMBH 1998 *Environmental Report 1997/98*, Germany.

Greene, D. 1992 *Lifecycle Analysis: A View of the Environmental Impact of Consumer Products Using Clothes Washing Machines as an Example*, Australian Consumers Association, Sydney.

Miele 1996 *Environmental Report 1996*, Germany.

Pears, A. 1998a 'Shifting from "no regrets" to "win-win": The next phase of greenhouse response', *Greenhouse: Beyond Kyoto Conference*, Bureau of Resource Sciences, Canberra.

——1998b *Rating Energy Efficiency of Non-residential Buildings: A Path Forward for New South Wales*, Report for the Sustainable Energy Development Authority, New South Wales: www.seda.nsw.gov.au

Romm, J. 1994 *Lean and Clean Management*, Rocky Mountain Institute: http://www.rmi.org/gds/Book/wholesys.htm

Rosenberg, N. 1995 'Why technology forecasts often fail the futurist', *World Future Society*, July–August.

State Electricity Commission of Victoria (SECV) 1993 *Energy Saving Kit for Schools*, SECV, Melbourne.

von Weizsäcker E., Lovins, A. and Lovins, H. 1997 *Factor 4: Doubling Wealth, Halving Resource Use*, Allen & Unwin, St Leonards, NSW.

9

The technology strategy of the sustainable corporation

Hardin Tibbs

Introduction and overview

Corporate sustainability, the long term social and environmental viability of business activity, will be achieved in the context of crucial large scale changes occurring in society over the next few decades. These changes will reshape business by fundamentally altering the rules of the game for commerce and defining a new overall technology strategy business will need to adopt.

The nature of the future sustainable corporation can only be fully understood in the context of developments happening at a global scale. The basic dynamic which shapes the agenda of sustainability is the exponential growth of both the human population and the flow of materials through the industrial economy. When both nature and industry are analysed in terms of flows of materials, it becomes clear that industry is now approaching (and even exceeding) the scale of the natural environment, setting the stage for accelerating large scale environmental pollution and degradation.

Nevertheless, there is reason to believe that human population growth will decelerate and stabilise during the next thirty years. This deceleration will accompany and invoke changes in social values and will, in any optimistic scenario, be accompanied by a deceleration of linear (non-cyclic) flows of materials through the industrial economy.

A deceleration of materials flows will be achieved by recasting the basic architecture of industry, converting it to a system of cyclic flows. As this happens, the mass intensity of industrial production can be expected to decline (dematerialisation) and the carbon intensity of energy supply will complete its long run historical decline (decarbonisation). These developments will be guided by industrial ecology, an emerging field of applied research aimed at adapting industry to the unique bio-geochemical systems of planet earth.

As these developments occur there will be parallel shifts in business logic. Business thinking will shift from the concept of the value chain, based on the traditional model of linear materials flows, to the concept of the value loop, based on the sustainable model of cyclic materials flows. Value will be created and recreated endlessly as the same materials flow in a continuous loop, from manufacturing to consumption, then to reprocessing and back to manufacture. As firms become sustainable, they will have to relocate from the value chain to the value loop and many will have to redefine themselves in the process.

This sequence of changes, described in detail in the rest of the chapter, can be expected to determine the overall use of technology in the sustainable corporation after the whole socio-economic system achieves sustainability and increasingly during the transitional phase we are now entering.

A technology meta-strategy for the sustainable corporation

It is useful to think of the sustainable corporation as having a generic sustainable technology strategy, as distinct from the detailed sustainable technology strategy of a specific corporation. This 'meta-strategy' for technology is an overall framing of technology itself by the sustainable corporation and by a future sustainable society. It relates the detailed commercial goals of a corporation to the larger social and environmental goals of society. It sits beyond or behind the strategies of individual firms, shaping their individual strategies and being expressed by them through their detailed technological programs, product development, manufacturing systems and support infrastructure.

The traditional corporation also has a technology meta-strategy, although it almost always remains implicit and is seldom consciously acknowledged. It is useful to compare the prospective sustainable meta-strategy with the largely unconscious prevailing technology meta-strategy of society and its institutions.

The modern limited liability company—in which the liability of the owners is limited to the capital they invest no matter what losses the company incurs—came into being in Europe in the eighteenth century at the beginning of the industrial revolution. Their purpose was to limit the risk of investors in long and hazardous sea voyages that were nevertheless seen to benefit indirectly the whole community. In the nineteenth century, after the introduction of the joint stock company in the US, additional legal developments defined the company as a legal person with an indefinite lifespan, thus opening the way for enormous concentration of wealth and technological power by corporations. The modern corporation is thus a key socio-economic innovation of global industrial development, intended to achieve maximum economic output and growth by offering the dual incentive of maximising personal gain while limiting personal risk.

The technology meta-strategy of the conventional corporation is an expression of the wider social program of maximum industrial growth. Essentially it holds that any feasible technology that can be devised is available to any company to exploit how and where it likes without restriction. The social role of the firm is to maximise the use of any given technology and the supply of resources needed to operate it. As an incentive to develop the maximum range of possible applications as well as fundamental new technologies, the company can be granted a legal monopoly during the first couple of decades of exploitation of a new technology. Should the technology turn out to be physically harmful to people or the environment, provided this can be established on the basis of avoiding a Type I error of proof (discussed later), use of the technology may, after some period of time, be limited or legislated. If the technology simply causes social dislocation or personal stress, this is tolerated. The overall aim of this meta-strategy is straightforward: to maximise the development and growth of industry—a socially acceptable objective during the exponential expansion phase following the industrial revolution.

By contrast, the sustainable corporation[1] is the prospective future form of the corporation after the physical expansion phase of industrialisation decelerates, and the material throughput of the global economy levels out. The technology meta-strategy of the sustainable corporation brings a new set of values to the application and development of technology. The new perspective accepts the existence of highly advanced technology, and assumes that there is a high level of technological capability and scientific literacy in society. The meta-strategy favours technologies that enable the reuse of materials, cooperatively creating and maintaining a cyclic materials economy. It also favours the use of materials that exist abundantly in nature, and that are readily reprocessed and regenerated in nature. And in general it favours technologies that slow and reduce materials flows in the cyclic loop, particularly toxic elements and chemicals.

The sustainable corporation will therefore ensure that its use of materials contributes to an overall cyclic flow through the economy. It will also use energy technologies that have minimum, preferably zero, bio-geochemically active collateral materials flows or accumulations (such as CO_2, NO_x, SO_x, radioactive waste, etc.). It will avoid technologies and practices that degrade the informational integrity and genetic diversity of the biosphere. Since the overall technology program of society is no longer maximum physical growth, the products and services of the firm tend to relate to the creation and maintenance of complex physical systems. When there is a potential for technologies to cause physical harm to people or the environment, the sustainable corporation will adopt a precautionary approach, endeavouring to avoid Type II errors (discussed later) in establishing reasonable proof. The definition of harm is likely to expand, leading to avoidance and minimisation of technology that contributes to personal and social stress.

The thesis of this chapter is that this technology meta-strategy for sustainability will emerge from the sequence of future developments described here. Other outcomes are of course also possible: this account is in that sense only a scenario (Schwartz, 1991), but it is a particularly important one because an optimistic outcome is difficult to project without it.[2] Put another way, the optimistic scenario—in which the worldwide challenges of unsustainability[3] are overcome—appears to depend on major changes of the kind described here.

Materials flows

A basic assumption of the sustainable technology meta-strategy is that advanced technology need not be harmful to society and the environment, but that specific uses and applications of technology certainly can be. One of the main unsustainable impacts of technology is its ability to support an exponential increase in the linear throughput of materials through industry and the human economy.

Human population growth is the context for the exponential rise in materials throughputs, and the basis of the technology meta-strategy of the conventional firm. The growth to today's global population level of 5.8 billion was sudden and historically anomalous. Some time around 1750, at the onset of the industrial revolution, the population began to grow at an unprecedented exponential rate. Exponential growth is growth that results in a doubling of size with each given unit of passing time.

Exponential growth in a finite system is extremely deceptive psychologically, as it appears to be reassuringly slow at the outset, but later accelerates suddenly to use up remaining space or resources with surprising speed. This is particularly dangerous for political and other decision

Figure 9.1 Global population growth

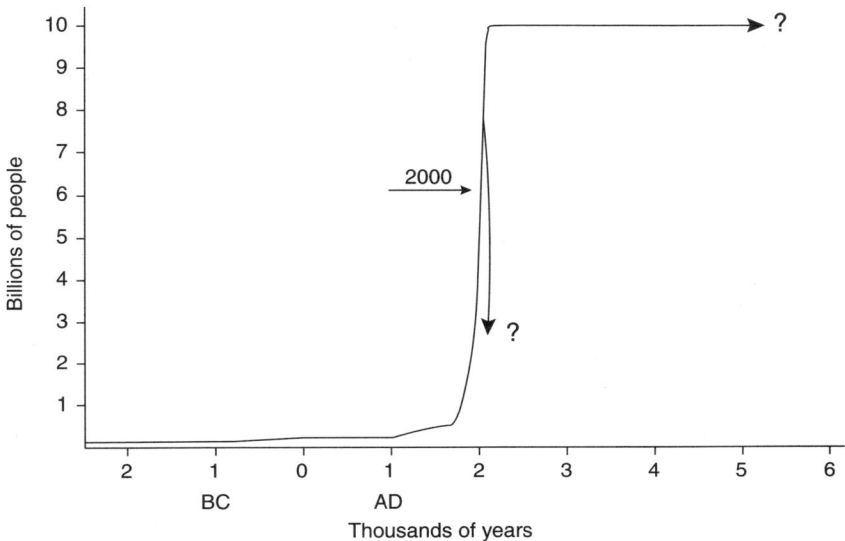

Source: Historical data based on Cohen, 1995

making, as it is notoriously difficult to take exponential change seriously until it is too late.

Figure 9.1 shows a simplified view of world population for the past several thousand years. It also shows the extraordinary jump that has taken place in the last 250 years. For thousands of years, the human population bumped along at a few hundred million people worldwide, growing slowly. In fact, the increase was not steady during this period— there were alternating surges and contractions—and there was no consistent exponential growth towards present levels as many people assume. The average growth rate from 1650 to 1950 was about 12 times greater than during the previous 10 000 years, and it more than doubled again after 1950.

Today, the world population is still growing extremely fast, even though the growth rate is slowing slightly. More people have been *added* to the world population in the 1990s than existed in the entire world in 1750. The world population has doubled during the life time of anyone now over 40, and if present rates of growth are maintained, the total population will double again within the next 40 to 50 years.

The overall graph for the flow of materials through the industrial system over the same time frame looks similar to Figure 9.1, except that growth is twice as fast—during the last few decades it has been doubling every 20 years. Figure 9.2 shows the expansion of materials consumption

Figure 9.2 Consumption of materials in the US, 1900–89

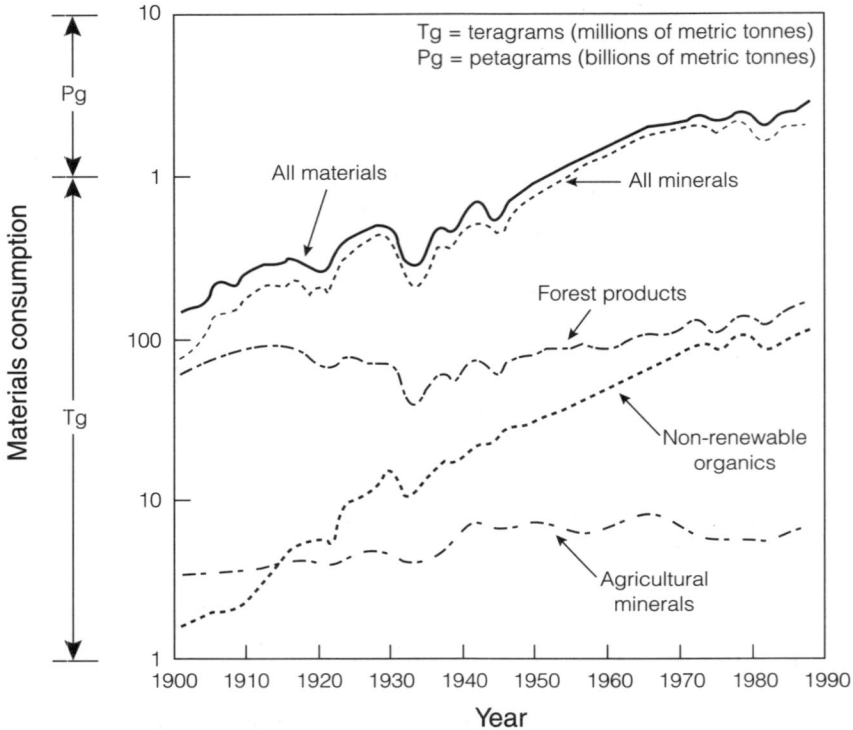

Note: On average, overall consumption of materials in the US has doubled every twenty years during the twentieth century

Source: Graedel & Allenby, 1995: 147

in the US during the last hundred years (the vertical scale is logarithmic, so the upward sweeping curve of increase appears as a roughly straight line). Total materials use in the US has ballooned from 140 million metric tonnes a year in 1900 to 2.8 billion metric tonnes a year in 1990, up from about 1.6 tonnes per person to 10.6 tonnes per person. Environmental impact is determined by industrial throughput, so, for example, the amount of carbon dioxide released into the atmosphere every year has also doubled twice over since 1950.

The result of exponential growth is that the industrial production system has now reached planetary scale. The volume of materials flowing through the industrial system into the human economy worldwide is now at roughly the same scale as the flow of materials occurring naturally through global bio-geochemical processes.

In the case of some materials, industry is already larger than nature.

Table 9.1 Worldwide emissions to the atmosphere (thousands of tonnes per year)

	Artificial flows	Natural flows	Ratio
Lead	332.0	28.0	11.9:1
Zinc	132.0	45.0	2.9:1
Copper	35.0	6.1	5.7:1
Arsenic	19.0	12.0	1.6:1
Antimony	3.5	2.6	1.3:1
Cadmium	7.6	1.4	5.4:1

Source: Nriagu, 1990

The global industrial flow of almost all toxic heavy metals is much greater than the natural background flows (natural flows occur because of geological processes such as the weathering of rock). The anthropogenic (human-caused) flow of lead into the atmosphere is 11.9 times greater than the amount of lead naturally mobilised through the biosphere. This is because internationally lead is still used in petrol (gasoline) as an anti-knock additive. For almost all the other toxic heavy metals, such as cadmium (5.4 times) and arsenic (1.6 times), the industrial flows into the atmosphere are greater than the natural flows (see Table 9.1). The metals are then dispersed into the biosphere—for example, 13 million pounds of mercury (a neurotoxin) falls in rain every year.

Another well-publicised example is the release of carbon dioxide into the atmosphere from burning fossil fuels. In this case, the natural flow is very large because carbon is one of the major nutrient substances (one of the so-called 'grand cycle' elements) in the biosphere. By the early 1990s the burning of fossil fuel and deforestation were releasing roughly eight billion tonnes of carbon into the atmosphere every year (in the form of 30 billion tonnes of carbon dioxide). This anthropogenic flow of carbon is equal to about a sixth of the natural background flow, and is increasing the total atmospheric 'reservoir' of 750 billion tonnes by some four billion tonnes a year (only half of the excess carbon is being successfully absorbed by the biosphere and ocean every year).

Why are these global-scale flows a problem? One concern is that industrial flows of materials are now so large that they can destabilise natural global systems because of their sheer scale compared to natural flows. Climatologists believe that the increasing (but non-toxic) level of atmospheric carbon dioxide is changing the world's climate. Another concern is that global-scale flows of pollution will lead to chronic toxification of the entire biosphere. Finally, the flows and their effects are not only large but they are growing exponentially.

The exponential growth of industry is now reaching levels that risk a global ecosystem breakdown. According to an estimate in 1986

(Vitousek, 1986), the human economy was then using 40 per cent of the entire annual growth of land surface biomass. If this percentage is increasing in line with growth in the use of materials—which is doubling every 20 years—it could reach the 80 per cent level by 2006. Increasing the human share this much is inherently risky as it means that much less than half of the total natural ecological processes and habitat will remain, which may compromise their viability as a planetary life-support system (Baskin, 1997). The so-called 'ecosystem services' provided by the natural environment include water and air purification, and a recent study by Stanford University researcher Gretchen Daily (1997) has valued their contribution to the world economy at over US$33 trillion a year.

An inevitable deceleration

In any optimistic global scenario, it is inevitable that population and materials flows will decelerate in the relatively near future. In part this is because population growth is now decelerating as an underlying driver. Although the population is still rising rapidly, the underlying exponential growth rate has been falling since its peak at 2.2 per cent per year in 1963. It may double once more during the first half of the twenty-first century, but is officially expected to have levelled off at around ten billion people worldwide by around 2050. The other cause of deceleration is the unsustainability of exponentially rising materials consumption. In any optimistic outcome, a combination of technological and social change would lead to a reduction in materials flows. (The alternative pessimistic outlook is that the exponential growth of materials flows leads to a global level ecosystem crisis and breakdown.)

This double deceleration—of population and materials flows—marks the end of the physical growth stage of industrialisation. For the first time since the onset of the industrial revolution there will be a net per capita dematerialisation of economic output internationally. This 'turning of the corner' from the historical growth phase of the planetary industrialisation process to the 'sustained development' phase will involve very significant social, technological and economic change. This may happen through voluntary policy change, spontaneous change induced by the market, or possibly be triggered by a crisis of unsustainability—or by a combination of all three.

The outcome of this transformative change will be a completely new kind of economy. It will be able to deliver prosperity equitably around the world, in balance with the natural environment, without depending on exponentially growing materials flows. It would simultaneously cope with the slowing and stabilising of population growth.

Figure 9.3 Ecological succession from J–curve to S–curve population growth

Numbers

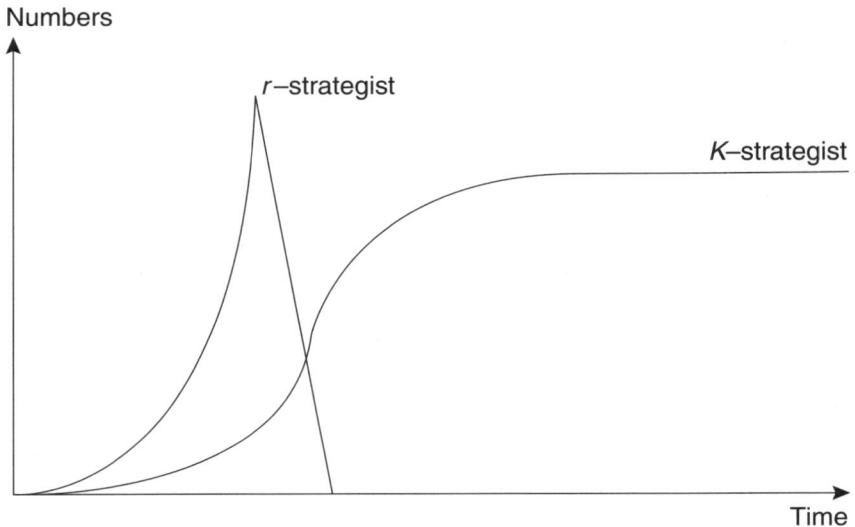

Source: Lawlor, 1994

The overall concept of a transformation, or 'transition to sustainability', itself has an analogue in a simple model of ecological development known as ecological succession. It is broadly equivalent to the shift that occurs as an ecosystem matures—as, say, forest regrows on cleared land—and makes the transition from a 'pioneer' to a 'mature' ecosystem (see Figure 9.3). The characteristic strategies of organisms that thrive in each of these two phases are particularly relevant.

The earliest plants to establish themselves on cleared land are called *r–strategists* because they emphasise high rates of reproduction (high *r*) and dispersal ability. Most of their biomass goes into reproductive structures, and they grow rapidly and produce large numbers of seeds. These pioneer species survive by their ability to find new open terrain and move on. Their populations increase rapidly and become locally extinct quite rapidly, a J–shaped curve of population that climbs steeply, hits a limit and falls away. Many short-lived annual weeds are *r*–strategists.

The *r*-strategists are followed by *K–strategists*—species that are adapted to stabilise their populations at a steady level. *K* is the term used in the equations of population ecology to denote the upper carrying capacity—the maximum sustainable density in an established ecosystem. The *K*–strategists grow slowly, put most of their biomass into non-reproductive structures (stems, roots and leaves), and produce few seeds. The K–strategists follow an S–shaped curve of population growth that smoothly levels out and extends on into the future at the carrying capacity. The trees in a mature forest are K–strategists (Odum, 1989).

The industrially-assisted population growth of human society has been the result of an r–strategy, with an emphasis on rapid growth, high rates of reproduction and wide dispersal. The r–strategy is well suited to an initially unlimited environment, such as cleared land being colonised by weeds, or a large planet with only a handful of industrialised countries. Our social institutions, just like the genes of the biological r–strategist, are adapted to this rapid growth mode. The challenge we now face as a society is to begin to adopt a K–strategy—which in ecosystems is one better suited to a sustained role in a crowded environment and implies a greater energy investment in the maintenance and survival of the adult.

This is a substantial challenge. Put in another way, it would mean moving from our familiar r form of capitalism, to an entirely new K–capitalism. In terms of the ecological analogy, this means completely reinventing the genetic makeup of our institutions, government and business. New K–organisations and K–industrialisation would replace older r–organisations and r–industrialisation (Lawlor, 1994).

By analogy, we could argue that human society has been behaving like a pioneer species, but unlike other pioneer species, our frontier has now been pushed out to include the entire biosphere and we have nowhere else to go. The hope is that we will use our unique self-awareness to adapt and consciously modify our behaviour, so avoiding the fate of other pioneer species when their environment gets too crowded.

The overall message is that any optimistic view of the future must contain very significant transformational change, as materials flows and population growth decelerate. Whether we view these changes defensively or proactively, it is apparent that most industries and activities will experience a deep shift of perspective and values, and a parallel shift to a new legislative, economic and technological base. Put simply, either there will be a system-wide crisis, or a solution will emerge. But the solution will not be an incremental modification of the way we do things now—it will be an entirely new kind of economy.

The role of technology

How can this outcome be achieved? We will have to learn new ways of doing things, and this implies new attitudes and ways of behaving, new laws, and new technology. Technology is a particularly important source

Figure 9.4 Sustainability requires changes in both values and technology

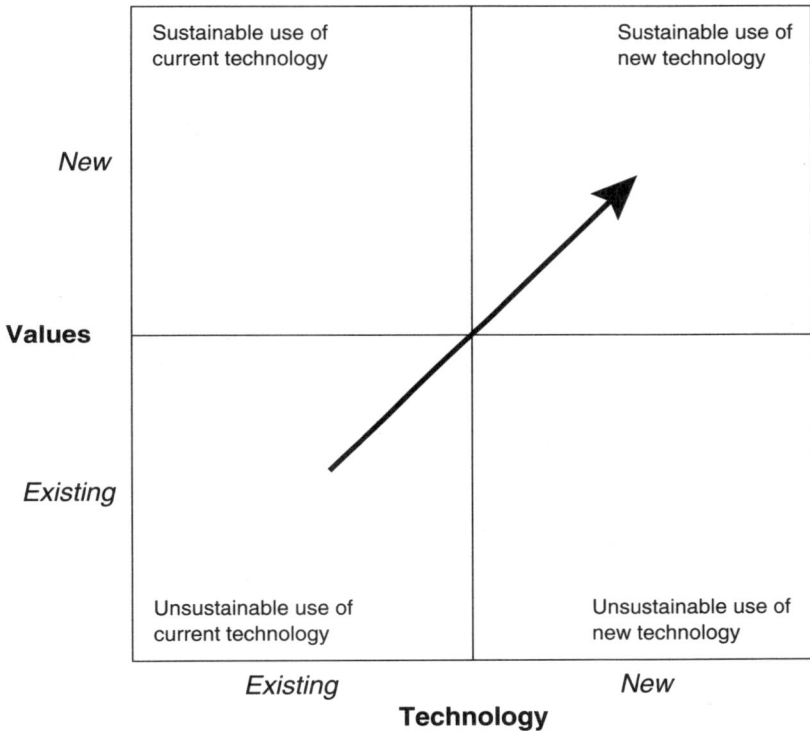

	Sustainable use of current technology	Sustainable use of new technology
New		
Values		
Existing		
	Unsustainable use of current technology	Unsustainable use of new technology
	Existing	New
	Technology	

of change, because it most directly determines the scale of materials flows through industry, but it is not the whole story.

Figure 9.4 shows the contribution technology can make. The path of viable future development in any optimistic scenario is from the bottom left quadrant of the matrix towards the top right, as the arrow indicates. Change in either values or in technology alone is not enough: the two must happen in conjunction. One of the reasons for this is that technology—and new technology in particular because it is more powerful—can either help provide solutions or make the situation worse. What makes the crucial difference is human intention.

Technology and scientific knowledge are advancing extremely rapidly and are now providing the capabilities we need to create an economy that does not depend on ever-increasing physical growth. If underlying social beliefs shift—with a growing interest in less materialistic personal values and deeper meaning—this can be expected to lead to greater concern about global issues and the environment, leading in turn to new

priorities in technological design. In this way, new technological poten-
tials can be directed along a path of development that is part of the
solution rather than part of the problem.

For example, if biotechnology in agriculture is applied in a narrow
reductionist way (bottom right quadrant), it could contribute to ecosystem destabilisation. Yet exactly the same technology applied within
an ecosystemic paradigm (top right quadrant) could result in increased
food production and improved ecosystem health. (Another way of
expressing this would be to say that just because biotechnology is
biological, that does not mean it is also ecological.)

Equally, expressing new social values using only today's technology
is likely to mean unnecessary austerity. For example, a sustainability
outlook might lead people to choose to give up heating and air con-
ditioning and shiver or swelter in conventional houses (top left
quadrant). But by expressing their new intent in terms of technology
they could choose instead to be comfortable in houses with passive
heating and cooling (top right quadrant). Behaving less wastefully is
praiseworthy, but why ignore the potential of new technology?[4]

The matrix in Figure 9.4 does not tell the whole story of the
technology meta-strategy—but it does illustrate why we cannot simply
rely on the emergence of new technology on its own to enable the safe
deceleration of exponential growth. Technology must be actively managed and designed to achieve this outcome, which is the purpose of the
meta-strategy.

Technology to reduce the impact of materials flows

The global scale of industry implies that the existing architecture of the
industrial system is obsolete, as it will not be able to support environmentally sustainable development into the future. Industrial ecology is
the emerging response to this challenge (Frosch, 1992; Tibbs, 1992;
Graedel & Allenby, 1995). It sets out systemic design principles for
harmonious co-existence of the industrial system and the natural system.
Two of the most important foundation concepts are the 'cyclic economy'
and the 'industrial ecosystem'.

At the moment, the industrial 'system' is less a system than a
collection of linear flows. Industry draws materials from the earth's crust
and the biosphere, processes them with fossil energy to derive transient
economic value, and dumps the residue back into nature (see Figure
9.5). For every 1 kilogram of finished goods we buy, about 20 kilograms

Figure 9.5 From linear to cyclic economy

Linear flow pattern
of existing industrial
system

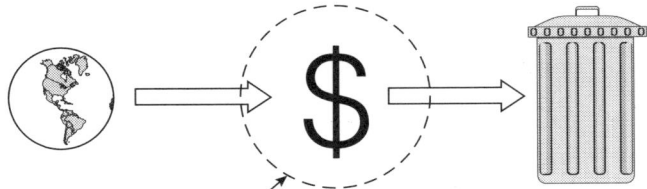

Market
domain

Future industrial
system based on
ecological principles
(cyclic flow system
with fully internalised
environmental costs)

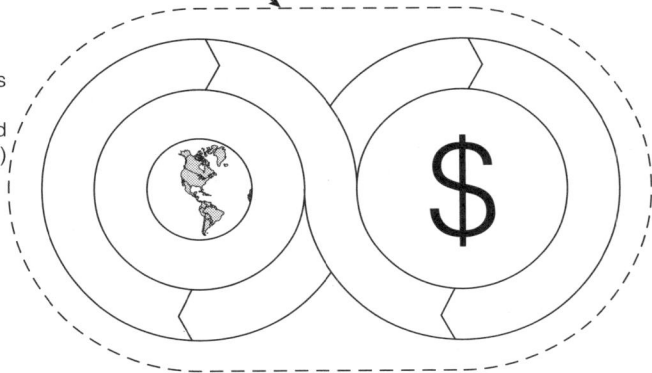

of waste have been created during production, and within six months 0.5 kilograms of our average purchase is already waste. This 'extract and dump' pattern is at the root of our current environmental difficulties.

The biosphere works very differently. From its early non-cyclic origins, it has evolved into a truly cyclic system, endlessly circulating and transforming materials, and managing to run almost entirely on solar energy (Lovelock, 1979). There is no reason why the international economy could not be redesigned along these lines as a continuous cyclic flow of materials. Such a 'cyclic economy' (see Box 9.1) would not be limited in terms of the economic activity and prosperity it could

Box 9.1 Characteristics of a cyclic economy

- Industrial system seen as a dependent subsystem of the biosphere
- Economic flows decoupled from materials flows
- Environmental costs fully internalised into the market domain
- Cyclic flow of materials
- Virgin materials use minimised
- Information substitutes for mass
- System entropy kept as low as possible

Box 9.2 Characteristics of natural ecosystems

There are many features of natural ecosystems that can be emulated by industry:

- In natural systems there is no such thing as 'waste' in the sense of something that cannot be absorbed constructively somewhere else in the system.
- Nutrients for one species are derived from the death and decay of another.
- Concentrated toxins are not stored or transported in bulk at the systems level, but are synthesised and used as needed only by individual species.
- Materials and energy are continually circulated and transformed in extremely elegant ways. The system runs entirely on ambient solar energy, and over time has actually managed to store energy in the form of fossil fuel.
- The natural system is dynamic and information-driven, and the identity of ecosystem players is defined in terms of processes.
- The system permits independent activity on the part of each individual of a species, yet cooperatively meshes the activity patterns of all species. Cooperation and competition are interlinked, held in balance.

generate, but it would be limited in terms of the input of new materials and energy it required. Pollution would be reduced close to zero. At the time of writing, Germany is the first country to begin seriously experimenting with the legislation needed to create a cyclic economy.

At a finer-grained level, the design principles embedded in natural ecosystems (see Box 9.2) have given rise to the idea of the 'industrial ecosystem'. This involves more than simple recycling of a single material or product. In effect, industrial ecosystems are complex 'food webs' between companies and industries to optimise the use of materials and embedded energy. They involve 'closing loops' by recycling, making maximum use of recycled materials in new production, optimising use of materials and embedded energy, minimising waste generation, and re-evaluating 'wastes' as raw material for other processes. They also imply more than simple 'one-dimensional' recycling of a single material or product—as with, for example, aluminium beverage can recycling. In effect, they represent 'multi-dimensional' recycling, or the creation of 'food webs' between companies and industries. A complex of indus-

Figure 9.6 The industrial ecosystem at Kalundborg

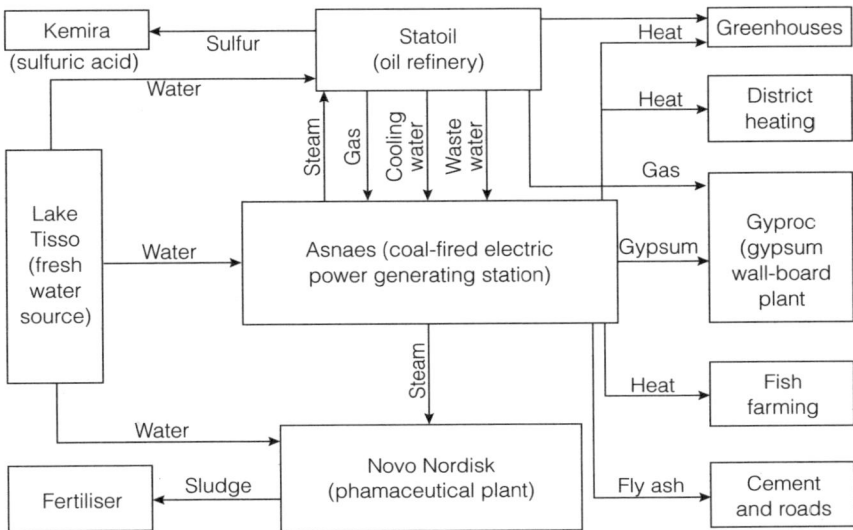

trial producers applying these principles has been referred to as an 'eco-industrial park'.

The best known example of an eco-industrial park is in Denmark (Tibbs, 1992). A network of independent companies in the town of Kalundborg has created a permanent waste exchange system in an area about 16 kilometres across (see Figure 9.6). The waste transfers are across industries, so that the by-product of one company becomes the raw material for another. The cooperation involves an electric power generating plant, an oil refinery, a biotechnology production plant, a plasterboard factory, a sulfuric acid producer, cement producers, local agriculture and horticulture, and district heating. Among the 'wastes' that are traded, some by direct pipeline, are water at various levels of heat and purity, sulfur, natural gas, industrial gypsum and fly ash.

This cooperation was not required by regulation; the earliest deals were purely economic. Recent initiatives have been made for environmental reasons, yet have also paid off financially. In some cases mandated cleanliness levels, such as the requirement for reduced nitrogen in waste water, or the removal of sulfur from flue gas, have permitted or stimulated the reuse of wastes, and helped make such cooperation feasible. Most of the exchanges are between geographically close participants since the cost of infrastructure, such as pipelines, is a factor. But proximity is not essential; the sulfur and fly ash are supplied to distant buyers. Ultimately, this kind of industrial ecosystem could be extended into a large scale network that might include the entire industrial system (Frosch & Gallopoulos, 1989).

Dematerialisation, decarbonisation and industrial metabolism

If large scale industrial ecosystems are established, resulting in a continuous cyclic flow and reuse of materials, this would largely eliminate the direct environmental impact of industry. But to be fully effective, additional steps would be needed.

Dematerialisation

The amount of materials in the closed loop, or web, can either be increased over time, kept stable, or decreased. Keeping it the same would avoid use of virgin non-renewable resources. But the system needs energy to run and leaks are possible (see below), and minimising these means reducing the volume of material in the loop over time.

If the global population doubles and becomes more affluent during the time the closed loop is established (within the next twenty to forty years), reducing or just holding the amount of material steady will require accelerated dematerialisation.

Dematerialisation refers to a decline in the materials- and energy-intensity of industrial production—an existing trend in industrially developed economies. Both materials and energy use (measured as quantity per constant dollar of gross national product (GNP)) have been falling since the 1970s (Larsen, Ross & Williams, 1986). This is because the market for basic products has saturated, while the weight and size of many other products has fallen. Information technology increasingly allows embedded information to reduce product bulk. New technologies such as nano-technology—assembling materials atom by atom—promise to accelerate dematerialisation.

Industrial ecology would aim for miniaturised, lower-mass products with longer life. This would decouple economic growth from growth in materials use, enabling a fixed flow of materials in the cyclic loop to provide goods for many more people.

Industrial metabolism

The efficiency of materials use is a key focus of industrial ecology. Industrial metabolism refers to the type and pattern of chemical reactions and materials flows in the industrial system. Potential improvements could yield significant environmental benefits. Compared with the elegance and economy of biological metabolic processes, such as photosynthesis and the citric acid cycle, most industrial processes are far from their potential ultimate efficiency in terms of basic chemical and energy pathways.

Similarly, the cyclic flow of materials, like any engineered system, would suffer from leaks. But the most serious 'leaks' come from design, not accident. Many materials are 'dissipated' or dispersed into the environment as they are used, with no hope of recovery for recycling. This problem can be overcome by designing differently. For instance, car brake pads leave a finely distributed powder on our highways as they wear down. This can be avoided with frictionless electrically-regenerative braking, as in the latest hybrid electric cars like the 1998 Toyota Prius.

Decarbonisation

Energy would be required to move materials through the cyclic loop and periodically reprocess them for reuse. To minimise its environmental impact, this energy will need to be progressively decarbonised—contain less carbon over time. Energy sources have been decarbonising for more than 150 years, as industrialised countries move away from high carbon fuel sources such as firewood and coal, to oil and low carbon sources such as natural gas (Ausubel, 1989). Because carbon dioxide from industry is a major dissipative flow of material, industrial ecology would aim for decarbonisation of energy. A completely carbon free energy supply could be provided using pure hydrogen gas produced from renewable energy sources. A possible future hydrogen electric economy would combine hydrogen (the lightest element) to provide a clean, low mass carbon free store of renewable energy, and electricity to provide precision and control in energy delivery.

Planetary physiology

The overarching concept behind industrial ecology is the need to place the whole global industrial system in the context of planetary physiology. The ultimate aim of industrial ecology is to create a planetary order of technology for the long haul—a deployment of technology planet-wide that is suited to the special characteristics of planet earth. Put another way, this means the emergence of a technological infrastructure that can harmonise with the unique bio-geochemical processes and cycles of this planet. One of the main reasons for thinking on such a large scale is precisely that industry itself has now reached planetary scale—its throughputs and waste flows are so large that they are disturbing the large scale planetary life support systems on which we all depend.

This means that industrial ecology is focused not only on the structure of industry, but also on the systems and structures of planetary physiology. The appropriate long term structure of industry cannot be determined until we have a good understanding of the way the planet works, at both large and small scales, both in time and space. Since the whole concept of looking at the physiology of the earth itself is relatively new, industrial ecology has important contributions to make in this area, focusing study to provide the insights needed for the design of industry.

The British scientist James Lovelock coined the term Gaia (Lovelock, 1979) (the name of the ancient Greek goddess of the earth) to express the idea of the entire planet as a single living super-organism, with homeostatic feedback loops that create a physiology comparable to that of a regular organism. Lovelock pioneered the study of planetary physiology, or geophysiology as he calls it. Geophysiology can be understood as including geological processes, climatic and hydrological cycles, and ecology, all of which are responsible for materials flows in the natural environment. As we begin to uncover the intricately interlocked workings of geophysiology, the implications for industry become clear. We contain within our bodies biochemical processes that not only serve our own life, but also enable the bio-geochemical processes of Gaia. In a very literal sense, we are a functional part of the planet. Industry needs to be structured the same way—to serve human needs as well as planetary needs. Industry must become a cooperative part of the planet, of the life of Gaia.

Needless to say, it is far from that today. So how do we make a bridge between geophysiology and the design of industry? The keys to geophysiology are to understand the cycles of matter, the way feedback loops regulate the cycles, the key stocks and flows in the system, and the way living and non-living elements in the entire system interact. We can study how industry works on the large scale by mapping it in much the same way. The study of industrial metabolism, pioneered by scientist Robert Ayres, is a natural complement to geophysiology—indeed, given the scale on which we are doing things, it is rapidly making a significant impact on it. Industrial metabolism involves looking at the way elements flow from the environment into and through industry, and back out into the environment. The elements or molecules of most interest are those that flow in the greatest volume, and those that are the most toxic— either to organisms or to Gaia—carbon, sulfur, nitrogen, heavy metals such as cadmium and mercury, CFCs, etc.

Once we have understood better how Gaia works, and once we have a good grasp of today's industrial metabolism, we will be in a position to devise a new form of industry. At that point, we may find we have to redefine the concept of industry itself. The trouble with the word 'industry' is the image it typically evokes of gloomy grey buildings with saw-tooth roofs and tall stacks belching grimy smoke. We need a different conception of industry.

This is why the idea of industrial ecosystems and eco-industrial parks, like the one at Kalundborg in Denmark, although vital, are not enough on their own. The heart of the industrial ecosystem at Kalundborg is a large—1500 megawatt—coal-burning electricity generating station called Asnaes. While it is true that many valuable savings in the use of materials and water have been achieved by linking Asnaes to other industrial facilities in the surrounding area, it seems unlikely that burning coal for energy production can be acceptable for very much longer.

In short, industrial ecology is more than simply a combination of best practice environmental management tools, such as life cycle analysis (LCA) and design for environment (DFE). Defining it in these terms fails to grasp the larger intent of industrial ecology. It is not just another tool, nor is it even another environmental management system (EMS). Industrial ecology is—or at least aspires to be—the emerging field of knowledge that interrelates the various environmental tools and management systems that have been devised so far. It generates an overall context and gives the whole set of tools and systems a coherent objective—aligning industry with geophysiology.

From value chain to value loop

Business analysis focuses on the concept of the value chain, which represents the 'idealised form' of the linear materials throughput economy. Industrial players define themselves according to their roles and interactions in the value chain. The technology meta-strategy of sustainability requires this conceptual map to be revised. Instead of a value chain, sustainable corporations must come to see themselves as part of a cyclic value loop (see Figure 9.7). This will require a strategic redefinition for firms in many industries—particularly those at the beginning and end of the traditional value chain. Mining companies, for example, will no longer be able to view themselves as a one-way source point for materials in the industrial economy. They will need to re-perceive themselves as being in the materials management business, responsible for the post-use reclamation and reprocessing of the materials they specialise in. As today, they will supply concentrated, purified materials in specified physical forms to manufacturers who will convert these

Figure 9.7 Relocating from the value chain to the value loop

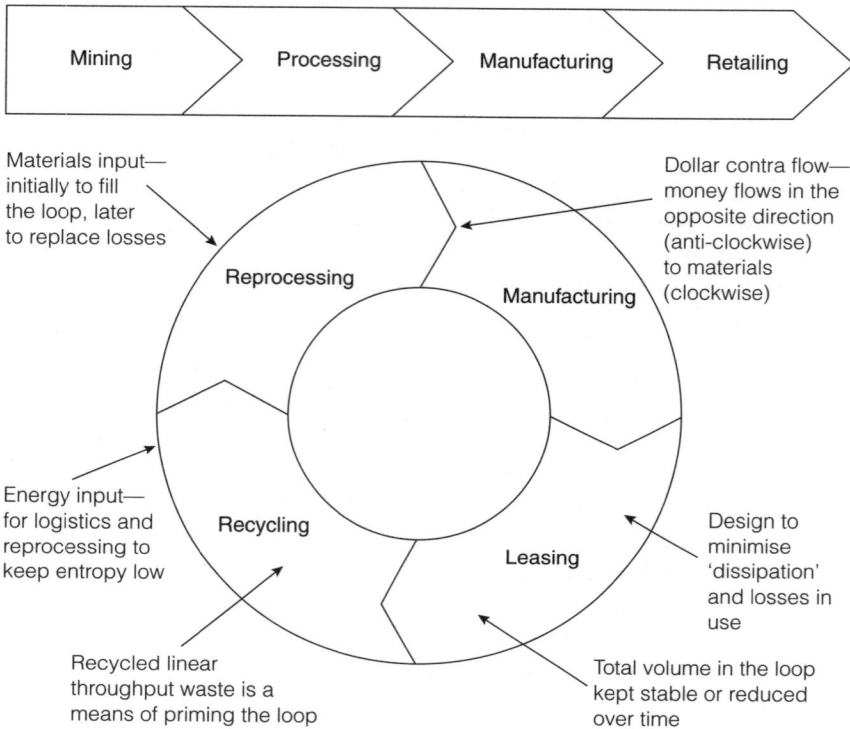

materials into finished goods. But the new materials managers will source the raw materials they need not from the earth's crust, but from the urban industrial ecosystems in the materials catchment areas where their plants are located. This is not such an outlandish concept, since it is essentially how steel mini-mills already source materials from urban catchment areas, reclaiming scrap steel from old automobiles and reprocessing it.

Seeing the cyclic economy from a business perspective as a value loop highlights a number of important points about the detailed operation of cyclic materials flows.

An important question for industrial players committing to component infrastructure for the cyclic economy is the resilience of the resulting system. If an industrial ecosystem is created to reduce materials use and waste, what happens if or when one of its component processes becomes obsolete? Does the whole industrial ecosystem then become unviable? Or can structures of interlock be designed which allow for change, such as cleaner future technology, without creating increased dependence on such things as coal-fired power plants? Put differently, can interlock be achieved without unwanted lock-in?

The answer is likely to depend on working through a sequence of steps. One approach would be first to identify a set of materials that have long term geophysiological compatibility. A fairly small set of acceptable materials could probably be used to supply 80 per cent or more of all production needs. The next step would be to devise clusters of production processes that use some or all these materials, and which can be interlocked ecosystem-style.

Once this is done, the resulting industrial clusters or industrial ecosystems should stand a reasonable chance of being stable over time. Gunter Pauli of the Zero Emissions Research Initiative (ZERI) at the United Nations University in Japan, has shown that focused industrial clusters of this sort, based on biomass inputs and zero waste, can make very good sense in business, social and environmental terms (Pauli, 1996).

Once closed loops of materials flows are established, the next question is whether the volume of materials flowing in the loops can be allowed to grow or not. Linear throughput growth (in which materials flow through the economy as if through a straight pipe) places a double burden on the environment—once during the production of virgin materials, and again when wastes are ultimately dumped—and about 95 per cent of all the materials we use end up as waste before the finished product is even purchased. But if all materials flow in a loop, does the volume in the loop matter? At first sight, it would appear not, but on closer examination, it is an issue.

The first concern is the exponentially growing demand for materials as global population and relative affluence increase. If all materials flowed in a closed loop and demand continued to grow exponentially, ever more virgin materials would need to be poured into the loop to meet the growing demand. Suppose this growth was offset by dramatic dematerialisation of the useful products created, to the point where the volume of materials in the loop could at least be kept stable. Would this be enough? The answer depends on the level of leaks from the loop, and the characteristics of the energy used to keep materials moving round the loop. Even in a loop, materials need to be transported and processed repeatedly to keep them useful, and this requires energy. If energy production still has a high environmental cost—for example, because it still results in high carbon dioxide emissions—then the volume of materials in the loop would have to be reduced over time to lower the energy consumption. Simply folding linear flows into webs and loops is not enough.

Avoiding harm

The emphasis in the meta-strategy for sustainability shifts from avoiding Type I to avoiding Type II errors when dealing with the possible negative impacts of technology (Lee, 1993).

During the growth phase of industrial development, the emphasis was squarely on the development of new scientific knowledge as a basis for acquiring technological capability. The scientific method calls for caution in advancing ideas as new knowledge unless they are well grounded in empirical evidence. The emphasis in science is to avoid what are called Type I errors—the error of affirming propositions as true that later turn out to be false. Over time this bias in science and engineering has become the predominant influence in environmental policy making and strategy setting.

In a world which now has a high level of scientific knowledge and which is saturated with technology, another kind of error becomes more important, but is less well recognised. This is the Type II error—the error of rejecting propositions as false that later turn out to be true. This is the kind of error that fire brigades try to avoid—which is why firefighters always respond even to what may be false alarms.

When the concern is merely the development of abstract knowledge, society can afford to emphasise the avoidance of Type I errors. But when new technologies with potentially harmful effects are about to be commercially introduced, or when technologies with suspected harmful effects are proliferating rapidly, it can be dangerous to be obsessed only with Type I errors. The time it takes for definitive proof may be precisely the time during which critical harm is done. Far better, in these circumstances, to be much more concerned with avoiding Type II errors.

By emphasising Type II errors, the technology meta-strategy takes a precautionary approach. In this respect it is similar in intention to other sets of systems principles for sustainability. One well-known set of such principles was created by Dr Karl-Henrik Robèrt, a leading Swedish cancer researcher, with his nationwide initiative in Sweden, *Det Naturaliga Steget* (*the Natural Step*). These principles were arrived at by a consultation process involving Swedish scientists and academics, with 22 rounds of drafts and corrections, so they represent a refined technical consensus. The Natural Step consists of four principles:

1 nature cannot withstand a systematic build-up of dispersed matter mined from the earth's crust (for example, minerals, oil, etc.)
2 nature cannot withstand a systematic build-up of persistent compounds made by humans (for example, polychlorinated biphenyls (PCBs))

3 nature cannot tolerate a systematic deterioration of its capacity for renewal (for example, harvesting fish faster than they can replenish, converting fertile land to desert)

4 therefore, if we want life to continue, we must (a) be efficient in our use of resources and (b) promote justice—because ignoring poverty will lead the poor, for short term survival, to destroy resources that we all need for long term survival (for example, the rain forest).

The Natural Step has been criticised because it does not address the full range of possible unsustainability. For example, it may not preclude possible negative impacts of biotechnology—probably because the four principles were developed before biotechnology emerged as a major commercial force. The technology meta-strategy for sustainability would address such gaps—in this case by explicitly calling for the protection and preservation of the informational integrity of the biosphere and ecosphere.

The sustainable corporation

The sustainable corporation needs a clear framework for its strategic thinking. This chapter has attempted to show that the necessary framework can be rooted in an understanding of the sources of unsustainability, the technological responses necessary, and the business translation of these responses. However, the sustainable corporation cannot be considered as an isolated phenomenon—it must be closely related to changes in society as a whole.

Sustainability of corporations cannot be achieved independently of the socio-economic system as a whole, but their level of unsustainability can be reduced and this is an important near-term and transitional goal for corporate strategy. True sustainability can become a goal for corporations only as the whole socio-economic system moves towards sustainability.

The true future 'sustainable corporation' will emerge from this larger process of change. This can be expected to include a revision of international company law, redefining the goals of the private company and introducing a 'multiple bottom line': accountability to a wide range of present and future stakeholders, and a commitment to avoiding negative environmental and social externalities and maintaining social and natural capital stocks. These changes would no doubt be supported by changes in tax legislation, probably along the lines currently being discussed as 'ecological tax reform', in which the tax burden is shifted away from payroll to the consumption of virgin materials (Weizsäcker, Lovins & Lovins, 1997). This would accelerate the shift away from intensive materials use and tend to reduce unemployment—in the terminology of strategist Michael Porter (1995) the emphasis in the search for productivity would shift from labour productivity to resource productivity.

A significant new paradigm of personal belief and social values would also be needed to accompany and enable the changes envisaged in the socio-economic system, since they will not be accomplished by technology advance alone. It can be anticipated that the result would be the emergence of a less materialistic, and hence less materials-intensive way of living. Such a shift may well be catalysed by major disruptions or crises, whether social, economic, ecological or climatic.

Conclusion

The meta-strategy for the sustainable corporation addresses our total use of technology around the world and our ability to make it serve both society and individuals. It includes our need to work within geophysiology on both the large and small scales, the need to do this equitably, and the ability to keep doing it over time. The meta-strategy aims at ensuring that human application of technology can meet the needs of all peoples and exist in harmony indefinitely with natural bio-geochemical systems, based on the creation of large scale technology ecosystems specifically adapted to this planet we call home.

As it happens, the ecosystems metaphor is already becoming influential in corporate strategic planning. Strategists are increasingly talking about 'business ecosystems,' about 'value webs' rather than value chains, and about 'co-opetition', a balance between competition and cooperation as is found in nature. This amounts to a realisation that business is more successful when it adopts a 'live and let live' orientation rather than when it attempts to destroy all competition, and that the 'survival of the fittest' is best understood in terms of the 'survival of those that fit best'. This shift of outlook is an ideal grounding for the next step, which is to relate business strategy and survival not only to adaptive fit with other businesses, but also to adaptive fit with the natural environment. If strategic ideas and an ecosystemic technology perspective flow together—a convergence whose time may be just about to arrive—it could well open the way for industry, and indeed all human technology, to become truly sustainable.

Endnotes

1 The term 'sustainable corporation' can be understood in a 'strong' sense, as a future form of the corporation reframed by new company law and supporting new tax and other legislation that refocuses its fundamental motivation, or in a 'weak' sense, as a transitional form of today's conventional corporation which is seeking voluntarily to reduce its contribution to unsustainability.
2 For a global sustainability scenario framework see Tibbs, 1998.
3 For a discussion of unsustainability see Tibbs, 1999.
4 Strictly speaking, the example given is not new technology, but since it is not mainstream its widespread adoption would be a major new development.

References

Ausubel, J. H. 1989 'Regularities in technological development' in J. H. Ausubel and H. E. Sladovich (eds), *Technology and Environment*, National Academy Press, Washington, DC, pp. 70–91.

Baskin, Y. 1997 *The Work of Nature*, Island Press, Washington.

Cohen, J. E. 1995 *How Many People Can the Earth Support*, W. W. Norton, New York.

Daily, G. 1997 *Nature's Services*, Island Press, Washington.

Frosch, R. A. 1992 'Industrial Ecology: A philosophical introduction', *Proceedings of the National Academy of Sciences*, vol. 89, pp. 800–3.

Frosch, R. and Gallopoulos, N. 1989 'Strategies for manufacturing', *Scientific American*, September, pp. 144–52.

Graedel, T. E. and Allenby, B. R. 1995 *Industrial Ecology*, Prentice-Hall, NJ.

Larson, E. D., Ross, M. H. and Williams, R. H. 1986 'Beyond the era of materials', *Scientific American*, pp. 24–31.

Lawlor, L. R. 1994 'The ecology of corporate re-engineering: Is business leading us to a sustainable future?', Unpublished paper and personal communication.

Lee, K. N. 1993 *The Compass and the Gyroscope*, Island Press, Washington, pp. 74–5, 173.

Lovelock, J. E. 1979 *Gaia: A New Look at Life on Earth*, Oxford University Press, Oxford.

Nriagu, J. O. 1990 'Global metal pollution', *Environment*, vol. 32, no. 7, pp. 7–32.

Odum, E. P. 1989 *Ecology and Our Endangered Life-Support Systems*, Sinauer Associates, Sunderland, MA.

Pauli, G. 1996 *Breakthroughs: What Business can Offer Society*, Epsilon Press, Haslemere, UK.

Porter, M. E. 1995 'Green and competitive: Ending the stalemate', *Harvard Business Review*, September–October, pp. 120–34.

Schwartz, P. 1991 *The Art of the Long View*, Currency Doubleday, New York.

Tibbs, H. 1992 'Industrial ecology: An environmental agenda for industry', *Whole Earth Review*, no. 77, winter, pp. 4–19 also available from Global Business Network, Emeryville, CA, USA: http://www.sustainable. doe.gov/articles/indecol.htm

——1998 'Global change and the future of transport', *Road and Transport Research*, vol. 7, no. 2, pp. 70–83.

——1999, 'Sustainability', *The Deeper News*, Global Business Network, vol. 3, no. 1.

Vitousek, P. M. 1986 'Human appropriation of the products of photosynthesis', *Bioscience*, vol. 36, June, pp. 368–73.

von Weizsäcker, E., Lovins, A. and Lovins, L. H. 1997 *Factor 4: Doubling Wealth, Halving Resource Use*, Allen & Unwin, St Leonards, NSW.

Part IV

Towards the sustainable corporation

10

New organisational architectures: creating and retrofitting for sustainability

Andrew Griffiths

Introduction

What do companies as diverse as Volvo, Monsanto, Proctor & Gamble and Interface have in common? Apart from all being players in global competitive markets, they have introduced and are implementing significant corporate environmental strategies and programs. All have started retrofitting their corporations—that is, developing new organisational architectures to support and capitalise on these emerging strategic imperatives.[1]

Interface, for example, specialises in the production and provision of modular carpets and office refitting services and has a production presence in 27 countries. Interface has developed a corporate environmental management program that sits alongside its other corporate programs for growth, profitability and efficiency. Unlike many other firms, Interface has a commitment to ecological and human sustainability which moves beyond rhetorical platitudes into powerful programs of organisational reconstruction.

The Interface story is an interesting one. In 1994 Ray Anderson, the company's CEO and founder, instigated QUEST—a corporate program designed to address the environmental consequences of manufacturing commercial carpets. QUEST was aimed at waste minimisation through a variety of processes including the recycling of carpet. However, for QUEST to succeed as a program, the organisational members needed to be strongly motivated to address the negative environmental impacts of key elements of the Interface value-adding chain. This required a dramatic shift in the mindsets and motivations of everyone in the organisation, from Ray Anderson to shopfloor workers.

While QUEST was a company-wide program, decisions on how the program was to be undertaken were delegated to each of the individual production facilities. Plants in individual countries were given the autonomy to pursue the QUEST program according to local needs. Under these conditions, the Australian plant went from being number 27—or worst in the organisation—to number 1 by 1997.[2] In facilities across the world, small teams were established to address internal issues, such as waste reduction and minimisation, and external issues, such as customer and supplier requirements. Company processes were then altered so that they aligned with the new focus on quality, waste reduction and recycling. For example, individuals and groups of employees were rewarded for attaining these goals. At Interface, the distinction between human and ecological sustainability issues has been removed—new structures and processes have been established that reward progress in both areas and encourage the pursuit of excellence in each.[3] As companies like Interface assume responsibility for their impact on the lives of their workforce, the society and the ecological environment, they are discovering that significant changes need to be made in their corporate architectures.

While there exists an impressive and growing literature on corporate 'green' strategies, there is very little research, or even anecdotal evidence about which architectures and organisational change processes assist organisations to enact these strategies. An interesting analogy can be drawn between the current efforts to institutionalise green strategies and earlier corporate experiences with the implementation of flexible manufacturing systems and new technologies. For instance, at the height of competition between US and Japanese manufacturing firms, Jaikumar (1986) showed that Japanese firms outperformed US firms using the same or similar technologies. Why? It appears that traditional organisational structures and processes hindered US firms from taking full advantage of the new technology. The Japanese not only introduced the new technology, they also changed their structures and organisational processes to secure maximum advantage from it.

This story serves as a powerful reminder of the importance of organisational architectures in enabling strategic outcomes. It should also act as a warning that, in our haste to develop corporate sustainability strategies, we should not overlook the need to identify activities and architectures that could impede or facilitate the adoption of such strategies at the corporate or business level. This chapter therefore presents a positive agenda for designing and retrofitting corporate architectures in order to support sustainable practices. It attempts to answer the following key questions:

- How can current organisational architectures, practices and routines impede the development of sustainable organisations?
- What kinds of corporate architectures will characterise the sustainable corporation? In particular, what kinds of architectures will generate and utilise human capabilities? Are these the same as or different from those that will generate and utilise ecological capabilities? What principles underlie architectures that support sustainability?
- How do we transform corporate architectures to create sustainable practices?

Architectures that generate human sustainability outcomes

Dunphy and Griffiths (1998) document the history of the Organisational Renewal Movement (ORM) in Australia—tracing the movement from its emergence in the mid 1960s to its acceptance as orthodoxy in the 1990s. Over its thirty year history, the ORM focused on generating organisational structures that contributed to human satisfaction, growth and development while also contributing to the profitability and productivity of the enterprise. This movement developed capabilities and knowledge relevant to the effective conduct of the micro- and macro-elements of organisational change. While early change agents focused on interventions at an individual and/or group level, the focus moved subsequently to the management of large scale corporate restructuring and to forging links between change management practices and the emerging discipline of corporate strategy. So, over thirty years, the change movement generated a wealth of information on how to redesign and renew organisational architectures from the individual level to the total organisation.

For instance, at the level of the individual, jobs were redesigned to enhance an individual's autonomy in decision making and to link individual employee's work to the organisation's central purpose. Jobs redesigned in this way generate greater organisational commitment and employee satisfaction. However, a focus on job redesign alone, which was typical of early ORM interventions, while altering the responsibilities of individuals was often not enough in itself to generate sustainable benefits for people in organisations. These initiatives had to be supported by more encompassing organisational structures and systems for the fullest range of human potential to be released. Therefore, while job redesign, skills training, human development and culture change workshops frequently succeeded in enhancing individual skills, if such initiatives were not backed up with organisational systems and architectures that rewarded people for using these skills the initiatives would fail to generate sustainable positive outcomes for individuals and for the organisation.

At the level of the work group or business unit, the ORM focused on designing architectures that would both benefit individuals and produce outcomes, such as improved productivity and profitability for the organisation. Such initiatives came mainly from the organisation development (OD) and socio-technical systems (STS) traditions and focused on the establishment of team based organisational architectures. These architectures were designed to address the stifling and oppressive structures in large bureaucratic organisations that impeded creativity and innovation in organisations and led to widespread employee alienation and industrial relations conflict.

Team-based organisations were implemented, in which smaller business units were created and in turn broken down into semi-autonomous work teams. These were teams made up of skilled individuals who could take responsibility for planning, scheduling, quality and customer service in the production of goods and services. Such organisational architectures proved to be as effective or more effective than their mechanistic counterparts in producing high levels of performance and significantly raised employee work satisfaction. However, they were also fragile. Factors such as changes in management, the introduction of new corporate regulations, removal of resources and corporate power games could easily marginalise these innovations and cause them to fail despite their proven benefits for team members and for the organisation. Team based organisational architectures required supportive organisational systems such as particular approaches to recruitment and selection; the remuneration and the distribution of resources to value-adding activities. They also required significant modification of hierarchal management structures (Lawler, 1992).

More recently, the ORM has contributed to the creation of large scale organisational changes to corporate structures. So we know a great deal more about how to go about corporate change. The key question now, however, has become how to create high performance organisations that can survive under turbulent economic conditions. That is, how do we make change stick and create organisations that continue to adopt to new environmental developments?

Unfortunately, some organisations, in their quest to become more competitive, have become stuck in a cycle of downsizing and cost-cutting—losing important human and organisational capabilities in the process. Such large corporate restructuring exercises can create potential problems such as survivor syndrome. Survivor syndrome refers to the impact of downsizing on those who do not lose their jobs; the effects include increased cynicism and decreased work motivation. Downsizing and re-engineering can also destroy the firm's core competencies and capabilities—capabilities that may be more expensive to purchase back in, or that may take years to develop again. While the human sustainability tradition advocates the use of large scale restructuring tools such as process re-engineering, downsizing and restructuring, in cases where organisational architectures are significantly out of alignment with their competitive environment, the ORM warns that the reckless application of these techniques can also have devastating consequences for organisations. However, despite radical changes in competitive environments, some organisations have proved quite adaptable to change. The next section of the paper explores the characteristics of long living organisations and the implications for the pursuit of human and ecological sustainability.

Long living organisations and characteristics of ESOs

In recent years researchers have investigated the characteristics of organisations that survive for long periods and show sustained productivity. If organisational longevity is taken as the criterion of sustainability, some organisations have consistently managed to outperform their rivals (Collins & Porras 1994; De Geus 1997). There are limitations to adopting longevity as a measure of sustainability, principally because longevity is no indicator of whether an organisation is pursuing goals that are either/or human and ecologically sustainable. However, the characteristics of these long living organisations provide insights into how organisations adapt to changing environments. De Geus (1997b: 52) argues that many companies perish early because 'their policies and practices are based too heavily on the thinking and language of economics'. By focusing exclusively on the production of wealth, through creating goods and services, managers ignore the fact that their organisations are also a collective community of individuals engaged in business. De Geus (1997a) identifies four characteristics of long living companies, including, first, fiscal responsibility—these companies are not high risk takers in the financial arena; they create a store of capital for investment to take advantage of future opportunities as they present themselves. Second, long living companies are aware of and in tune with their environment. They scan it constantly and respond quickly to emerging consumer demands. Third, long living companies have developed ways to experiment and to examine peripheral ideas and turn these into core activities or important side businesses. Finally, these companies have a sense of identity—a strong sense of community—and they work at maintaining the integrity of their communal relationships.

The authors we have discussed to this point are predominantly concerned with 'human sustainability' in corporations. Another set of authors, such as Korten (1995), von Weizsäcker, Lovins and Lovins (1998) and Shrivastava (1995) have identified the characteristics of ecologically sustainable organisations (ESOs). A definition of ESOs is provided below:

> The test of an organization's ecological sustainability is the degree to which its activities can be continued indefinitely without negatively altering the limiting factors that permit the existence and flourishing of other groups of entities, including other organizations. Limiting factors determine the carrying capacity of a given ecosystem for a type of entity and these include, food, water, shelter, breeding and rearing sites, predators, competitors, disease organisms and toxins . . . for living species. Sustainable organizational activities would not alter physical, chemical and biological factors (or political, economic, social or cultural conditions) such that carrying capacity for otherwise sustainable entities would be dramatically reduced or eliminated (Starik & Rands, 1995: 909).

These authors note some of the characteristics of future ecologically sustainable organisations and the conditions that will generate them. These characteristics include, first, small is beautiful, or that smaller corporate entities and structures will be more responsive to environmental concerns and will be less powerful and less inclined to dismiss government and societal attempts to regulate them. Second, these authors note that government regulation can be used to shape corporate environmental behaviour in order to adopt programs for environmental management, such as TQEM—total quality environmental management—to reduce waste and pollution. Third, increased power should be devolved to individuals and local communities in order to create a citizens-inspired agenda for local ecological sustainability. Finally, that future ESOs will play an active role in creating self-sufficient communities where production and use align with community needs.

However, some proponents of sustainability, such as Korten (1995), argue that first, it is beyond the capacity of large corporations to adopt ecologically-friendly practices and second, that the structures, strategies and decision making processes in large corporations are incompatible with some of the ideal characteristics of ESOs identified earlier. In his view sustainability will depend heavily on the creation of small, self-reliant communities and a citizens' agenda for change, rather than a corporate change agenda. It is the argument here, that if corporate structures and strategies are a significant part of the problem of sustainability, that they will also be a significant part of the solution.

Shrivastava (1995) and von Weizsäcker, Lovins and Lovins (1998) adopt a different perspective. Both argue that corporations can play a key role in creating sustainable economies. Both authors argue that organisations can become much more efficient at modifying inputs, throughputs and outputs to reduce their negative impact on the ecology. Shrivastava (1995: 942) argues that there are several key components to ESOs. These include first, TQEM—a set of techniques used to solve organisational problems from a whole systems perspective. Application of the techniques ensures that an organisation's inputs, throughputs and outputs have a minimal environmental impact. Like TQM (total quality management), TQEM requires structural and cultural changes, which enable an organisation's employees to take on greater responsibilities in solving problems if its full benefits are to be utilised. Second, there exists a range of corporate strategies that organisations can pursue that have consequences on the structure, content and sophistication of corporate environmental programs. Some strategies, such as those at Interface, have impacted significantly on how that organisation views and approaches the issue of sustainability. Other corporate strategies, such as the introduction of environmental marketing programs, may require little change to an organisation's structure and orientation.

Finally, these authors argue that ESOs will be characterised by an ability to influence and impact on population control and balance. For instance in developed countries, it is possible for corporations to establish and locate facilities in rural areas to assist with the development of sustainable local communities; while in developing countries, corporations can use their extensive networks to disseminate information on family planning and other ecologically important issues (Shrivastava, 1995). Lying at the heart of these studies on ESOs is the notion that ESOs will require internal structural changes, such as the implementation of TQEM programs, and a broader understanding of what constitutes social and environmental 'best practice'.

Limitations of current corporate architectures

What can these studies tell us about the corporate structures that contribute to or impede the attainment of sustainability? These studies indicate three ways in which current corporate architectures impede sustainability. First, current corporate architectures insulate organisational systems and processes from a broad range of environmental information. This is because they have no structural elements, such as specialised departments that have the expert knowledge to recognise, act on and transfer to other parts of the organisation information of an environmentally relevant nature. Current initiatives tend to rely on inspired leaders who pursue human and ecological agendas as a consequence of their own value system. Systems that rely on inspired leaders rather than establishing structural and systemic solutions are vulnerable. When the leader moves on, the function can be lost.

Second, the established routines and organisational systems of many organisations seek to promote and protect the status quo. Schon (1971) refers to this as the dynamic conservatism of social systems. As a result new practices and theories are defined as threats to established ways of working. In particular the organisational innovations which support sustainability are a threat to command and control style management systems. Managers who have risen to power in command and control systems frequently resist the transition to alternative structures.

Finally, current architectures limit or deny access to a range of stakeholders whose participation is vital for the pursuit of sustainability agendas. Traditional organisations tend to be focused on a limited set of stakeholders, in particular, boards of directors and shareholders. The initiatives of other stakeholders—particularly the workforce, unions and 'greenies'—are seen as hostile forces that may harm the basis of current organisational performance. In response to initiatives from these interest groups, some corporations adopt aggressive and defensive practices which undermine the development of the broader stakeholder accountability and involvement needed to support moves to create more sustainable practices (Beder, 1997).

The points we have made in this section primarily refer to large traditional corporations that are hierarchical in design and that have developed systems of managerial practice based on a strong centralised command and control style of management. Such corporate practices are also supported by broader institutional systems. For example, economic systems that encourage and reward for the creation of pollution and waste; vested financial interests which block the radical restructuring of organisations for the achievement of sustainable goals. However, the economic, political and social context within which corporations operate is changing. New corporations are moving into prominence and old corporations are reorganising, so as the world shifts, an active search for new organisational forms is taking place. In the next section of this chapter therefore, we discuss alternative architectures for sustainability.

Alternative architectures for sustainability

The previous section identified ways in which traditional corporate architectures hinder moves to create more sustainable organisations. In this section, three alternative organisational architectures are identified: the network; the virtual organisation; and the community of practice. Each of these architectures is an ideal type. In reality they vary and appear in hybrid form. However, we identify their general characteristics, and the prospects that they provide for enhancing human and ecological sustainability will be discussed. It is important to keep in mind that these forms can be replicated at the level of groups, business units and whole organisations, making it not only possible to create new organisations based on these ideal types, but to also retro-fit existing organisational architectures to capture the sustainability benefits of these new forms.

Network organisations

In recent years, the network organisation has emerged as a powerful alternative to traditional vertically integrated organisational architectures. Network organisations may take a variety of forms but fundamentally they are organisations that give the advantages of larger size, while remaining small.[4] In these organisations, the centre retains some key areas of decision making, for example, major strategic moves, ceding considerable autonomy to smaller relatively independent units. Such organisational forms exist in Australia. For instance TCG, a company that operates in the technology and software support and services industry, is a small network of 24 independent firms that cluster together to provide the advantages of size while maintaining the flexibility and innovativeness of small firms (Mathews, 1992).

Quinn (1992) refers to network organisations as 'spider web' organisations, noting that they typically have dispersed service nodes. He describes them as spider web organisations because of the lightness and multiple interconnectedness. Such organisations tend to have flatter hierarchies and minimise the use of formal rules. Individual units obtain more information by acting as a collective and can also attain economies of scale and scope as a result of their interconnectedness. Clusters of small firms, such as TCG, represent one form of network. But a network can also form around a large firm that seeks to outsource parts of its production or service value adding chain or that enters into strategic alliances. Joint ventures, partnerships and strategic alliances may also provide firms with the benefits associated with networks, if managed appropriately.

A major strength of network architecture lies in its ability to grow (by adding on new firms) while keeping the constituent units small, flexible, responsive and innovative. Networks are sustainable primarily because of their ability to respond quickly to changing market conditions, to be flexible in meeting customer requirements and to transform markets through the speedy development of new products and services. However, networks have to be coordinated differently from traditional hierarchical organisations—they often appoint network 'brokers' who coordinate the various elements of a network value adding chain. Alternatively, networks may form in infrastructurally strong regions, such as Silicon Valley (electronics and software) or in Italy (furniture, textiles and ceramics). Networks are strongly dependent on the skills, dexterity and knowledge base of their employees—while traditionally associated with craft work, new network forms have emerged in the new 'craft industries' of biotechnology, software and information technology. Networks are relevant to sustainability in at least two key ways. First, networks are increasingly recognised as a major source of innovativeness in new product and service developments. In Germany and Denmark clusters of small firm networks have been leaders in green technology developments. Second, network structures are reliant upon free flowing information and communication—they are therefore appropriate structures for capturing and diffusing through the network information that is relevant to sustainability outcomes.

Virtual organisations

Another alternate organisational form that can support sustainability is the virtual organisation. The concept of the virtual organisation has received increasing attention in both popular press and academic journals. The virtual corporation can be seen to be designed on several levels. At one level the virtual corporation can be interpreted as an organisation with a limited life. At first appearances, this does not appear to be a 'sustainable practice'. In these cases, the issue is not about sustaining the organisation in terms of longevity, but rather recognising that in the pursuit of sustainability there will be a need for limited term projects—organisations—that will come together to solve or address important issues and disband once they have been addressed.

Alternatively, a virtual organisation can give the impression of size, yet be small in terms of numbers of employees. In other words, corporate sustainability is not just about large corporations but can and will also include smaller more nimble corporations that have a virtual facade.

Organisations such as Amazon.com (an Internet book retailer) and Lands End (textile and clothing manufacturer) can service via the Internet and electronic commerce and operate globally with a small number of employees. Such organisations require structures that are flexible and that compete on speed.

New information technologies are revolutionising industries—such as retail and publishing—by operating with a small yet committed core of staff with high levels of technical and information systems expertise. Typically these organisations form strategic alliances for their distribution and warehousing activities. Such activities may be undertaken inhouse but more often are outsourced. These organisations will tend to leave a minimal environmental footprint, however they will need to be responsible for the environmental impacts of their suppliers and distributors rather than take the attitude that it is none of their responsibility how suppliers/distributors operate.

Some organisations have adopted a virtual approach throughout the entire organisation. In other cases, the virtual organisation may be used only for organising particular functions and/or projects. Townsend, DeMarie and Hendrickson (1998) have discussed how virtual teams are best managed. As these commentators have pointed out, the creation of such teams raises new challenges in terms of the structure, technology and functioning of work. For instance, virtual teams will more than likely have members operating in diverse geographical regions and possibly members who are peripheral to or even outside of the formal organisation. Such teams can already be found in organisations such as Anderson Consulting where project members may be working on the same change programs while based in different countries. However, the successful operation of such teams requires significant investments in information technology and in the skill sets of employees so that they can effectively use the new communication technologies. Virtual teams also require the reconfiguration of reward systems and resourcing arrangements. Traditional cost centre approaches to accounting may also impede the innovative focus and development of such teams. As virtual teams will not belong to a unit or division, but rather draw together a range of experts across an organisation, traditional cost accounting and management systems will need to be modified to adapt to the flexibilities offered by virtual teams and technologies.

Organisations as communities of practice

Unlike the previous two organisational forms, communities of practice are not clearly defined entities. Communities of practice have amorphous and in some cases fluid structures that form around areas of interest, expertise and/or project orientation. An example of a community of practice may be a community of professionals who gather information, pass on knowledge and contribute to the development of their field of expertise. Such communities generate the diffusion and acceptance of explicit and tacit knowledge that can be transferred into innovative solutions and actions within formal organisations. Increasingly, communities of practice and knowledge groups rely on and are assisted by cutting edge information technologies that provide the potential for innovation, rapid response and the ability to generate solutions quickly.

Brown and Duguid (1991) have stated that communities of practice have few hierarchies—member status is based on expertise and contribution to the development of leading ideas rather than on position or authority. They go on to state that: 'The communities that we discern are . . . more fluid and interpretative than bounded, often crossing the restrictive boundaries of the organization to incorporate people from outside' (Brown & Duguid, 1991: 49). Such communities of learning may be difficult to design, but rather emerge organically and are continually being formed and reformed.

Whether they are located within formal organisations or arise independently, communities of practice are characterised by the following features. They are reliant upon architectures which enable them to take on new members, acquire new information and which bind people to each other through common interests, desire for learning and an enhanced ability to achieve collective and individual goals. Second, such organisations are characterised by a reliance on both formal and informal processes for skills development and learning. Finally, communities of practice establish a core or nucleus of people who are responsible for creating and sustaining the community's collective memory. Their contribution to the attainment of sustainability outcomes for organisations lies in their ability to collect, process and diffuse knowledge of a technical and specialised nature and translate this knowledge into innovative and rapid solutions.

Architectures for building human and ecologically sustainable corporations

The previous sections examined the contributions that the literature on human sustainability, long living corporations and ESOs can make to our understanding of architectures for sustainability. In this discussion we described some alternative organisational forms and how they can support sustainability. This section draws together these characteristics to create an ideal set of structural attributes for human and ecologically sustainable corporations.

Architectures for utilising employee knowledge

Both the human and ecologically sustainable literature emphasise the importance of employee knowledge in generating adaptive and responsive organisations. Hierarchies are killers of initiative and innovation and impede the effective utilisation of employee knowledge. Other alternative organisational forms are more conducive to fostering the generation of employee knowledge and to using it effectively. Team-based organisational architectures enable employees to have input, discretion over decision making and provide them with the information and resources to deliver organisational outcomes. Such strategies are long term, not a quick fix, for team based organisational architectures require large investments in time and energy. As a consequence, managers need to make the shift from a short term orientation to the longer term strategies of developing these people-centred, service-oriented architectures (Quinn, 1992). Team based organisational architectures, which include project teams and virtual teams based on new communication technologies, provide the basis for capturing and utilising the employees' knowledge needed to create effective sustainable corporate strategies.

Architectures for capturing and making use of ecological information

An important element in the generation of sustainable corporations is the creation of organisational architectures and systems that are capable of capturing, processing and making sense of environmental information. King (1995) notes that organisations with limited access to environmental information are more likely to make ecological and environmental blunders. For an organisation to avoid this and capture the benefits of environmental awareness, there must be multiple and diverse information entry points into the organisation. If critical information about the environment is confined to specialist units it will fail to diffuse throughout the organisation and is unlikely to be used in strategic decision making processes. Communities of practice can help assist with the diffusion and acceptance of such vital information. Creating a broad range of information entry points helps to reinforce the creation and generation of corporate wide environmental strategies (Maxwell et al., 1997). The challenge therefore is to create corporate architectures that effectively internalise the environmental information needed to meet regulatory standards and corporate competitive strategies based on sustainable practices. For example, in Volvo environmental programs were established by creating four corporate-wide 'working groups' focused on addressing a broad environmental agenda. Specifically, project teams examined first, structures and systems that could capture the benefits of product recycling; second, structuring organisational systems for acquiring and diffusing environmental information; third, reviewing production processes for environmental efficiencies and, finally, meeting European Union regulatory standards on environmental management (Maxwell et al., 1997: 122).

Architectures for speedy change and adaptation

Paul Shrivastava (1995) argues that 'The challenge facing organizational scholars is to flesh out organizational pathways to ecological sustainability'. The structures for achieving this need to be ambidextrous. On the one hand, they need to maintain the day-to-day operational activities that create valuable products and services. On the other, they need to support the ongoing transformation of these activities to move them inexorably in the direction of human and ecological sustainability. Speedy change in corporate architectures is required—delay in this agenda means continuing damage to the quality of our community life and the ecology of the planet. It is in this area that the organisational renewal movement can make its greatest contribution to date—by providing the critical knowledge and skills needed for the transformation of traditional product and service organisations to the sustainable effective organisations of the future.

Hart (1997) has advocated the use of a sustainability portfolio; this tool enables organisations to diagnose whether their corporate strategy is consistent with sustainability, and whether they require drastic action to rectify an 'unbalanced approach'. Similarly, Shrivastava (1995) has argued that slow and gradual investments in green technologies, products and creation of markets will spread the cost of corporate environmentalism over time, enabling companies to meet or develop balanced sustainability portfolios. Some corporations have already created organisational architectures that position them to take advantage of these processes by creating supportive networks, virtual organisations and communities of practice. For example, Monsanto, the chemical company, has modified its structure through the establishment of sustainability teams which include an eco-efficiency team, a full cost accounting team, the index team, the new business new products team, the water team, the global hunger team and the communication and education team.[5] Robert Shapiro, the CEO of Monsanto, states that (Magretta 1997: 87):

Part of the design and structure of any successful institution is going to be giving the people permission to select tasks and goals that they care about . . . I don't mean to romanticise it, but, by and large, self regulating systems are probably going to be more productive than those based primarily on control loops.

Conclusion

While a significant amount of time and energy has been devoted to the creation and generation of environmental corporate strategies, there has been virtually no attention given to understanding the ways in which different corporate architectures impede or facilitate progress toward human and ecological sustainability. We have tried to fill this gap by bringing together knowledge from several traditions. The basic approach has been that traditional architectures will not support the adoption of the changes in business practices necessary to achieve human and eco-logical sustainability. Corporations, large and small, will need to experiment with alternative organisational structures and systems. Such experimentation is already occurring. Many emerging organisations will never become large traditional bureaucracies. Existing bureaucratic organisations will need to adopt in part these new corporate forms or modify the rigidity of their current structures.

It is useful to view these alternative organisational forms—which are more people responsive, fluid and open to a range of information sources—as nested organisational forms. They can fit within each other or operate alongside each other compatibly. Such architectures may also be grafted onto traditional organisational structures. But such grafting of alternative organisational forms—be they network, virtual or commu-nities of practice—represents only the first step in retrofitting traditional organisational structures.

Endnotes

1 For a summary of these programs see Hart, 1997; Maxwell, et al., 1997.

2 The strategies used at Interface are influenced by the philosophy and approach developed in the Natural Step (Robèrt, Daly, Hawken & Holmberg, 1997).

3 While Interface are proud of the achievements in addressing sus-tainability issues, their corporate philosophy suggests that they have

only just started on the path to becoming an ecologically sustainable organisation (ESO).

4 Some authors use other terms, for example, Charles Handy (1990) refers to networks as federated organisations.

5 Monsanto is an interesting example. Hart (1997) uses Monsanto as an example of a company that is moving towards sustainability and developing competencies in this area. However, Monsanto also is attempting to dispel consumer fears and environmental activists' concerns over its use of genetically engineered and modified food products and the corporate strategies they have adopted in developing this range of new genetically modified products.

References

Beder, S. 1997 *Global Spin: The Corporate Assault on Environmentalism*, Scribe Books, Carlton, Victoria.

Brown, J. and Duguid, P. 1991 'Organizational learning and communities of practice: Toward a unified view of working, learning and innovation', *Organization Science*, vol. 2, no. 1, pp. 40–57.

Collins, J. and Porras, J. 1994 *Built to Last: Successful Habits of Visionary Companies*, Century, London.

De Geus, A. 1997a *The Living Company: Habits for Survival in a Turbulent Business Environment*, Harvard Business School Press, Cambridge, MA.

——1997b 'The living company', *Harvard Business Review*, March–April, pp. 51–9.

Dunphy, D. and Griffiths, A. 1998 *The Sustainable Corporation: Organizational Renewal in Australia*, Allen & Unwin, St Leonards, NSW.

Handy, C. 1990 *The Age of Unreason*, Harvard Business School Press, Boston, MA.

Hart, S. 1997 'Beyond greening: Strategies for a sustainable world', *Harvard Business Review*, January–February, pp. 66–76.

Jaikumar, R. 1986 'Postindustrial manufacturing', *Harvard Business Review*, November–December, pp. 69–76.

King, A. 1995 'Avoiding ecological surprise: Lessons from long standing communities', *The Academy of Management Review*, vol. 20, no. 4, pp. 961–85.

Korten, D. 1997 *When Corporations Rule the World*, Kumarian Press, CT.

Lawler, E. 1992 *The Ultimate Advantage: Creating High Involvement Organizations*, Jossey Bass, San Francisco.

Magretta, J. 1997 'Growth through global sustainability: An interview with Monsanto's CEO, Robert B. Shapiro', *Harvard Business Review*, January–February, pp. 79–88.

Mathews, J. 1992 *TCG: Sustainable Economic Organization Through Networking*, UNSW Studies in Organizational Analysis and Innovation, Industrial Relations Research Centre, University of New South Wales.

Maxwell, J., Rothenberg, S., Briscoe, F. and Marcus, A. 1997 'Green schemes: Corporate environmental strategies and their implementation', *California Management Review*, vol. 39, no. 3, pp. 118–34.

Pfeffer, J. 1996 'Why do smart organizations occasionally do dumb things', *Organizational Dynamics*, Summer, pp. 33–44.

Quinn, J. 1992 *Intelligent Enterprise*, Free Press, New York.

Robèrt, K., Daly, H., Hawken, P. and Holmberg, J. 1997 'A compass for sustainable development', *International Journal of Sustainable Development and World Ecology*, pp. 79–92.

Schon, D. 1971 *Beyond the Stable State*, Norton, New York.

Shrivastava, P. 1995 'The role of corporations in achieving ecological sustainability', *The Academy of Management Review*, vol. 20, no. 4, pp. 936–60.

Starik, M. and Rands, G. 1995 'Weaving an integrated web: Multilevel and multisystem perspectives of ecologically sustainable organizations', *The Academy of Management Review*, vol. 20, no. 4, pp. 908–35.

Townsend, A., DeMarie, S. and Hendrickson, A. 1998 'Virtual teams: Technology and the workplace of the future', *Academy of Management Executive*, vol. 12, no. 3, pp. 17–29.

von Weizsäcker, E., Lovins, A. and Lovins, L. 1998 *Factor 4: Doubling Wealth, Halving Resource Use*, Earthscan Publications, London.

11

Guiding principles:
the way ahead

Molly Harriss Olson and Phillip Toyne

Introduction

Sustainability is not a science but rather a new social and economic paradigm. Consequently, corporations on the cutting edge of developing sustainable practices, processes, products and services require some beacons to guide their efforts. This chapter will discuss the important concept of guiding principles for corporate sustainability, and illustrate how guiding principles can be used as a compass to steer a course toward a sustainable corporation through the twenty-first century.

Why guiding principles?

Civilisation has witnessed more radical and profound change to the earth in the last eighty years than in all the rest of human history combined. In 1904 the first airplane flight took place and by the 1960s we had landed a man on the moon. The pace of global change has accelerated at an even faster rate since the 1960s—so fast in fact that technologies can be eclipsed by new advances before you get them to the office.

The pace and scale of the change is more than the human brain has evolved to comprehend. Paul Ehrlich and Dr Robert Ornstein discuss this issue of how the brain evolved and its difficulty in responding to long term earth threatening trends (1989). According to Ehrlich and Ornstein

> our 'mental structure' evolved in large part to deal with environmental opportunities and dangers. The human brain, like that of the crocodile

and the tarsier, promotes the survival and reproduction of individuals, but it evolved to help individuals living in circumstances very different from today. Our evolutionary history equipped us to live with a handful of compatriots, in a stable environment, with many short term challenges . . . (Ehrlich & Ornstein, 1989: 29).

So what does the evolution of the brain have to do with the need to develop principles for corporate sustainability? Because our brains evolved to meet short term, localised environmental problems, we are not designed to function in the context of rapidly changing high risk and global scale problems. This is true for both corporations and for society at large. Principles guide us. They are the ultimate source, origin, fundamental truth and modifying force that informs our actions. Principles are essential to assist corporations and civilisation as a whole to move quickly to understand the new rules of the sustainability paradigm. The principles should ensure that the actions we take are not violating the basic conditions that make life, as we know it today, possible on earth. A clear and concise set of guiding principles can enable groups to act where otherwise chaos would reign. It also enables all of us as individuals, in corporations and in society, to participate in creating the solutions. The problems inherent in the current unsustainable paradigm of development mean that no existing government, community or institution on earth is powerful enough to unilaterally make society or industry sustainable, or even require others to do so. If we wait for government or consumers or corporations to solve these problems in the absence of a set of guiding principles they may not be solved.

The challenge for corporations is to do business and provide services in a sustainable way that does not contribute to the deepening social or ecological crisis and thus does not violate the basic survival prospects for humanity and other species. Corporations are not the only ones with an interest and obligation to act sustainably. This is a whole-of-society concern. But business controls most of the world's capital and is a key contributor to the unsustainable use of the world's resources. Business must therefore be a critical player in the move to a new paradigm. On a more basic level, it is in the interests of business to sustain a market demand for products and services and fundamental to this is sustaining humanity. The challenge is for business to profoundly reconsider its basic mode of operating to include social and environmental impacts as well as profitability.

Humanity's great triumph, starting with the dawn of the agricultural revolution, has been to transform the world so that many of us can meet our most immediate needs. These changes have had many impacts, both good and bad, upon people and the world within which we live. Some of the indisputable, negative consequences have been the rapid deterioration of the natural environment and a widening of the gap between rich and poor. There is widespread and growing social concern about both.

It is widely recognised that the nature of environmental problems has changed radically in this last thirty years. Rachel Carson's book *Silent Spring* was the first, widely read, study that recognised that many of the environmental problems we faced were due to a systemic failure to predict the non-target impacts of our actions (Carson, 1962). Carson looked at manufactured pesticides like DDT—its profound impact on wild bird populations was pushing the California condor and the bald eagle to the brink of extinction. Carson's book was a key catalyst for enacting the major environmental laws in the US. As Vice President Al Gore has said, 'thanks to Rachel Carson's clarion call, we developed new and vital protections for the American public' (Gore, 1996: i).

In the early 1960s, we thought the nature of environmental problems was localised and derived from a few largely identifiable sources. There was generally a short time delay between cause and effect and thus a relatively low level of complexity involved in finding a solution. It was easy to tie the dead fish in the river to the chemical spill from the factory. Thirty years later, Theo Colborne takes up where Carson began. Today many of our problems are global, like climate change, land based sources of marine pollution, and the hole in the ozone layer. These problems are diffuse, coming from many sources, and there is often a long time delay between cause and effect. The inventor of DDT, touted as a miracle pesticide, was given the Nobel Prize. Decades later, in 1972, DDT was banned in the US. We now have environmental problems facing civilisation that are highly complex and it is often impossible to identify the cause and effect relationships.

In the book *Our Stolen Future* we start to see the full extent of the systemic damage we are causing to the reproductive capability of life on this earth (Colborne, Dumanoski & Myer, 1996). A vast array of manufactured compounds is inadvertently disrupting the basic endocrine systems of wildlife and humans. Thus, reduced sperm counts and defective reproductive organs have been documented from Florida to Denmark. They are found in penguins in Antarctica and polar bears in the Arctic and in humans everywhere. There are already some 14 000 pages of EPA regulations in the US that are meant to protect the US public from the unintended impacts of pollution. However, almost none of them deal with any endocrine disrupting compounds; just cancer-causing ones. We are only beginning to see the extent of the damage we are creating on the planet and it is unlikely that legislation or regulations are going to be effective in addressing problems of this magnitude in a timely way.

Another example is genetic engineering. There is little effective regulation of this rapidly expanding area of science, yet the dangers are real. Recently it was discovered that genetically modified corn pollen is lethal to one of the species of butterflies which has historically eaten the pollen safely. The implications of this for the manufacturer and for society are enormous. Technology, which was strenuously promoted as failsafe, has had unanticipated negative impacts on the health of the environment. Its use and evaluation are now being re-thought by farmers, consumers and corporations around the world.

Issues such as these will determine the future profitability or even viability of companies. Only those companies that have adopted a truly sustainable development approach will survive and thrive. In the case of genetic engineering, it may well be the consumers who will determine which products and companies are accepted. The widespread objections to genetically modified foods and the insistence that these are labelled, presage an increasing community activism about what will be acceptable and what will not. Greenpeace has pulled up genetically engineered crops in Europe. Australian consumers have won the right to label those foods that contain modified genes. Consumer choice may well be the ultimate regulator of these activities, as governments become increasingly incapable of establishing timely, regulatory frameworks to deal with newly emerging technologies.

Companies that ignore the environmental and social costs of their activities are likely to fail if their activities offend the communities upon which they ultimately depend for their survival. Exxon is still remembered for the Alaska oil spill disaster. Shell experienced international public condemnation in the face of its attempts to sink the Brent Spar oil platform into the ocean and also because of its perceived role in human rights abuses in Nigeria. Similarly, Monsanto lost 20 per cent market share due to the controversy over GMOs and found that the brightest and the best university graduates do not want to work for the company identified as the largest polluter under the US government's 'Community right to know' (Toxics Release Inventory) legislation. Nike has come under increased attack because of the use of child labour in overseas manufacturing plants. Companies failing to act responsibly will be judged harshly, not only by the law, but also by the markets. The response now is often immediate, global and spontaneous, as groups, once isolated, communicate on the Internet. For example, BHP's environmental problems at Ok Tedi in Papua New Guinea were understood by the Dene Indians of Canada's North-West Territory as soon as the company attempted to negotiate access to tribal lands for diamond exploration.

A growing number of investors have insisted on having their funds screened to ensure they are only invested in socially responsible ventures. Ethical investment was once limited to exclusions such as on tobacco, alcohol or gambling, but increasingly environmental and human rights considerations are at the forefront. By the end of 1997 there was over a trillion US dollars invested in socially screened investment funds. This has grown by 85 per cent between 1995 and 1997.[1] Funds managers now actively engage the companies in which they invest, over issues such as clear-felling forestry or activities in undemocratic regimes like Burma.

The visionary companies

What kind of companies are likely to thrive in the face of these increasing pressures? What kind of companies are likely to be the ones able to set this forward looking path which will take into account the new sustainability agenda of social responsibility, profitability and environmental stewardship? This is also known as the 'triple bottom line'.

A fascinating study has been done of a group of visionary companies that have been extraordinarily profitable over a long period of time. These companies have shown resilience when confronted by difficulties and are marked by the capacity to meet new issues successfully as they emerge. In studying 1700 years experience of successful corporations, Collins and Porras (1994) from Stanford Business School, identify some of the fundamental principles on which 'visionary' companies operate. They asked the question: 'What makes truly exceptional companies different from other companies—and what might explain their enduring quality and prosperity?' They compared the top companies to similar companies in their sector that did not achieve the same success. The study defined visionary companies as:

> Premier institutions—the crown jewels—in their industries, widely admired by peers and having a long track record of making a significant impact on the world around them. The key point is that a visionary company is an organization—an institution. All institutional leaders, no matter how charismatic or visionary, eventually die; and all visionary products and services—all great ideas—eventually become obsolete . . . Yet visionary companies prosper over long periods of time, through multiple product life cycles and multiple generations of active leaders (Collins & Porras 1994: 1–2).

What distinguished the visionary companies in the Stanford University study was that the companies had core values and ideologies that drove the company—not profits. For example, they cite Johnson and Johnson, 'The company exists to alleviate pain and disease. We have a hierarchy of responsibilities: customers first employees second, society third, and shareholders fourth' (Collins & Porras, 1994, p. 59). Another example was Merck: 'We are in the business of preserving and improving human life. All our activities must be measured by our success in achieving this goal' (Collins & Porras, 1994, p. 481). They were, in Collins and Porras' terminology, 'clock builders', not 'time tellers'.

What they found was remarkable. The visionary companies were fifteen times more profitable than the general market, even though profit was not their primary objective. For example, if you had invested US$1 in the general market in 1926, you would have received a return on investment of US$415 in 1996. If you had invested in the comparison companies you would have had a US$955 return on investment. But if you had invested in the 'visionary' companies, you would have earned a US$6356 return on investment.

There were other significant differences. All of these elite companies have a core ideology that gives guidance and inspiration to the people inside the company. They place great store in a company culture and in inculcating all staff with common values. They also have stable management and tend to recruit their CEOs from within the company. Perhaps most importantly, they set audacious goals for the organisation such as DuPont's aim of becoming a 'zero waste' manufacturer.

A recent study extended Collins and Porras' work by examining whether the visionary companies also outperformed their competitors in their treatment of primary stakeholders other than their owners (Graves & Waddock, 1999). It included employees, customers, society and the environment. This study concluded that there is a link between positive social performance, especially as it relates to stakeholders, and other types of performance, particularly financial.

This study did not look at sustainability specifically. However, we believe that in the next century, sustainability will be a defining issue for profitable business enterprises. The businesses that survive and thrive will be those that can produce goods and services needed by society in a way that does not fundamentally violate the health and productive capacity of the earth and humanity.

Visionary companies in the next century will recognise the need to enlarge their corporate mission to include the sustainable development agenda. But what are the principles corporations will need to achieve sustainability? For all that has been said and written, sustainable development remains an elusive concept. As Brundtland claims, 'to meet the needs of the present without compromising the ability of future generations to meet their own needs is a vision, not a blue-print for action' (Brundtland, 1987, p. 8).

Some companies are attempting to design their own principles and base their action plans upon them. BMW, for example, has adopted the sustainable development agenda early and is now a leader of activity in its sector. It was the first car maker to construct its cars so that they can be deconstructed at the end of their life and the components recycled. It has introduced innovations to dramatically curtail energy use in all its plants—a measure which has included the transport of its new cars between factories by water. It has long placed a high priority on producing cars that minimise pollution and maximise fuel efficiency. It is well advanced in the development of natural gas and electric cars and continues to see hydrogen-fuelled vehicles as the long term solution to transport related pollution. BMW has a set of ecological guidelines to set its direction, undertaking in them to 'use resources in an efficient and conscientious manner and . . . protect the environment in the long term' (BMW, 1997, p. 9).

The guidelines speak of going beyond compliance with regulation in the avoidance of impacts on the environment and to introduce environmental evaluation into every aspect of product design and development. There is particular emphasis on the recycling capacity of products and processes. BMW is a vigorous adherent to ISO14000 and other quality standards.

Shell is another multinational making huge strides in introducing sustainability thinking into its global activities, initiated in response to increasing criticism of some key aspects of its global operations. It has established a worldwide consultative process including external stakeholders that are invited to critique Shell's operations and performance. They have produced a series of strategic documents based on a commitment to sustainable development. One of these documents is a 'Statement of General Business Principles' that identifies the company's responsibilities to shareholders, customers, employees, business associates and society. The last is cast in terms of respect for human rights and a commitment to contribute to sustainable development. There are specific principles relating to the economy, business integrity, political activities, the environment and other areas. Of particular significance is the requirement that regional chairs report annually on progress towards the company's stated goals. Shell is now following BP in acknowledging the seriousness of climate change and investing substantial amounts in the research and development of renewable energy technologies.

All companies seeking to adopt a sustainable development path would benefit from a set of immutable principles known as the Natural Step, which set out the parameters of sustainability. Dr Karl-Henrik Robèrt started the Swedish based movement, by developing such a set of principles. These principles are designed to be a conceptual framework and compass for organisations trying to achieve sustainability. They are based on fundamental scientific understandings and have been endorsed by many scientists worldwide including Nobel laureates. They are simply stated, but have profound implications for companies seeking to apply them (see Chapter 9).

These principles are based on four basic scientific understandings. The first is that matter and energy cannot appear or disappear (the conservation law). The second is that matter and energy tend to spread spontaneously (the second law of thermodynamics). Together the first and second laws of thermodynamics tell us that everything in the universe and on earth spreads, but nothing disappears. The third scientific understanding is that biological and economic value is in the quality, concentration and structure of materials. Substances such as ink, petrol, coal, gold and water are only of value to us in so far as they are pure and concentrated. None of the above are of any value if they are dispersed into the environment. And finally, green plant cells are essentially the only net producers of concentration and structure through photosynthesis. Humans can and do produce high quality concentration and structure, however for every 100 lbs (45 kg) of product produced in the US today, 3200 lbs (1450 kg) of waste is generated (Hawken, 1997).

These principles have been successfully used by over 100 major corporations worldwide with some very impressive results. Among them are Electrolux, Ikea and Interface. Interface alone is saving over US\$167 million per year on their sustainability initiatives. This is enough to fully fund their remaining sustainability initiatives.[2] Being a principled company may involve extra costs but it can also generate extra profits that more than cover the costs.

By using a set of guiding principles, a corporation can provide its people with a sort of compass or rule book so that all parts of the organisation are moving in the same direction. This is particularly important for the designers of processes and products within any corporation. In addressing the vital issue of design for sustainability, William McDonough, Dean of the University of Virginia School of Architecture, has said: 'There are four R's not just three . . . Reduce, Reuse, Recycle and Redesign'. McDonough has developed three simple principles to use in his design work. They are:

- waste equals food—this principle encourages the elimination of the concept of waste in industrial design so that the products themselves, as well as leftover chemicals, materials and effluents can become food for other processes
- rely on current solar income—use only non-carbon fuels, and redesign energy use to be highly efficient

- respect diversity—this requires the evaluation of every design for its potential impacts on all aspects of the biosphere.

McDonough has used these principles in the design of many buildings such as the Heinz Foundation Headquarters in Pittsburgh, which include extensive energy efficiency designs like the use of natural light and fresh air, as well as sustainably produced tropical hardwoods for the furniture. In the redesign of an upholstery plant in Switzerland, McDonough is famous for the fact that the water coming out of the plant is now cleaner than the water going into it.

The Ethical Investment funds, discussed above, have also been active in the development of sustainability principles through the establishment of the Coalition for Environmentally Responsible Economies (CERES) in 1989. The idea for CERES came from the socially responsible investment community's need to procure reliable information about companies' environmental performance and impact. Companies have been invited to adopt the CERES principles as an indication of their commitment to sustainable development. The principles are as follows:

- Protection of the biosphere—Reduction and progress toward eliminating the release of substances that may cause environmental damage to the earth or its inhabitants. Protecting open spaces and preserving biodiversity.
- Sustainable use of natural resources—Sustainable use of renewable natural resources and conservation of non-renewable natural resources through efficient use and careful planning.
- Reduction and disposal of wastes—Reduction or elimination of waste through source reduction and recycling.
- Energy conservation—Conservation of energy and improved energy efficiency of operations, goods and services. Use of environmentally safe and sustainable energy sources.
- Risk reduction—Minimise the environmental, health and safety risks to employees and communities.
- Safe products and services—Reduce or eliminate the use, manufacture or sale of products and services that cause environmental damage or health or safety hazards.
- Environmental restoration—Promptly and responsibly correct conditions that endanger health, safety or the environment and redress injuries to persons or damage to the environment.
- Informing the public—Inform everyone affected of conditions caused by the signatory that might endanger health, safety or the environment. Regularly seek advice and counsel with communities and refrain from actions against employees for reporting dangerous incidents or conditions.

- Management commitment—Implement and sustain a process that ensures the board and CEO are fully informed about pertinent environmental issues and are fully responsible for environment policy.
- Audits and reports—Conduct an annual self-evaluation of the implementation of these principles, including annual completion of CERES report, which will be made available to the public.

The 'Earth Enterprise Tool Kit' produced by the International Institute for Sustainable Development (IISD, 1994), provides a framework checklist that corporations can use for procurement and product development. While the checklist is not in itself a set of principles, it is a working application of principles. Put another way, it would be possible to draw principles from the checklist. The key questions they pose include the following:

The first and overriding question is whether the product or service is truly necessary. More specifically:

- Does the product use fewer polluting byproducts than competing products?
- Is the product durable and easily, safely and economically serviced?
    - Are any components of required maintenance environmentally damaging?
    - Are all the features of the product necessary?
    - Is the company producing the product in compliance with all environmental laws and regulations?
- Are you aware of any product alternatives that are more environmentally responsible?
    - Is the product designed to reduce consumption?
    - Is the product designed to minimise waste?
    - Is the product reusable?
    - Is the product technically and economically recyclable?
    - Do facilities exist to recycle the product?
    - Are recycling collection systems in place at the point of end use?
    - Can the product be returned to the supplier at the end of its useful life?
    - Is the product compostable?
- Are recycled materials used in the product? If so, what percentage? What percentage of post-consumer materials is used?
- Is the product energy efficient?
    - Can the product be recharged?
    - Can the product run on renewable fuels?
    - Does the product reduce water use?
- Does the product require special disposal?

- Is the product free of any banned substances? Heavy metals?
- Is the product free of toxic or endangered materials?
- Does the product emit volatile organic compounds or other air pollutants?
- Does the product require special use instructions for health and safety?
- Can the packaging be eliminated?
    - Is the packaging designed to be minimal?
    - Is the product packaged in bulk?
    - Is the packaging reusable or recyclable?
    - Are recycled materials used to produce the packaging?
    - Can the packaging be returned to the supplier?
    - Is the package compostable?
- Has a life cycle analysis of the environmental burdens associated with the product or packaging been conducted by a certified testing organisation?
- Is the company producing the product equipped to bid and bill electronically?
- Does the company have an environmental policy statement?
    - What is the company's history on environmental and safety issues?
    - Can the company verify all environmental claims?
    - What waste reduction programs does the company have in place? Planned?
    - Has the company conducted an environmental or waste audit?
    - Is the company responsive to information requests from stakeholders?

'The Earth Enterprise Tool Kit' continues with Characteristics of Sustainable Technologies. These are:

- Low environment impact—These are technologies which have very low or benign emissions to the environment in production, use and disposal. They have no toxic releases and benefit the environment indirectly through their use and/or inherent efficiency.
- Resource efficiency—These are technologies which have efficient utilisation of material resources, often using recycled material, based on renewable resources and energy (or minimal use of non-renewable resources). They feature efficient consumption of energy in production and use and are durable, reusable and/or recyclable.
- Economic advantages—Sustainable technologies are also economically cost effective compared to conventional product or service, incorporating externalities in market price. They can be financed by

the user through various financial saving streams, and they improve productivity or competitiveness of industry and commerce.

■   Social advantages—Sustainable technologies also enhance or maintain living standards or quality of life. They are readily available and accessible by all classes and cultures and are consistent with themes of decentralisation, individual control and democracy.

These guidelines or principles have obvious embedded values, as is the case with any set of principles. Collins and Porras found that a key strength of each of their visionary companies was a clearly articulated set of values that drove the business. The values inherent in any set of principles need to be transparently related to the overall mission and objectives of the corporation using them. This is an essential part of the integration of a corporate sustainability philosophy. Principles such as the Natural Step ones described in Chapter 9 only have meaning when applied to the activities and circumstances of the corporations using them. They are not a blueprint, but a framework for creating one.

It is apparent when examining the development of principles articulated above that they are 'works in progress'. There is ongoing work to refine and expand them. One obvious conclusion to be drawn is that there is greater focus to date on principles relating to the environment. This is not completely unexpected, given the intense focus given to problems in this arena. But it is not true to say that social issues have been ignored. The fourth of the Natural Step principles is a 'social' rather than scientific one, pointing to the hopelessness of seeking sustainable practices if fundamental inequities in the allocation of the world's resources remain. We will never achieve our goal of commerce, nature and society in equilibrium if 80 per cent of the earth's people live in abject poverty.

The socially responsible investors have begun to place increasing attention on the 'social' agenda by rejecting companies that invest in undemocratic regimes, such as Burma. They black-list companies making products using child labour or discriminatory employment practices. It was, after all, anti-apartheid campaigners who initiated shareholder activism in the 1970s, which has led to the massive ethical investment market of today.

It is comparatively easy to extrapolate social principles for the sustainable corporations of the future. Shell, for one, is working on its own, which refer to openness, transparency, respect for human rights, the rejection of bribery and so on. One can create a simple checklist of prohibited activities, such as employment of child labour. It is the adoption of these shibboleths, not their formulation, which constitutes the real challenge.

Martin Bennett and Peter James (1999) identify fourteen key factors in evaluating social performance. They include: human rights; labour conditions (including child labour, collective bargaining); supply chain and overseas suppliers (including fair trade and factory monitoring); consumer products (including safety and quality); technology transfer and investment in emerging economies; trade with oppressive regimes; defense and weapons; alcohol, tobacco, gambling and pornography; animal testing; philanthropy and volunteerism; community development; downsizing and restructuring; employment policies and empowerment (including affirmative action, sexual harassment); and stakeholder relations and accountability.

The pressure on business to adopt some form of principles as a framework for future activity is now irresistible. At the Davos meeting of the World Economic Forum in February 2000, President Clinton, Prime Minister Tony Blair, World Bank President Jim Wolfensohn and UN Secretary-General Kofi Annan all called on the CEOs assembled to meet the needs of a much broader set of stakeholders than just their shareholders. Annan released the UN's own principles in the form of a Global Compact and challenged world business leaders to 'embrace and enact' the Global Compact, both in their individual corporate practices and by supporting appropriate public policies in three major areas, as follows:

1 Human rights
   Principle 1: support and respect the protection of international human rights within their sphere of influence; and
   Principle 2: make sure their own corporations are not complicit in human rights abuses.
2 Labour standards
   Principle 3: freedom of association and the effective recognition of the right to collective bargaining;
   Principle 4: the elimination of all forms of forced and compulsory labour;
   Principle 5: the effective abolition of child labour; and
   Principle 6: the elimination of discrimination in respect of employment and occupation.
3 Environment
   Principle 7: support a precautionary approach to environmental challenges;
   Principle 8: undertake initiatives to promote greater environmental responsibility; and
   Principle 9: encourage the development and diffusion of environmentally friendly technologies.

Conclusion

There are now many hundreds of examples of corporations and civic organisations developing and applying sustainability principles. Of the plethora of examples we could chose from, we selected a diverse range to demonstrate the value of using principles in achieving corporate sustainability.

We began with the question: Why Guiding Principles? The answer is simple. There is insufficient time for each corporation to develop its own philosophical framework and principles. There is no need for each corporation to reinvent the wheel. Billions of corporations and communities around the globe must transform their activities to achieve sustainability. To assist them in the task, we must develop principles to guide actions, which are transparent and easy to understand and apply. From these, individual corporations and communities can develop their own plans of action, which if well found, will produce the quantum leap needed for the new commerce of the sustainable future.

Endnotes

1 Susan Davis, Capitol Missions Company, personal communication.
2 Ray Anderson, Interface, personal communication.

References

Bennett, M. and James, P. 1999 (eds) *Sustainable Measures: Evaluation and Reporting of Environmental and Social Performance*, Greenleaf Publishing, Sheffield.
BMW 1997–1998 *The BMW Environment Report*, BMW, Munich, p. 9.
Brundtland, G. H. 1987 *Our Common Future*, World Commission on Environment and Development, Oxford University Press, Oxford.
Carson, R. 1962 *Silent Spring*, Fawcett-Crest Books, Greenwich, Connecticut.
Colborne, T., Dumanoski, D. and Myers, J. 1996 *Our Stolen Future*, Penguin, New York.
Collins, J. C. and Porras, J. I. 1994 *Built to Last*, Harper Collins Publishers, New York.
Ehrlich, P. and Ornstein, R. 1989 *New World New Mind*, Doubleday, New York.
Gore, A. 1996 'Forward' in T. Colborn, D. Dumanoski, J. P. Myers, *Our Stolen Future*, Dutton, New York.

Graves and Waddock 1999 *'Built to Last and Then Some'*, Unpublished paper.

Hawken, P. 1997 'Natural Capitalism', *Mother Jones*, March–April, pp. 40–53.

International Institute for Sustainable Development (IISD) 1994 *Earth Enterprise Tool Kit*, Winnipeg, Manitoba, Canada.

12

Implementing the sustainable corporation

Dexter Dunphy

Introduction

In this book we have created a debate about the nature of sustainability. Sustainability is more a symbol than a scientific concept. Like an icon or a flag, it is a focus for a cluster of related values, aspirations and knowledge in the making. It is the rallying point for an emergent ideology and a new social movement. We have asked the question: 'What is the sustainable corporation?' and our various authors have given differing answers. There is significant overlap but there are also contrasting emphases and divergent opinions. It is vital that this value-based debate proceeds and this book is a contribution to that debate.

Action, however, cannot be delayed until the debate is resolved. Ideas without actions are like birds without wings—they never get off the ground. The urgency of the ecological and social crisis that faces us demands that change begins now. In fact the change is already underway and will not wait upon the reasonable resolution of our differences. Differences in social ideologies are never resolved through value debate alone but rather through a dialectic of dialogue and action, of trying to put ideas into effect, of experimenting, observing and reflecting on experience. We work out our ideologies in the hot human process of engaging with the issues, and with each other, in the complex and messy world of shared hopes and conflicting interests.

So this chapter deals with strategies for implementing the sustainable corporation, suggesting ways in which we can bring the new organisational forms into being. This chapter also touches on the social context required for change, for corporations are not isolated entities but integral cells of the wider society. For this reason, they are critical to the broader move toward sustainability. The core of modern society is the economy and that core is composed of corporations. Any transformation of our relationship to each other and to the planet must take effect at the organisational level or our efforts to create a sustainable society will prove futile. The corporation is not the only arena for action but it is an important one.

Our authors make it clear that the kind of corporate change needed will be no easy transition marked by minor modifications of our current lifestyle and ways of doing business. They argue for the need to change fundamental values and beliefs about ourselves and the world, to thoroughly overhaul and redesign the central production processes of society, to modify market capitalism so that it meets social and ecological objectives. Overall, this is transformative rather than evolutionary change.

Nevertheless, renewing the corporation to ensure that it exemplifies the principles of sustainability will involve both evolutionary and transformative change. There are a number of reasons for this. Some corporations, because of their history, the nature of their industry or their leadership have already made moves toward sustainability. For example, the zero emissions movement and the Natural Step movement have engaged a large number of organisations around the world in sharing ways of dramatically reducing their footprint on the planet (Nattras & Altomare, 1999). For those organisations that are well down this path, the further changes needed will be evolutionary rather than transformative. In some industries, such as those using organic materials, recycling and new environmentally-friendly technologies may make the transition to more sustainable practices relatively easy and painless.

In addition, the social context of organisations is not standing still but is also changing. As the sustainability movement takes hold, the overall social, economic and political environment of corporations will increasingly facilitate the transition to sustainable corporate practices. For example, the elimination of government subsidies which currently support unsustainable practices will create a significant shift in corporate production processes. As these subsidies are currently estimated to be globally US$700 billion a year, their progressive removal will have a significant impact on the behaviour of firms and government instrumentalities (Strong, 1999). There are and will continue to be significant changes to the context in which organisations operate and many of these changes will support the progressive implementation of corporate sustainability.

However, there are corporations whose business practices still plunder and pollute the planet, weaken critical links in the biosphere and degrade and debase the lives of employees and the community. These corporations face either transformation or extinction for human society can no longer tolerate such massive assaults on the web of life or on the social fabric. Increasingly the community will abandon their products and services, they will be unable to attract bright, competent employees and governments will legislate crushing penalties for the negative impacts they make on the ecological environment. There are, however, other organisations where some key practices are not sustainable but where there is commitment to change and to finding a viable way forward that does not threaten the existence of the organisation. Sometimes, however, it is difficult to find practical, easy alternatives to current production methods or wasteful procedures. Where this is the case, these organisations typically face transformative change. So we are in need of intervention strategies of two kinds: those that produce incremental, evolutionary change and those that produce transformational, revolutionary change. In this chapter we review both.

Creating the enabling context

Many corporations are already being radically reshaped by economic, political and social forces. To the extent that these forces are compatible with and even encourage the changes we need to put in place to achieve sustainability, we can work with them. Just as the carver of jade seeks the 'grain' of the jade and works with it rather than against it, the agents of corporate change can align their actions with powerful social forces that are already reshaping and renewing corporations. For example, modern communication technologies allow knowledge to be shared instantly, facilitating exchange of information between and within organisations about the application and implementation of sustainability principles. What are some of the enabling forces favourable to corporate sustainability and how can they be used to move organisations more rapidly down the sustainability path?

One of these enablers is the widespread realisation that we are reaching the limits of the politics of greed. When international figures such as George Soros become critics of key aspects of market capitalism and argue for the imposition of social restraints on its operation, there clearly is need to reconsider the virtue and beneficence of the 'invisible hand' of market forces (Soros, 1998). Similarly, when the President of the New York Stock Exchange advocates that companies listed on the exchange undertake systematic human resource accounting, it is clear that people are indeed being increasingly viewed as a potential resource rather than simply a source of regrettable costs. Major moves to increase corporate accountability are taking place across the world and can provide a political platform for the introduction of sustainability measures.

Another major influence on organisations is the transition to the knowledge-based economy. The markets for knowledge and services are currently far more extensive than the markets for goods. Knowledge workers dominate the workforce in advanced economies. This dematerialisation of the economy—the move to intangibles—is creating a context more conducive to both ecological and human sustainability. From the ecological point of view, the move to intangible assets can support moves to reduce our impact on the natural world. It also provides a positive alternative and reward for moving away from non-sustainable practices. To quote Katrina Garnett, an Australian who is President and co-founder of CrossWorlds Software, a leading Silicon Valley software company: 'You want to cry "Come on, Australia, wake up, smell the coffee, get moving!" Digging stuff out of the ground to export seems, well, Dark Ages stuff.'

Building 'knowledge capital' and providing services are now more likely to create competitive advantage for a firm than being a supplier of raw materials or a traditional manufacturer of material goods. The increasing number of knowledge workers in the workforce also increases the likelihood that there are more people in organisations who can grapple with complexity and think in whole system terms—prerequisites for radically redesigning corporations for sustainability.

So the economic, political and social context of organisations will increasingly provide rewards for organisations to move to sustainable practices and bring pressure to bear on those organisations that fail to respond. However, we would be naive to imagine that the entire social context will be enabling—we can also expect powerful countervailing pressures to provide some skirmishes and stoushes along the way, particularly as the sustainability movement gains momentum.

As enthusiasm, support and commitment for the sustainability movement build up, opposing ideologies with a strong stake in the status quo or in alternative future scenarios will also be energised. Their proponents will actively seek to counter the values, discredit the champions and subvert the programs of the sustainability movement. Often a measure of the relative success of a social movement is the controversy and opposition it arouses. Significant shifts in social values rarely take place through consensus-seeking processes. Rather they occur through dramatic and symbolic enactments of conflict between the protagonists of opposing forces or through traumatic social experiences like the fall of the Berlin Wall, that shatter a prevailing but increasingly fragile world view.

In this chapter we are concerned primarily with corporate change strategies that can be consciously used by internal or external change

agents. However, we need to keep in mind that the sustainability movement as a whole needs to be operating on the broader fronts of economic,
political and social change so that we maximise the positive context
for corporate change. In addition, corporate change agents need to be
aware of and actively connect with enabling forces in the wider context.

Chapter 1 of this book outlined a model of the phases of corporate
sustainability. This model identified six phases in corporate progression
toward full sustainability. These are:

- rejection
- non-responsiveness
- compliance/risk reduction
- efficiency
- strategic sustainability
- ideological commitment.

(For more details see Chapter 1, particularly Appendix 1.1). These phases
emphasise that there is an enormous difference in the readiness of various
organisations to move toward sustainable practices. Some firms are highly
advanced in terms of having sustainable human resource practices; others
have scarcely given them a thought or actually pursue profit by exploiting
their workforce. The same is true in the area of ecological sustainability—some firms are actively working toward practices which sustain and
renew the environment while others continue to exploit the environment
as if there were no tomorrow. Because traditionally the two kinds of
sustainability have rarely been seen as connected, there can also be a lack
of conjunction between an organisation's current position on one dimension and on the other. So, for example, a firm may be highly advanced
in terms of having exemplary human resource practices and community
relations but be involved in environmentally destructive resource extraction or production processes. Conversely a firm may be highly
responsible in their environmental practices but make little or no investment in the capabilities, knowledge and skills of their workforce.

Ideally what we need to develop and institutionalise in corporations
is a fully integrated corporate philosophy of sustainability that abandons
the exploitation and degradation of both human and natural resources
for a positive commitment to pursuing the maintenance and renewal of
those resources. This life-affirming philosophy must be clearly evidenced
in consistent practices that are its embodiment and expression. Progress
on a single dimension is good but it is not enough—it is like trying to
walk the path of sustainability on one leg instead of two.

The ideal of a fully sustainable corporation is outlined in Figure
12.1. Figure 12.1 combines the scales of the two dimensions in the
phases of corporate sustainability on to a matrix. In the first cell (upper

Figure 12.1 A categorisation of corporate sustainability development profiles

Ecological sustainability

	Low Phases 1–3	Phases 4–6 High
Low Phases 1–3	1 The unsustainable corporation	2 The ecologically-concerned corporation
Phases 4–6 **High**	3 The people-concerned corporation	4 The sustainable corporation

Human sustainability

left hand quadrant) we have those organisations that are on the lower end of both human and ecological sustainability, being actively rejecting, indifferent or simply minimally compliant to both human and ecological sustainability issues. Clearly we want to move corporations that are in this quadrant out of it as rapidly as possible. The goal is to move more and more organisations to the lower right hand quadrant which represents varying degrees of active involvement on the bases of efficiency, strategic advantage or commitment (or some combination of these factors). The most challenging transformational change is to move directly from quadrant 1 to quadrant 4. By contrast, those organisations that have already made substantial progress on either ecological or human sustainability (quadrants 2 and 3 respectively) may be able to take a more evolutionary and incremental path to full sustainability. What we will explore in the next section of this chapter are the kinds of change interventions that may be suitable in these different kinds of transitions.

Taking charge of corporate change: an overview of evolutionary and transformative approaches

One major debate that has preoccupied theorists of organisational change for the last twenty years has centred around the issue of whether organisations should change incrementally or transformationally. The debate has been complicated by the search for the 'quick fix' to problems created by the rapid transformation of markets, economic deregulation and the globalisation of business. A very human response to new and challenging circumstances is to seek a quick, simple and ready made answer that will solve the confusion and burgeoning problems of a world that suddenly seems out of control. There has been no dearth of management gurus, particularly from the US, proffering, at a high price, the latest snake oil remedies—simple prescriptions for corporate change that represent a universal solution—the 'one right way' to change an organisation and solve all its ills in all situations. However, to quote H. L. Mencken, 'To every human problem there is a neat and easy solution—and it's wrong' (Mencken, 1996).

Over the last ten years, a colleague—Doug Stace—and I have conducted extensive field research to determine how corporate transitions can be successfully managed (Dunphy & Stace, 1991; Stace & Dunphy, 1994). The research has shown that there is no single path to successful change implementation that holds in all situations. However, we have found that we can define a small number of viable routes to success, each of which works in particular circumstances.[1]

The central model of organisational change arising from our research is shown in Figure 12.2, our original conceptual model of change. It features two dimensions. The lateral dimension defines the scale of change in terms of four levels: fine-tuning, incremental adjustment, modular transformation and corporate transformation. (Modular transformation is transformation of a significant part of the organisation, such as a division or a stratum of the organisation such as middle management.) The vertical dimension defines the style of change management in terms of four levels that relate to the way the organisation's executive leadership or dominant elite leads the process of change. This matrix allows us to describe any organisation, or organisational unit, at a particular time in terms of these two important dimensions and also use the matrix to track the organisation's path of change over its history.

The shaded area of Figure 12.2 is the position where corporate financial performance is maximised. In our research, we asked financial analysts to rate the performance of the organisations we studied. We found that performance was highest where the organisations were changing fast enough to keep pace with their commercial environment but not undergoing frame breaking change. Similarly, the most productive management styles were consultative or directive, or a combination of both, not collaborative or coercive. While frame breaking change and coercive change leadership might be necessary at times to bring an

Figure 12.2 The Dunphy–Stace change matrix

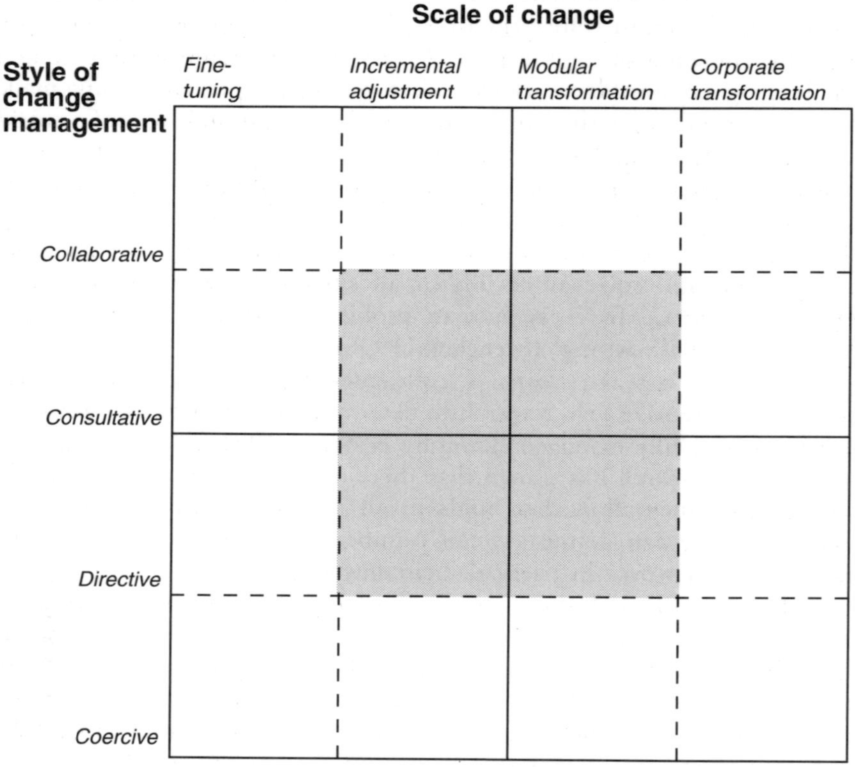

Scale of change

Style of change management	Fine-tuning	Incremental adjustment	Modular transformation	Corporate transformation
Collaborative				
Consultative				
Directive				
Coercive				

Source: Stace & Dunphy, 1994

organisation back into fit with its environment, its immediate impact on productivity is usually negative. Relentless mid-range change, led consultatively or directively, is the way to create sustainable success in business terms.

Despite this, we found that a majority of organisations went through at least one period of transformative change in a five year period. Such large scale transformative change generally arose from a crisis in performance as the organisation's traditional strategies failed in the face of massive environmental change. Often managers' initial instinctive response to such a situation is to work harder at the unsuccessful irrelevant traditional management practices that once brought success. Successful change was usually only initiated, however, when the board was reconstituted or a new, externally recruited CEO was appointed who immediately moved to make radical changes in the organisation's mission, strategies, structures, processes and values. Such change is usually painful for those involved, demotivating for the workforce, and initially only exacerbates the crisis in corporate performance.

By contrast there were some organisations that maintained consistently high performance levels without going through one or more periods of frame breaking change. These organisations constantly monitored their environments, progressively repositioning themselves strategically, making continuous innovations and improvements—not product innovation alone but also innovation in their structures, systems and workplace practices.

Continuous change of this kind is more and more replacing the old 'stop, reorganise, start again' approaches to organisational change. This can be seen most clearly in the newer high-tech industries. Firms like Hewlett Packard, for example, estimate that products such as printers will be overtaken by a competitive product within three to five months of being launched. In fact, they strive to 'eat their own lunch' by introducing the next competitive product themselves first. Similarly, the rapiconvergence of new technologies that is happening with increasing speed creates new industries. In the information technology field, for example, such a convergence can lead an organisation such as Ericsson to continuously reinvent itself.

Constant change is therefore the new norm and, paradoxically, while this is currently creating a plethora of new products, increasing waste and pollution, it also prepares the ground for the potential of a rapid transformation to new sustainable practices. The heavy determinism of traditional structures and practices is giving way to a commitment to opportunity driven change. The corporate world is being increasingly drawn forward by future vision rather than captured by precedent and past practices. Our task is to ensure that the new visions embody sustainable practices.

The central dilemma facing modern organisations is to achieve an appropriate balance between putting resources into maintaining current performance and into reshaping the organisation for future performance. This dilemma is clearly identified by another study carried out by Dennis Turner and Michael Crawford (1998). This statistically-based study of 243 cases of organisational change demonstrated that effective performance was dependent on the organisation investing in corporate capabilities that gave it competitive advantage. The authors identified two important kinds of capabilities. The first set they called *operational capabilities* and these provide the basis for current performance and results. The second set they called *reshaping capabilities* and these enable the organisation to change effectively, thus providing the basis for future performance. Clearly what we have been identifying above as incremental and transformative approaches to change are ways of building reshaping competencies. But effective change creates a productive balance between operational and reshaping capabilities. If the organisation concentrates on operational performance alone, it fails to make sufficient adjustment to its dynamic environment; if it is forced into organisation-wide transformational change, it is unable to put sufficient resources into maintaining current operations and its performance also declines. High performance comes from simultaneously managing for today while working actively to reshape the organisation for the future.

Currently most organisations are better at managing operational performance than managing organisational renewal (reshaping). The competencies involved in managing operational performance are familiar to most managers, are generally rewarded, and are readily gained through experience and/or formal training. The competencies for reshaping organisations are, by contrast, not nearly so familiar to managers, are often not rewarded and are not widely available through the experience and/or training. However, as we have moved into a much more dynamic world, reshaping competencies are more widely needed for effective corporate performance. And as we face the challenge of reshaping our organisations for ongoing sustainability, including ecological sustainability, the competencies involved in corporate reshaping will become central. These are precisely the competencies needed to make the shift to sustainable corporate practices and we must support the accelerated development of these reshaping competencies.

Evolutionary approaches to corporate change

We have noted that there will be some organisations that will be able to reach the ideal of the sustainable organisation through an evolutionary transition. We now return to outline the conditions under which such an approach is appropriate, the kinds of intervention strategies that are available to make the change, the characteristics of evolutionary change and its major advantages and disadvantages. We will then follow this discussion with a parallel one for transformational approaches.

In research previously referred to (Dunphy & Stace, 1991; Stace & Dunphy, 1994), Doug Stace and I distinguished two evolutionary approaches to corporate change. These we referred to as *developmental transitions* and *task focused transitions*. Both have in common a consistent and persistent evolutionary drive to make continuous innovatory change. They differ, however, in the focus of the change process and the way in which performance is addressed. Developmental transitions are characteristic of professionalised, service-based organisations such as banks or software companies, although they are not limited to them. In these organisations, the secret of maintaining high performance lies in building the competencies of the members of the organisation and developing voluntary commitment to a shared vision of continual improvement. Over time, they systematically build up the intellectual capital that is the driving factor in their success. Service industries favour this approach as people are so central to success. Consequently human sustainability issues are likely to dominate the change agenda with ecological sustainability being secondary. Organisations that employ this approach to move toward the ideal of sustainability will need to work actively to involve organisational members in developing a vision of what sustainability means for their organisation in their industry. Most service sector industries do not leave as heavy a footprint on global ecology as do capital intensive industries operating in areas such as mineral extraction and manufacturing, so their human sustainability policies and practices will dominate over the ecological.

Leadership of a developmental transition needs to be highly interactive, responsive to initiatives at all levels of the organisation and operate on a collegial and consultative basis. In this approach to change, vision is an emerging phenomenon, there is widespread involvement of people throughout the organisation in the change process and a great deal of bottom-up planning of ongoing change. Ownership of the change process is developed by creating shared experiences around the development of new organisational norms and values. As this occurs, the members of the organisation increasingly develop the skills needed to build a strong corporate capability for continuous corporate renewal—rganisational change becomes a way of life for everyone in the organissation. An organisation like Hewlett Packard, for example, has based its business strategy on constant corporate innovation supported by the recruitment and development of high calibre staff.

The major intervention strategies that are used in developmental transitions are listed in Box 12.1.

The strengths of this approach are the involvement and ownership that often develop, the number and variety of initiatives emerging in the organisation and the energy for change that can, over time, build sustained momentum. There are, however, also potential downsides. Even where there is a committed board, CEO and executive team, there is the potential loss of control and direction and the vulnerability to diversion from initial goals inherent in highly participative processes. There are high levels of skill needed to coordinate disparate initiatives and emergent leaders. There is also the time consuming nature of participative processes. The delays involved can lead to cynicism on the

Box 12.1 Major intervention strategies that are used in developmental transitions

Change intervention tools typically used:

- Vision/mission development (consultative)
- Culture enhancement programs
- Team building (self-managed work teams)
- Management and team leadership development programs
- Service quality programs
- Personal and professional development/skills formation
- TQM, process benchmarking programs
- Building corporate competencies
- Radical delegation/empowerment of staff
- Developing horizontal organisation structures

part of some organisational members about whether any real change will ever occur and can provide competitors with a window of opportunity to move more quickly and seize a significant advantage.

This brings us to the other major variant of evolutionary change—task focused transitions. Task focused transitions are more characteristic of organisations in industries with heavy investment in capital equipment—for example, mining, power production and telecommunications. In organisations of this kind, the secret of high performance is to maximise the return on the heavy investment in technology. Consequently change focuses on technology enhancement and systems redesign; it is task focused because high performance is secured by the effective deployment of people in technical tasks around the technology. Within most organisations there will be business units where the emphasis will be on cost containment and others where it will be on product innovation.

In capital intensive organisations making significant change, the main emphasis is likely to be on ecological sustainability with a secondary emphasis on human sustainability. Industries with heavy capital investment in plant and machinery will be increasingly the focus of external attempts from governments and community bodies to examine the ratio of 'goods' to 'bads' that they produce and to significantly decrease or eliminate the bads (for example, pollution and resource waste). There will be increasing inspection of supply, processing and distribution chains and demands for efficiency of resource use along the entire chain with the elimination, reduction and recycling of 'wastes'. We are learning that

Box 12.2 Major intervention strategies that are used in task oriented transitions

Change intervention tools typically used:

- Systems redesign
- Workforce planning/right-sizing
- Job redesign/business process redesign/re-engineering
- Productivity measurement and improvement
- Strategic and process benchmarking
- Objective setting/MBO/performance contracts/appraisal
- Strong technical skills training
- Management and team leadership development
- TQM, continuous improvement

one organisation's waste can be another organisation's resource. For example, the coal-fired Pacific Power Eraring power generating plant now converts the sewage from its surrounding community into clean water using a Memtech filtration plant. This is a win–win for Pacific Power and the community as Pacific Power no longer buys water for washing coal and the community has avoided the cost of building an ocean outfall (Dunphy, 1999).

The major change strategies used in task oriented transitions are shown in Box 12.2.

Change strategies in task oriented transitions focus on improving structures, systems and technical processes. Workplace redesign is central. Productivity benchmarking and measurement, quality control and technical skill training are also vital. Leadership is directed to planning, initiating and evaluating key system changes. Leadership is often top-down and directive, particularly in terms of business strategies, financial objectives and vision. There is, however, usually consultation and involvement in the implementation of technology and system changes at the workplace.

The strengths of this approach to change are the clarity of objectives and organisation-wide communication, the systematic plans and strategies used. However, the lack of involvement in setting the organisation's overall goals and strategies can reduce workforce commitment to the planned changes so that the changes are not fully implemented. As we move toward sustainability, this poses a dilemma. Sustainability will demand a new mindset on the part of all or most within the corporation. An important aspect of implementing change will be creating the conditions for this changed mindset. This is most readily achieved through people's participation in changes designed to foster corporate practices that increase sustainability. There is likely to be a disjunction here between the need for decisive executive action for reshaping of technical systems and processes and the need to involve and educate the workforce to win their commitment, shifting established attitudes and work practices. Managing this disjunction requires considerable behavioural flexibility on the part of change agents as well as workforce flexibility.

Transformative approaches to corporate change

We have discussed evolutionary approaches to change and when they may be most appropriate in moving organisations along the path to sustainability. But there will be many organisations where such gradualist approaches will be insufficient in scope or speed to meet the exigencies generated by the global crisis created by unsustainable ecological practices. In these organisations, change may need to be truly trans- formative— thoroughly dissolving old structures and processes and creating a new corporate identity fundamentally different from the old. A biological analogy may be useful: When a caterpillar creates a cocoon in order to transform itself into a butterfly, the process is not completed by minor or even significant structural modification of the caterpillar's body. Rather what happens inside the cocoon is a thoroughgoing transformative process—the caterpillar body dissolves into a biological 'soup' and the constituent cells regroup to form the new body whose characteristics are determined by the need for flight, mating and an entirely different way of feeding.

Transformative change in organisations is similar in that the new form taken by the organisation may be unrecognisable by anyone who has not witnessed the transition. The organisation often emerges with a new name, a new vision and business strategy, a new structure, a significantly different skill mix in the workforce; it may operate in a different industry or industries, have new suppliers, different products, new leadership and a new culture.

Transformative change is an imperative for most of those organisations we have located in the upper left hand quadrant (1) of Figure 12.1, that is, those organisations that have been actively opposed to introducing sustainable practices, have regarded them as irrelevant or have engaged in minimal compliance to legal requirements and community expectations. The move from a traditional culture based on an exploitative approach to both human and ecological resources to a new culture based on conservation, regeneration and renewal of those resources will not be achieved in an evolutionary fashion. The growing urgency of the environmental crisis on the one hand and the substantial shift to a knowledge-based society on the other mean that organisational survival will depend on a difficult journey through the melting pot of corporate transformation. What do we know about this process? This is the lesson that Skandic Hotels learned as it moved from initial bankruptcy to being the leading hotel chain in Europe (Nattras & Altomare, 1999).

We know a great deal about the process given the massive changes occurring in organisations worldwide in response to globalisation, tariff reductions and economic deregulation. The corporate changes consequent upon these massive changes in the economic and social environment have been painful for many but a useful training ground for the even more massive societal and corporate reorganisation that will be required by the move to sustainable societal and corporate practices.

Typically transformative change requires a rapid, radical redefinition of the organisation's core business, new business strategies, market redefinition, successive corporate and workplace restructures and reformulating the corporation's core culture. This is a paradigm shifting exercise requiring courageous and visionary leadership, a challenge to existing values and the management of an internal and external political process through which existing stakeholder perceptions and relations are altered.

Once again, we have distinguished two important variant approaches to transformational change. The first we have termed *charismatic transformation* and the second *turnaround*. In a charismatic transformation, the change can be led from the front by a charismatic leader who inspires and enthuses others to make dramatic changes in the way the organisation operates. A great deal of the change in mindset and behaviour is achieved through voluntary compliance, sparked particularly by the top team effectively involving organisational members in the creation of a new vision and then role modelling the new values and behaviours needed to move the organisation forward. Charismatic transformation can create high energy for change and maintain the momentum of change in difficult circumstances. The main intervention strategies used in charismatic transformations are shown in Box 12.3.

However charismatic transformation can only occur when the key interest groups and organisational stakeholders support the need for change and are willing to actively participate in or at least allow the process of transformation to go forward. It also demands one or more charismatic leaders with whom organisational members can create a strong sense of identification. Given that every move from an established status quo threatens someone or some group and that there is a shortage of leaders with the personality and skills to be charismatic, these conditions are rarely fully present.

Box 12.3 Major intervention strategies that are used in charismatic transitions

Change intervention tools typically used:

- New vision/mission
- Radical organic restructuring, right-sizing, voluntary redundancies
- New executive recruits, often from outside
- Top team building programs
- Cross-functional task teams
- Service excellence programs
- Symbolic communication (change of corporate name, logo and wardrobe, excellence awards)

In the absence of widespread support for transformational change, turnaround is the alternative path forward. Turnaround is a high risk strategy mounted by a committed elite, usually but not always the executive team. The radical new vision for the organisation's future either has to be imposed on those groups who are opposed to the change or negotiated with them. Some of the change interventions will be unilateral and confrontational and change will be in part a political operation. In the end, the committed elite needs to be able to create a political coalition with sufficient power either to impose a new order on those who oppose it or to remove the opposing elements from the organisation. Even if this is achieved, the elite still have the problem of building an expanded commitment on the part of those remaining in the organisation. The main intervention strategies used in turnarounds are shown in Box 12.4.

Box 12.4 Major intervention strategies that are used in turnarounds

Change intervention tools typically used:

- Strategy and market segmentation analysis
- Merger/acquisition/divestment of non-core business
- Restructuring/downsizing/right-sizing/forced retrenchments
- Reconstruction and development of the top team
- Cultural and industrial confrontation strategies
- Radical business process redesign
- Human resource strategy redesign

Key success factors in corporate change programs

Successful change programs share some common characteristics whether they are evolutionary or transformative. They are planned with care yet are opportunistic in remaining open to modification in the light of unforeseen events or developments. They are managed with an awareness that any significant change program is a political operation which must realistically assess and deal with the perceived interests of organisational stakeholders. Yet they need to exemplify integrity, openness and equity. They employ a range of intervention strategies that are integrated and 'bundled' for maximum effect—seldom is a single intervention enough to change a complex organisational system. Yet the overall strategy must be articulated simply enough to be widely understood by people at all levels of the organisation. Finally, change programs are only successful if initiated and led by skilled change agents who pay attention to the ongoing process of change as it affects the understanding, emotions and relationships of those who are involved in the change, both within and outside the organisation. The numbers of effective change agents of this kind are limited and, given the task ahead in moving to sustainability, we need programs to train and develop them in large numbers.[2]

This brings us to the question of who the agents of change are and how they can be deployed in bringing about significant change.

Agents of change

Any major corporate change program demands a variety of change agents who play differing but complementary roles. Central to effective change are the organisation's executives and managers. Subject to the limitations placed on their actions by boards of management, financial institutions and markets, these are the organisational members who have the most authority and power to move the organisation to adopt sustainability principles and practices. However, if they are primarily insiders, their knowledge and attitudes will have been shaped by the prevailing organisational culture. Cultures tend to perpetuate themselves with executives choosing others to replace them who share similar characteristics. While senior executives often have the greatest power to initiate change, they are often the least likely to do so. For this reason, in the last decade we have seen boards replacing CEOs at two to three year intervals, seeking to bring in cultural 'cleanskins' committed to the change program desired by the board.

It is vital to secure the commitment of senior executives to sustainability principles. One powerful lead has been set by former US Assistant Secretary of State Eileen Clauson who now heads the not-for-profit Pew Center in the US which addresses the business challenge posed by climate change. The Pew Center works actively with a consortium of 22 major multinational companies such as Toyota, BP, 3M and Boeing. Such consortia can provide the kinds of active and informed interchange across senior levels of influential companies that will create increasing commitment to sustainability at the point of organisational power where there is the greatest leverage for change.

It is also important that boards and financial analysts are subjected to similar influence attempts, for they write the core rules and rewards which influence the decisions of CEOs and senior executives. Here the power of ethical investment funds is critical. Such funds now control billions of dollars. Ethical investment funds can play an important role in convincing the financial markets that real commitment to sustainability principles at the senior levels of companies can lead to positive financial returns and that failure to act in accordance with these principles can lead to significant reductions in share price. At the moment, the financial markets often act as though issues of sustainability are irrelevant to a company's value, or worse, are simply a source of added costs. As we have seen in other chapters in this book, the reality is that sustainability policies can have major positive effects on key business outcomes.

Other internal change agents are so-called staff functionaries such as strategic human resource planners, internal organisation development (OD) and business process re-engineering (BPR) consultants and trainers. Effective change programs require coalitions of such change agents who work to a common agenda and coordinate the overall impact of their separate change interventions on the company as a whole. One important aspect of such a coordinated approach to change is the development of grassroots leaders in the organisation who act collaboratively with the guiding coalition of change agents to support the progressive implementation of change throughout the entire organisation. There is an immediate need for the creation of basic introductory courses in sustainability principles and practices, with many case examples, to help create an informed organisational 'citizenry' from which these grassroots leaders can be selected or, better still, self-select. Such courses are currently in the early stages of development but are available.

Important too for effective corporate change programs are external professional change agents who can provide skills and expertise beyond those readily available within the organisation. The practice of change management is already a substantial rising profession. (Anderson Consulting, for example, has over 3000 organisational change practitioners worldwide.) Issues of sustainability must be brought to the forefront of the attention of professional change agents. For them to be effective, there is a need to develop systematic techniques, interventions and packaged programs for analysing the current level of sustainability of an organisation's human and technical systems, setting sustainability development goals and designing suitable change programs to move the organisation closer to an ideal position. There are now professional consultants specialising in corporate sustainability. However, it is also vital that the mainstream consulting companies actively pursue a sustainability agenda.

Other change agents can be academics and community activists who generate new ideas, contribute to the emerging sustainability debate, popularise the emerging ethos and engage public attention, and create external pressure for change on specific organisations. Powerful social movements develop a mix of prophets, popularisers and practitioners who together advance the central debate, draw in more and more people, generate energy and enthusiasm and work out, test and evaluate practical workable options (Dunphy & Griffiths, 1998). The sustainability movement needs all of these kinds of change agents and needs to foster an appreciation that all have a part to play in advancing corporate sustainability.

How will we define success?

There is definitive research evidence that corporate change programs only succeed when they have clear goals and success criteria for change and systematically monitor their progress toward these goals (Turner & Crawford, 1998). Corporate change involves iterative feedback cycles rather like the guidance systems on ballistic missiles. Once the target is set and the missile launched, its forward movement is constantly monitored and continuously corrected to ensure it is on track to the target.

So what targets are appropriate for corporate change programs that seek to move an organisation toward sustainable practices? We suggest the following as guidelines:

1 elimination of societal, organisational, group or individual rewards for unsustainable practices
2 reduction or elimination of unsustainable practices, that is, the deterioration or waste of human and natural resources
3 cost savings from the elimination or recycling of 'waste' (waste here includes inefficient use of human resources such as high turnover of valued employees due to poor human resource policies)

4 increased competitive advantage through product or process innovation and the acquisition or development of corporate competencies for future enhanced performance

5 corporate contribution to overall community welfare.

All of these goals are worthwhile in their own right. However, they also have the capacity to make significant contributions to bottom-line performance in the short and/or longer term. For example, failure to eliminate unsustainable practices (1) can lead to costly conflict and litigation with environmental groups and/or government penalties. Contributing to overall community welfare (5) can enhance the organisation's corporate image in the short term and in the longer term lead to the reduction of taxes through decreasing the cost to the community of disposing of physical waste or controlling illness or crime.

Having defined the performance goals of their sustainability-related change programs, executives need to ensure that the pace and direction of change remains consistent with the chosen targets. Two kinds of monitoring are useful. The first is internal monitoring of the kind that effective strategically-oriented organisations currently use and often use well. Sustainability needs to be central to the business agenda of corporations and no new principles for performance monitoring need to be invented. The best practice currently used to monitor change of other kinds is equally appropriate for change in this area and needs to be the responsibility of those who are leading the change program and also of those whose worklife and behaviour is affected, wherever they are in the organisation. There is also a need for external monitoring. Just as governments and stock markets insist on independent auditing of financial accounts, so they will increasingly insist on independent auditing of the environmental impact of a corporation's activities (Dow Jones, for example, has instituted a sustainability index and is measuring companies on this basis). While work has begun in this area, there is a need for the development of innovative approaches to meet the requirements of different industries.

In the final analysis, most private sector organisations will institute sustainable practices in response to the prospect of a combination of achieving potentially improved business outcomes and avoiding penalties imposed by law or community pressure. There is, therefore, a need to document case studies of firms which have instituted more sustainable practices and achieved success according to these traditional criteria. Von Weizsäcker, Lovins and Lovins' 1997 book is a model in this regard.

Traditionally conservationists have remained critical of large corporations even when they have made major moves toward sustainability. It often seemed that even the most herculean efforts on the part of corporates were never good enough. There is an urgent need to celebrate significant steps made by corporations along the road to sustainability. This is not to argue for ignoring the fact that in many organisations there will still need to be greater efforts on new fronts. Nor does it imply that we should condone the ignorance, laziness, wilful greed and unbridled self-interest that characterise some corporate leaders. Such attitudes need to be consistently exposed, confronted and challenged. However, where challenging sustainability goals are set, appropriate action is initiated, performance is monitored and success can be demonstrated, that success should be widely publicised and celebrated. Setting out on the path to sustainability is a declaration of the value of all life on the planet and the pilgrims who tread that path need to support and encourage each other and joyfully celebrate progress along the way, particularly in the face of difficulties.

The inner transformation

Finally we will discuss briefly the role of individual consciousness and personal action in creating corporate change directed to sustainable outcomes. We have focused in this book on the important role that corporates can play in advancing the cause of sustainability. However, we want to emphasise that corporations are in the final analysis, as the sociologist Emile Durkheim noted years ago, merely 'social fictions'. They do not exist in the same way that we do ourselves; they have no physical reality apart from their appurtenances of land, plant, equipment and materials. They exist only insofar as we agree to act as if they exist, that is we collude to pretend they are real and to the extent that our pretences are shared, they do. On the other hand, if we remove our commitment from them, they collapse as surely as did the USSR when its peoples withdrew their commitment to that institution. All organisations are constructed realities, dependent on the consent of their stakeholders. While we have written of the importance of change leaders, ultimately the leader is dependent on the willingness of followers to accept leadership and to work to reinvent the organisational culture. The groundswell of public awareness, commitment and social action within and outside the corporation is as important as leadership by executives and managers in creating the conditions for instituting sustainable practices.

The outer reality of our social worlds is a mirror reflection of the dynamic reality of our inner worlds. Inner consciousness and outer reality are intimately related and co-create each other. It follows, therefore, that any significant transformation of the world about us depends in part on the transformation of our inner consciousness—our values and attitudes, the lenses of intellectual categories through which we view and understand our world, the meanings we give to our experience and the emotional commitment we bring to our actions. The most important change agenda is internal and intensely personal. There is no way that we will transform the world unless we are also profoundly committed to transforming ourselves. It is this agenda that is primary and more challenging than the external task of transforming organisations.

The continued well-being of the human species and of other species on this planet depends on the achievement of human and ecological sustainability. This demands the transformation of corporations along with other social institutions. However, none of this will be possible without the transformation of human consciousness. In the end, individuals make the difference in the course of social change—their convictions, awareness, knowledge and skills matter. Therefore the questions each of us must answer are:

- Are we willing to work for the regeneration and renewal of life on the planet?
- Will we pursue this commitment in the organisations in which and with which we work?
- Will we pioneer this new ideology ourselves by living the regenerative life with courage, compassion and joy?

Our answer to this last question will have most impact on the central agenda of the twenty-first century—transforming organisations so that they actively contribute to the creation of a society that truly sustains and renews the richness of life on this unique planet.

Endnotes

1 This is what is referred to in the social sciences as a 'contingency theory', that is, a theory or model that makes predictions on the basis of contingent situational factors.
2 Such a training program, the 'Change Management Qualification', has been instituted at the Australian Graduate School of Management, Sydney, Australia. It is available online.

References

Dunphy, D. 1999 'Sustainability: The secret of high performance', *AGSM Magazine*, Australian Graduate School of Management, Sydney, NSW.

Dunphy, D. and Griffiths, A. 1998 *The Sustainable Corporation: Organisational Renewal in Australia*, Allen & Unwin, Sydney.

Dunphy, D. and Stace, D. 1991 *Under New Management: Australian Organizations in Transition*, McGraw-Hill, Sydney.

Mencken, H. L. 1996 quoted in D. MacHal (ed.), *Wit*, Prion Press, Singapore.

Nattras, B. and Altomare, M. 1999 *The Natural Step for Business: Wealth, Ecology and the Evolutionary Corporation*, New Society Publishers, Gabriola Island, British Columbia, Canada.

Soros, G. 1998 *The Crisis of Global Capitalism: Open Society Endangered*, Pacific Affairs, New York.

Stace, D. and Dunphy, D. 1994 *Beyond the Boundaries: Leading and Creating the Successful Enterprise*, McGraw-Hill, Sydney.

Strong, M. 1999 Chairman of the Earth Council, Under-Secretary-General and Special Adviser to the Secretary-General of the United Nations in the Jack Beale Lecture on the Global Environment 'Towards a Sustainable Civilisation?', University of NSW, Sydney, 11 February.

Turner, D. and Crawford, M. 1998 *Change Power: Capabilities that Drive Corporate Renewal*, Business & Professional Publishing, Sydney.

von Weizsäcker, E., Lovins, A. B. and Lovins, L. H. 1997 *Factor 4: Doubling Wealth, Halving Resource Use*, Allen & Unwin, St Leonards, NSW.

Index